Trauma
PLOT

Trauma
PLOT

—— A Life ——

JAMIE HOOD

PANTHEON BOOKS
New York

FIRST HARDCOVER EDITION
PUBLISHED BY PANTHEON BOOKS 2025

Published by Pantheon Books, a division of Penguin Random House LLC,
1745 Broadway, New York, NY 10019.

Pantheon Books and the colophon are registered trademarks
of Penguin Random House LLC.

LCCN 2024056206
ISBN 978-0-593-70097-6
Ebook ISBN 978-0-593-70099-0

penguinrandomhouse.com | pantheonbooks.com

Printed in the United States of America
1st Printing

The authorized representative in the EU for product safety and compliance is
Penguin Random House Ireland, Morrison Chambers, 32 Nassau Street,
Dublin D02 YH68, Ireland, https://eu-contact.penguin.ie.

For Olive,

who is my heart

She had a perpetual sense . . . of being out, far out to sea and alone; she always had the feeling that it was very, very dangerous to live even one day.

—VIRGINIA WOOLF, *Mrs. Dalloway*

Contents

Introduction

xi

PART I

— She —

I

PART II

— I —

79

PART III

— You —

147

PART IV

— We —

197

Introduction

I began writing this book in 2016, a year after five men gang-raped me and around the time the *Access Hollywood* tapes were leaked to the public: "When you're a star they let you do it. You can do anything. Grab 'em by the pussy." A month later, Donald Trump would be elected to the presidency, another place where they let you do anything. Immediately, though, this framing misdirects. It intimates causality between "my" trauma and Trump's swaggering admission to Billy Bush on a hot mic—"locker room talk." By opening here, perhaps I imply that Trump, or in any case, "the Trump era," made my writing possible, that the perilous cultural moment just before #MeToo reanimated my life, or else gave language to my abjection. That isn't the truth, though, or not wholly.

There were other writings and other histories. I may as well say the gang rape wasn't my first experience of sexual violence, far from it—but it was the worst of them. It nearly killed me. Really, though, I guess I wanted to die then. In the weeks and months after, I'd catch myself laughing, thinking how funny it was those men hadn't killed me, and I was angry with them too, not because of what they'd done, but because they'd cheated me out of the death I longed for, one that would have tidied my loose threads, a death that had trailed and mocked me my whole life.

Until then, I'd never put a name to this longing. I wanted the end of it all, but no force lived behind my desire. I wanted total passivity. I wanted it to just happen. And then some airless Sunday in August, at the end of a long bar shift, I walked into traffic on Clinton Avenue and waited for death to come. I stared straight ahead. I saw two white orbs grow larger and larger: two impassive moons. Time broke open, but I didn't witness my life. God didn't come. I saw no angels. Only the suck of absence hovered over me. Some instinct must have kicked in, an involuntary motion, because next thing, I was heaped on the sidewalk. Or maybe it was that death refused me. Maybe death rolled me on its tongue and spat me back like a cherry pit. In any case, I lived, so I figured I had to go on.

I have never told anyone about that night. But then most of this book was unspoken before now.

My failed suicide is another origin of *Trauma Plot,* which became a bulwark against death, or perhaps death's opposite. Or, no—the book usurped death's eminence in my life. It functioned, as it were, substitutively, supplanting suicide. At the time, suicide was less a reversal of my position in the world than an elaboration of it. I was a zombie. I was death-in-life. Sure, I woke each morning, and most days I ate, usually I'd take my dog to the dog park, I went to work, I saw people and drank and did a lot of drugs. Despite the rapes, I still had sex—plenty, in fact, though most not very good. I didn't think there was anything exceptional about me. I'd grown up poor and wounded like a lot of people. Surely like most of the people I'd grown up around. My entrée into adulthood coincided with the 2008 financial crisis, and when Occupy happened in 2011, I was bunkered down in graduate school, convinced my education was the sole foothold above the quicksand of my mother's poverty.

But my life there had become untenable. I crawled out of it and ran to New York to transform myself. Everywhere I went, rape followed. Rape was the little phrase repeating through the score of my life. At last I gave up the possibility that my time on earth could be special, that I would be loved, or happy, or have anything good happen to me ever again.

I still don't know how much of this is unusual. For most of my life no one I knew talked about rape, so there were many years when I thought it happened to every heroine of every Lifetime movie and to me. From these programs I'd been led to believe rape was the inexorable terminus of a life's plot: that rape was so destabilizing and shameful it would stop a girl's whole world short, and then she'd be nothing but this awful moment that happened to her. So I thought if I said anything about what I'd endured, I, too, would have nowhere left to get to.

The *Access Hollywood* footage, and the reactions to it, laid bare a dynamic I'd long suspected but never confirmed: that most of the women in my life were at war, and the men around us—even or especially the ones we loved—couldn't see it, didn't want to, or worse, cared hardly at all. While people everywhere made the same feeble jokes Trump did, a feeling I'd shoved in a hole started to surface. I couldn't separate from it any longer, and when I looked—when at last I, unbending, *looked*—I saw the feeling was rage, the blinding kind, and it was bigger than I was—rage, undoing me from the inside. Silence had become impossible.

Once I began speaking about this history of violence, I found most of my female friends had survived similar and kept on. We shared this terror, that to talk about our victimization would mean being trapped in it forever, would mean being understood as *ruined*. To say anything at all was to be told you were wallowing—the sole signal of liberation, the proof you'd "gotten over" your "trauma," was shutting up and soldiering on. It was funny to me how much of this came from other women, some of whom had privately told me they'd withstood the same. Was it that I liked the attention? Why couldn't I just move forward? I'm trying to, I wanted to say, but then someone like you says something like this to me and I go all stubborn. Grief gets deferred.

And of course if I said anything about rape to a man, usually he'd clam up altogether, or act like I was accusing him of something.

Don't mistake me, though. It's not that I see all men as rapists, facilitators, or apologists, and I find it dangerous and infantilizing to position victimization as elemental to the "female condition." There's nothing biologically or metaphysically essential to my observation, and I put no faith in the impotent fantasy of savage men and helpless women. It's a matter of training: a question of social atmospherics. I have to go on believing sexual revolution is possible, even as I mourn how our erotic lives seem inextricable from patriarchal indoctrination. For the time being, rape culture contaminates us all.

But sometimes a crack in the aquarium glass yields a flood. In 2016, I didn't care that I was *too much*. It was nothing to me when some slick dickhead called me weak. If Trump epitomized a particular slouch of blustering misogyny at the heart of American life, he was also, and quite patently, a clown. Clowns, we supposed, we knew how to manage. That brassy braggadocio was its own Waterloo. Something in the air had shifted, and as being mute on the subject of violence never stopped it from happening, perhaps the opposite tack must be taken: perhaps the past must be made to surface. The stories were legion. Most women I spoke to had existing connections to the men: fathers or stepfathers, hookups or boyfriends, teachers, bosses, pastors, and other authority figures. I was an outlier but not alone. Most of us had kept the secret: threats of retaliation were too frightening. I found I knew a woman who took her rapist to trial and won, but she hated the process; it traumatized her more than the rape, she said. I never reported, and I'll name no man in these pages. My dream isn't any longer of vengeance, and if I know anything, I know what the carceral system metes out isn't justice. Policing is the opposite of futurity. Anyhow, all this talk among the women I loved was before #MeToo even. Our stories were whispered at first, just bar gossip. So many creeps moved through our circles. We were trying to protect one another. There was only so much we could do.

Like many women artists, I've been haunted for years by a story from Ovid's *Metamorphoses,* the myth of Philomela, an Athenian princess who is raped and mutilated by her brother-in-law, Tereus.* Her sister, Procne, asks Tereus to bring Philomela from Athens to the Thracian court so they may be reunited. But once they are back on Thrace's shores, Tereus

> *drags Pandion's daughter*
> *to a far cabin cloaked by ancient woods*
> *and locks her in—pale, panicked, terrified.*
> *She weeps and asks him where her sister is.*
> *He first confesses his unspeakable crime,*
> *then conquers her, a virgin all alone,*
> *through force. She calls and calls upon her father*
> *and sister—most of all the mighty gods.*†

But in vain. Still, Philomela does not go quietly:

---

* Among these works I extend particular gratitude to Nina MacLaughlin's *Wake, Siren,* Paisley Rekdal's *Nightingale,* Anahid Nersessian's *Keats's Odes,* and Jennifer Kent's *The Nightingale.* Love and solidarity forever.
† I'm indebted to Stephanie McCarter's 2022 translation of the *Metamorphoses.*

> *"If the gods see these things, if they have any*
> *power, if all things are not lost with me,*
> *one day I'll make you pay. I'll cast off shame*
> *and tell your deeds. If I can get to people,*
> *I'll go to them. Or if I'm trapped in forests,*
> *my voice will fill the forests—stones will know.*
> *Heaven will hear, and any god that lives there!"*

So Tereus cuts out her tongue and again annihilates her: "They say he often raped her mangled body." In Ovid's world, as in ours, Philomela is hardly alone. Rape, wrote the University of Buffalo scholar Leo Curran, is "the dirty little secret of Ovidian scholarship."[*] But was it secret? As Daniel Mendelsohn remarks in *The New Yorker*, rape is the central conflict of "about fifty" of the *Metamorphoses*' tales—something like one in five—but (he points out) many translators efface rape's brutality in the process of naming it. They say assailants "ravish" and "plunder,"and in so doing, as Curran further attests, their "elegant variation of nomenclature becomes either evasion of condonation" instead.[†] "Rape" is traceable to the Latin *rapere*: to seize, grab, or carry off, though I'm told *stuprare* was more usual in classical Latin—to defile or violate. In Roman law, the act of taking a woman by force was *raptus,* which often involved intercourse but remained extricable from it. Rape shares an etymological genesis, then, with "rapture," a word that was occasionally used to describe forcible sexual acts until the early seventeenth century, at which point its meaning shifted, forming an affinity with the mystics and mystical writings.

To experience rapture in 1624, say, was to come closer to

[*] "Rape and Rape Victims in the *Metamorphoses*," *Arethusa* 11, no. 1/2, 1978.
[†] "Should Ovid's *Metamorphoses* Have a Trigger Warning?," *The New Yorker*, November 7, 2022.

God. From Ovid, though, we know what gods will do when they come close.

The material event of Philomela's rape was not what shattered me. After all, I could have comfortably identified with any number of raped women in the myths of antiquity—Io, Orithyia, Europa, Proserpina, Thetis. Often I've dreamed of Daphne as a laurel, and Apollo slipping calloused fingers beneath her bark. In one vision of the story, a self-portrait, the photographer Francesca Woodman stands arms aloft in a dense clearing, her back to the spectator. Her hands and forearms are wrapped in dead tree matter. Her hair is knotted; she's observable and phantasmic at once. I have been her kind. For years, too, I was Medusa, ugly with the evil thrust on me: stone-eyed, untouchable, a hissing fury. But when I shed those selves, Philomela remained. Philomela and her pulsing little tongue stump; Philomela, stricken but ongoing, raving but righteous; Philomela, whose grief and wrath surface, again and again, above silence. Denied language, she learns the loom, weaving a witness into being, creating a tapestry to transmit her torment in a different design.* I became entranced by this ripple in the story, its provocative diagnosis of rape as a formal problem—something that exceeds or can be clipped by language. Something that may mandate a kaleidoscopic technique of narration. I had a need of my own to reckon with the ways rape resists testimony or explodes the containers of its own telling, without in turn surrendering to the convention that trauma is, as it were, altogether unintelligible. With tongue or without, the story will out.

As with many of Ovid's corporeal metamorphoses, a punitive shadow enwraps the transformation of Philomela into a

---

* Of the story woven there, McCarter points out that the "word Ovid uses (*notae*) can indicate generic 'markings' or 'figures,' or else 'letters.' It is therefore not clear if Philomela weaves in words or pictures."

bird. It stuck in me for years like a nettle. Three bodies changed by the end of Ovid's tale: Procne becomes a swallow, Tereus a hoopoe ("and he still looks armed"), and Philomela the nightingale. But the female nightingale is mute in nature—only the male sings. In my 2016 diary, I wrote, "Ovid told the first rape joke!" Really, I had to laugh.

The year 2017 came and we all went to the Women's March. For me this had little to do with electoral politics—a function of civic life I'd long been disenchanted by—and everything with needing to be among a crowd of mad women. It's fashionable now to poke fun at that moment, to mock renunciations of American totalitarianism as overly earnest, as "cringe." But in our present era, when increasingly well-funded and militarized police departments try (and often fail) to obliterate coalition building against fascist rule (at the time of my writing, I think especially of the student encampments standing in solidarity with the Palestinian people), it feels necessary to imagine and reimagine revolutionary dissent, and to seek out community and care wherever we are able, for as long as we are able. At that time, though, I had little sense of connectedness, and my life lacked some essential dignity. In thrall to my trauma, I refused to grant myself grace. The reality of my wound had never been acknowledged; that I was a person at all was not a serious proposition to me or anyone. To be beside others who'd known this absence, to find I was not alone, changed my way of seeing in some urgent, indescribable way. One day I held a sign with something scrawled on it about my gang rape. A group of pigs pointed at me and began laughing, so I screamed at them, feeling unloosed. Naturally, this made them laugh harder. I swam through a sea of pink pussy hats, not knowing if I was counted as their kin. But just then I didn't care: I'd caught the energy. I was molting. There were a lot of marches that year.

When #MeToo happened, everything women wrote about rape outside reportage was crowned by the same bloody image—*Judith Beheading Holofernes*—by the Italian baroque painter Artemisia Gentileschi. You'd think all of us were running around planning to cut men's heads off, but I'll admit, back then, I sort of was. I wanted my rapists dead. I boiled over with viciousness. Nothing satisfied me like escalating conflicts with the men who'd started them, the ones who called me names or touched my body when I didn't want it. In bartending, it's amazing how often a man thinks he can flick your tits or grab your ass while you struggle past him, arms full of other people's dirty pint glasses. I worked in a lot of dives then. It's worse in those, but at least you can tell someone to fuck off. My tongue became a blade, yes, but my body, too, burst with white heat. Everyone acts like you're a crazy woman for speaking out about your debasement, but sometimes you have to play the Cassandra, sometimes even Troy must fall. I kept waiting for the opportunity to throw fists. In southeast Virginia, most of the girls I grew up with knew how to fight. Earrings off, nails off, jewelry off. There were a lot of white girls named Krystal, a lot of heads getting slammed into a lot of lockers. If you were a trans girl where I came from, you needed grit to get by. Maybe it's why I've never been much good with court intrigue. For most of my life, violence came in the form of a fist.

With those men I never had the pleasure. But still, I told myself, what I'd failed at before—protecting myself from rape—wouldn't happen again. I was in training for the next time. I would be no Laura Palmer. I was J.Lo in *Enough*. I was Ashley Judd in *Double Jeopardy*. I honed my body, angling my whole life toward reprisal. I couldn't bear a closed space and never ate, but I was agile. My hunger left me edgy. Every part of me became a sharp point. My long hours at the bar gave me stamina, and what's more, I got a lot of practice kicking bastards out of the places I worked. A few of the women I hung around with then had the same patch on their jackets: DEAD MEN CAN'T CATCALL. One gave me a pocketknife after I told her my shit. She showed me how to flick it silently open.

Once I started talking about the rapes, words tore through me. I became an oracle of my self, I wasn't able to stop. Logorrhea is one name for this compulsion, a pathological need to divulge. At times the furious rhythm of my confessions felt like speaking in tongues. And my verbal irrepressibility was another rationale for the writing. I needed somewhere to stuff away all that speech. When I began to write, I arrived at a different condition: hypergraphia. Hundreds, probably thousands of pages over the years, amassed in three laptops, printouts scattered through old storage containers or folded inside favorite books on forgotten shelves.

By the time my little rape poems began getting published, I was told *Judith Beheading Holofernes* was cooked. Everyone had seen it by then and grown tired. As if it were possible to see that spurt of blood and not know freedom. I guess repetition can diminish the power of a thing for some people. What I loved best in the painting were Judith's and Abra's bored looks, like they were spraying Raid on a nest of roaches. With my fingers I traced photographs of Gentileschi's other paintings—not just her interrogations of violence and spectacle (the multiple Judiths, Jael, Susanna, Danaë, Bathsheba), but the self-portraits also, her allegories of melancholy, ecstasy, penitence. The scholar Mary Garrard remarks that you can separate a Gentileschi from its imitators by the hands of her women, which are muscular, mobile, and purposeful. Femininity in a Gentileschi is never passive. I read about the rape trial she withstood, the way her inquisitors bound her hands in thumbscrews during her time on the stand. She shouted "*È vero, è vero, è vero!*" ("It's true, it's true, it's true!") while testifying against her father's acquaintance, Agostino Tassi, who'd defiled her with the assistance of another man, Cosimo Quorli, and Tuzia, a female friend of the Gentileschi household. Artemisia might never have painted again. At a time I nearly abandoned this project, I read Anna Banti's novel of Artemisia, the original draft of which was destroyed after the Nazis detonated mines they'd planted along the Arno in occupied Florence. Susan Sontag dreamed of Banti stunned among the rubble, grieving the "death all around her [and] the manuscript that exists now only in her fragile memory." I went on.

Then the man who'd coordinated my gang rape began haunting the neighborhood again. Probably he'd been in jail awhile: he was a drug dealer, small-time, but had circulated enough cocaine through the area to be known to the cops, and locked up a couple years, which was about how long it'd been since I'd seen him. This was my guess anyhow, as I knew where he lived with his mom—it was where the rape took place, a couple blocks from where I worked—and I couldn't think where else he'd have gone. Now I'd pass him on the streets and his face tore through me like a nuclear blast. I'd be in a debilitating panic attack for days. Shell-shocked, I remember thinking, though of course I'd never been in war. The rapes were on me: total immediacy. I found myself on all fours. One of my best friends then was an ex-con, a huge guy, and when I told him of these encounters he said he'd kill the man for me if I only asked him to. He had no issue going back in, he said. Prison didn't frighten him anymore. I said homicide was a different beast than copping a drug charge, but he was a man of honor, a true gentleman. "Damaged" women like me tended to flock to him. His offer put things in starker terms.

My revenge found form, then. It was paint on an easel. Clay

in my hands. I dreamed of John the Baptist's oozing head on Salome's silver plate. Judith returned to me, imperturbable, with her glittering sword. I pictured Jael and Sisera—the fatal tent peg; that supple temple. Now my bloodlust was not mere fantasy. Death was in my hands. The trouble was, I loved my friend and didn't want him going anywhere. His family needed him free. I needed him here. First of all, he was the only man who'd ever protected me. He walked me home at the end of late bar shifts, and when he visited me during them, he played bodyguard. When men fucked with me, I didn't have to be the Medusa, because he'd cool things off. One night I eighty-sixed two guys who threatened to kill me while they walked out the door. An hour later they were back, three other men in tow. All five sat in a parked car just outside the entrance to the bar for hours. My friend waited through the long night with me. I felt sure nothing bad could happen with him around. But being protected by another person isn't the same as living beyond fear, and at last I saw I couldn't let anyone forfeit their life or liberty for mine, or for my "honor," whatever the fuck that was. Besides, if someone was to kill my rapists, it ought to be me. The desire vanished. I saw what I really wanted was that no one else get hurt.

It was obvious as #MeToo unfolded that the movement was fallible—that to achieve mainstream recognition, it would leave a lot of people out. Nevertheless, its revelations exposed the immensity of the problem: sexual violence was everywhere, and all the time. This knowledge freed me from ego, I guess, and something I needed in that moment was to surrender centrality. Until I was able to look outside the fractured self, I would never refashion it. What a relief to find I wasn't special. And how devastating. It's banal to say, but my sense that I was an aberration was what made me so sure I'd deserved all that had happened. Shame particularizes. Shame isolates. Now I no longer see my trauma as exceptional, which is a strange thing to confess at the beginning of a memoir about it. But if I am singular in some way, it's not through my endurance of violence. I refuse that naming. Rape seems to me only a trouble I am writing about, a trouble I've been better at managing lately.

Where Tarana Burke's 2006 vision for #MeToo prioritized procuring resources for low-income Black and brown girls who'd survived sexual trauma, 2017's reboot was animated chiefly by storytelling. It rallied an ambient solidarity through supposed collective recognition, gathering force through an infinite chorus of voices bearing witness. Whose voices were amplified as the plot coalesced was another matter altogether. It seemed the stories that gained the most traction were the most glamorous, or else the most gruesome. That the movement's narrative status quo mirrored the broader culture's warrants thoughtful, rigorous critique, but it doesn't discredit the watershed moment entirely. In *Dissent,* Sarah Jaffe remarked that #MeToo's orientation toward first-person narrative disproportionately invested energy in "naming and shaming" over material action. Hers was a useful rejoinder: no viral tweet will end rape. Nor will a memoir—not mine or anyone else's. "Bearing witness" doesn't produce liberation from thin air. Even still, casting traumatic testimony as politically inert or even ideologically regressive is the duty of the contrarian, the reactionary, the dictator. Such demobilizations transform nothing and no one. They aren't worth our time.

That the #MeToo movement of 2017 became clarified in the confessional mode made it fertile ground for cultural critics, even if the backlash itself took more time to root in our sedate groves. The long pop-cultural tail of Hanya Yanagihara's *A Little Life,* for example, wasn't properly cut and cauterized by books media until nearly six years after its meteoric success. But once it coagulated, *A Little Life* came to be seen as the ur-text of what Parul Sehgal would name "the trauma plot" in a December 2021 issue of *The New Yorker*. Some identified Yanagihara by name—Sehgal, Brandon Taylor, Andrea Long Chu, and Christian Lorentzen, who wrote an early pan of the novel for the *London Review of Books* ("What real person trapped in this novel wouldn't become a drug addict?" What person indeed?). For others, her "agony novel" was the unacknowledged and invisible nucleus of a diseased literary organism that had rendered fiction psychologically cheap and narratologically flat. Trauma, in these readings, had become the tiresome explanatory bedrock beneath all contemporary writing. As Sehgal argued, unlike the marriage plot, which opens the novel searchingly toward an unknowable future, the trauma plot is anchored only in the recursive muck of the past. For many, this plot was a uniquely modern marvel—the freeze-dried and vacuum-sealed by-product of a cultural market dominated by Bessel van der Kolk's *The Body Keeps the Score,* Lena Dunham's Brooklyn autofiction *Girls,* reality TV, and a decade of personal essay verticals at digital pubs like *Gawker, xoJane, Jezebel,* and *Thought Catalog.* For *Slate* in 2015, Laura Bennett named this the era of the "first-person industrial complex," classifying a parasitic dynamic between writers, editors, and audiences that (usefully) generated space "for underrepresented viewpoints" while consequently creating an ecosystem in which writers felt (to cite Jia Tolentino, quoted in Bennett's piece) that the "best thing they have to offer is the worst thing that ever happened to them."

Trauma plots are not above evaluation, and I respect the work of some of these critics quite deeply, but what troubles me in this increasingly consolidated recoil is its wholesale exile of authors from self-knowledge—the subterranean, insidious idea of our relation to writing as unexamined, crude, and lacking competence with self-reflexivity, humor, and play. Like there's no reason to write about trauma except to make a buck. Like if you talk about having lived through something awful, that's all you've ever talked about or ever will. Like you have no agency inside a story you yourself chose to tell. It's an old trick, the same used to argue autobiography is antithetical to art; that confessional writing is without tradition; that it's hack, just bloodletting on the helpless, virginal page. It damns trauma as only ever individual, and so functionally apolitical, even when texts position trauma as inextricable from systemic injustice—indicting class exploitation, for example, the continuing historical aftershocks of the Atlantic slave trade, or rape as a tactic of war (really even: rape as a war against women in its own right). These stories are rendered dismissible as "identitarian" cudgels, weaponized against lone perpetrators and taken on to lay claim to a de facto moral authority that, apparently, attends bodily harm. Which is news to me.

What remains funny about many of these arguments is how they paint writers of trauma as inartful—dupes of the market—while at the same time calling us con artists and tricksters. We're somehow too stupid to see we're selling our souls to the god of publicity, even while we leverage our nightmares against a defenselessly porous reading public and cash out. The ethical crime of storytelling is handily shifted back onto the person recording their victimization: *you* are the vector of damage. Trauma, in this frame, becomes a contaminating force. We infect others with our shameful sob stories, and what we take from those people is their time, their attention, and all the money in their pockets. The world over, readers can do nothing but go on buying and consuming our exhibitionist displays. We are succubi. We are Plath's Lady Lazarus, unwrapping ourselves before the "peanut-crunching crowd" for little more than a Buffalo nickel.

I should say I think it's perfectly fine to loathe *A Little Life*.

For a while, I'd see those flimsy tote bags all over the New York City subway, the ones with

JUDE&
JB&
WILLEM&
MALCOLM.

stacked on taupe canvas. I'd think how odd to bear their names like a fashion brand on your body, and how terrible it would be to realize *you* were the Jude of your friend group—until I remembered *I* was the Jude of several of *my* friend groups. I have a soft spot for the novel. There's something in its excess that rang true to me when I first read it. Although it's fiction, *A Little Life* understands it's possible to spend most of a life reckoning with sexual trauma. I surely have. One of the troubles with the dominant narrative of #MeToo was that it continued to imagine the experience of rape as an anomalous event in the usual order of a life, even as it underscored the overwhelming breadth of rape culture itself. But for women without support networks or safety nets, without certain social privileges or legibilities, I suspect the repetition of this trauma is commoner. If you don't have the money to get away from a partner who's beating or raping you, you could spend years in it. Some of this I watched right up close. One disquisitional frame against *A Little Life* had to do with *quantity*: the *amount* of trauma Jude suffered was understood as inexorably unbelievable. But for me, it was one of the only novels I'd read that saw how pervasive intimate violence is in our lives, and how shadowy, how stigmatized, how great the pressure to stay stoic in facing it, to weather violence without complaint.

A Little Life worked for me, too, I guess, because I love a Gothic fairy tale, and I'll always jump in the ring for the earnest, the cringe, the sentimental, the too much. I write for the messy bitches. I write for girls who haven't given their grief language. In the era of the Hater, it's no surprise to me that a dozen critics decided a book so many people were reading was undeserving of its audience and accolades. But to crucify a novel that never claimed to be *Middlemarch* for rank literary pretension seemed to me sort of strange. What's more, I found it thin how so many of these quarrels with "the" trauma plot seemed to be about *A Little Life* with maybe one or two other novels thrown in, which isn't so much a canon trouble as it is a problem of three books some person with a byline didn't like. Many critics I know are working writers, and most of us love books, are curious about art, and want conversations that expand the world rather than shrink it. Then some critics have too much damn time on their hands, so everything they read they read paranoid. Call it Terminal Op-Ed Brain. Call it a salaried position. They like the thrill of the takedown without the rigor of generosity, which sounds a little like what they accuse all us sellout trauma morons of, no?

In her diaries, the French writer Annie Ernaux remarks that "desire, writing, and death have always been interchangeable" for her, that, in these happenings, the self is ejected from time, evacuated of it, that there, time dissolves. I have sometimes thought of rape as another such rupture. Or perhaps: an event in which sex and death inflame and consume each other. They wear each other's faces. I am, I confess, not a theorist of rape, only an archivist of my own. *Trauma Plot* is the odd body of this archive: dusty, disordered, a Babel of memory. The first words I ever wrote of it live in a tattered notebook: RAPE IS AGAINST THE POEM. Beside it I sketched a self-portrait, my face hardly an outline.

Rape severed me from time, of which I lost much, in terms

of memory and self-presence, yes, but also in the sense of just living—I don't know if I was doing that until recently. In an early poem I wrote for the book, I described myself as a "persistence of biology." The years passed through me. Was this like life? The way trauma annihilates time seems to me one reason we consider it "unspeakable." What we mean, perhaps, is that it disorders narrative, for what is a story without time? How can a woman made into meat speak? Does abjection have its sort of character? These are irrevocable absences. They snip plot's thread.

The project settled into its current form just after the Brett Kavanaugh confirmation proceedings. Like countless women, I watched Christine Blasey Ford's testimony in horror. We knew what would happen after: retaliation, brutish and swift. Kavanaugh's ascension to the Supreme Court seemed to me the first meaningful death knell of #MeToo. Not because Ford's legitimacy as a witness of her own life was well challenged—it was obvious she was credible; even Trump yielded the point—but because it served to show no one much cared if a woman was violated or not, particularly if the perp was a man turning any special wheel of power. In her memoir, Ford writes that it "didn't feel like I hadn't been heard. It felt like I had been believed, [and] the response was a proverbial shrug." Like Anita Hill before her, testifying "hadn't solved the problem . . . I couldn't fix the fundamental injustice of that." Many felt he shouldn't be disqualified even if he *had* done it. That Kavanaugh would subsequently determine the rule of law governing women's bodily autonomy for decades to come didn't (the argument went) have all that much to do with his individual denial of one woman's authority over her own body. Rape, again, imagined as the private business of a few fucked-up women. A squabble between us and the beleaguered, brilliant men sucked into our vortexes.

The blow of the confirmation stalled *Trauma Plot* for a time.

What use, I felt, would this story have for so inhospitable a public? Maybe, I thought, I'll write the book for myself: a rape journal, some place I can lay all my suffering down in a heap. I saw if I didn't get it out of my body and into words, I'd die. I remembered Annie Dillard, who reminds us one plight of the writing life is knowing "your work is so meaningless, so fully for yourself alone, and so worthless to the world, that no one except you cares whether you do it well, or ever." It's indispensable advice, something I've often said again to myself—because I write for myself, first, and then for all the other reasons and everyone else. What was in me needed saying. It blazed there, then rotted. I required exorcism. So I wrote, and wrote, and then kept writing. After, I threw everything out. I burned some of the notebooks, and don't regret it. I started again. It was a book of poems, it was a novel, it was a memoir in redacted fragments. A cento of lines from survivors throughout literary history. No form held. I'd come to the end of ninety pages and face another demolition. Again, Dillard:

> Some of the walls are bearing walls; they have to stay, or every-
> thing will fall down. Other walls can go with impunity; you
> can hear the difference. Unfortunately, it is often a bearing wall
> that has to go. It cannot be helped. There is only one solution,
> which appalls you, but there it is. Knock it out. Duck . . . You
> can save some of the sentences, like bricks. It will be a miracle
> if you can save some of the paragraphs, no matter how excel-
> lent in themselves or hard-won. You can waste a year worrying
> about it, or you can get it over with now. (Are you a woman,
> or a mouse?)

Her schema of the well-built house offered a different lesson, perhaps, than intended. What wasn't working, I saw, was not my manner of seaming things properly together. Trauma annihilated me, it split me from my life and sent me floating out into dead space. Trauma ripped out all my delicate little stitches, all the work I'd done to get by. What I needed was to sit among my rubble and weep. I allowed chaos, and not its tidying, to be the book. None of the usual walls or fixtures sufficed. Nothing fit. I had to let go of it: my desire for order, for control. Three rapes outline the shape of this book, which moves, slantwise, chronologically across the span of a decade. These happened in quick succession: June 2012; February 2013; August 2015. Each I write in a different form. I refuse to reconcile them. I leap over time, and flit between styles, through multiple narrative positions in relation to my "self." My rapes aren't unspeakable, but my speech shifts, it metamorphoses, it refracts. I wanted my account to wrestle with rape's dis-ordering, how it turned my cells against themselves. I was undone, and I couldn't fix it sweeping the fragments into a dustpan. The shards *were* the book, violent and strange. I dance among them.

Part I

— SHE —

Boston, October 2012

S he came to in the kitchen and found the oven on. She didn't remember igniting it, but then, she couldn't seem to remember rising from bed that morning at all, not dressing, nor plodding—barefooted, she saw now—down the hall from the bedroom. This was not a shock. For months she'd been losing time. *Losing time,* she'd say, as if time were an object, a set of keys, say, or a passport, a thing one held and could, in turn, misplace, though it felt rather that time had lost her, had slipped its noose somehow and fled somewhere she could no longer see.

Her head was wooly; her limbs stiff. She stooped to peer through the oven door, carefully dodging her reflection in the glass. Empty. How queer.

Edie? she shouted.

Maybe her roommate had set it going and forgotten. Edie often rushed things—always late, but an otherwise sensible woman, generous and warm. Despite being born and raised in Boston, Edie had faith that the world arced toward goodness. The women had been up late the night before, drinking and cleaning and gossiping, but Edie was on a self-improvement kick this month, some October challenge she'd joined in solidarity with her colleagues at the museum, amiable divorcées all thirty years older than she was. Better, she'd said, to improve the mess now—more to work with at my age. Pliable flesh. She'd winked.

She'd have left for the gym an hour ago. Anyhow, the apartment had that eerie, unpeopled feeling. The air was humming to itself.

Jamie blinked against the sun where it crept through the window. It lay a shroud over the table. Outside, an oak shuddered, casting shade, causing the light, where it landed, to thicken and attenuate; to converge and again disengage. Like a shadow play, she thought, except she couldn't see any story in it. Something about this horrified her immensely.

She'd had the dream again. The grinning mouth, that shadowy stoop, a place of force. Its outline was clear but the specifics impossible to situate. It was just a haze of violence: odorous, goopy, exhausting. When she'd sat up it was three a.m.—it seemed always to be three a.m.—and the sheets were damp, her skin slick with night grease. The light was left on. The room had a weight to it, a fullness. She knew what she would find.

Floating there in the corner, that enigmatical nebula of atoms: the presence she'd come to call the Specter. A ghost, maybe, or just a hallucination. At any rate, it arrived in her life when the dream had, after that awful night in June, the one that had been thieved from her memory. For a time the Specter only appeared to her in the wake of the bad dream, as if part of the plot somehow, like it came from the same world.

But then it began to split apart, and she'd find it coagulating at the foot of the stairs in the middle of the day, a home invader, seeming now to move through her life at its leisure. A drifter. Autonomous. Unpredictable.

Turning her face from it, she shut off the light. She didn't like to look at the Specter in darkness—it was more threatening then. She'd lain still, breathing shallowly, and listened to her heart thud against the lockbox of her chest. At night, yes, she was unable to deal with it, the Specter's inscrutable watchfulness, so she closed her eyes and waited, and waited, and waited.

And then drifted, after what seemed a long while, into sleep once more.

Now the day entered her, and the vision dissolved. She felt only a tenseness, a kind of a vague, wiry condition. She stretched her arms up and yowled, feeling she hadn't slept at all.

Where the sun warmed the table she lay a palm on the wood and dragged her flesh against the grain—seeking friction, thinking to snag the thread of the dream and unspool it, scry its meaning, and so trace a path out from the center of the labyrinth to where— Her alarm shrieked, splitting her. She slammed a hand on the phone. Now a throb stirred behind her temples.

Vacant there before the stove, she was a girl in a fairy story, perhaps her favorite, the one about the sleeping beauty. As a child she'd watched the movie dozens of times, rewinding and replaying it so often the tape wore out, spitting its reels at her in tragic, weary ribbons. She'd loved the fairies and their trilling voices, as all little girls did, and admired the princess's forested solitude, the way she seemed always to be embraced by trees and smiling woodland creatures.

But what transfixed Jamie above all else was the scene where the princess wandered like a zombie through the castle toward fate—the hidden spindle, deadly and expectant. How beautiful she looked, and how fragile—Jamie had dreamed of one day brandishing that liquid mix of grace and delicacy, she longed to have such sexless breasts, the thick cascade of golden hair. And she had hated the wicked fairy, who set such horrors in motion, and for what—jealousy over a baby?

It didn't seem fair death had come to call on the princess. Through no fault of her own, she'd had, then, to answer, walking straight at it, her gaze cavernous. Her death was reversible, sure, undone by true love's kiss, but even as a girl Jamie had thought it funny how you always needed a man to dig you out of the hole of other women's envy, and no one ever seeing it was a man's fault there was any envy there to begin with.

Still, she couldn't stay mad at the prince; he was so handsome, and when he waltzed with the princess between the clouds— her gown flitting between shades of pale blue and rose—Jamie thought the place they'd ended up must be heaven, and wondered, if it was heaven, where God stood in the scene, why he'd brought them up there so early, only to remain out of frame. But then she thought how maybe God was really just a room made of clouds, accumulating there beneath you, around you, and all above your head. Maybe what God was was a soft holding cell. And what waited for you in the ever after, that heaven, was just a dull sense of weightlessness.

The stove clock glared at her: 7:30, then. A defenseless hour. The sun pulsed and climbed its blank ladder. The sky was glorious: a clean, uninterruptible blue. She cracked the window to air the room. A rush of cold. No more, the summer stench of city garbage; no cacophony of honks or shouts from the street below, or not yet. Autumn had arrived in the night. Here, now, its disintegrations. Already the leaves of the neighbor's maple were deepening and shifting in tone, Pilgrim colors: pumpkin and chestnut, shy goldenrod. Coronas of rouge at the leaves' centers pouted. Bruised mouths.

This, then, Boston's lone pleasure, its fall splendor. Though soon it would be winter. The gray threat loomed. And then a diminishment would set in, a hibernation, and her delight in clamming shut against the world would be followed by the long boredom, that half year of night, the city an underworld, cloaked and cramped in snow, in silence. Everyone miserable, and her thick depression. The sky birdless. The oxygen sucked from each room.

What was it she'd been doing.

She turned the oven off.

On her ring finger she noticed, now, the sliver of a hangnail. She suppressed an urge to suck and chew at its omen of disorder. Lately she'd been battling this habit, for she could squander whole afternoons picking absently at the wounds of her cuticles, the soft skin on the ends of her fingers. This occupied her while she read or graded papers, scrolled Facebook or stared emptily through the window of the bus, the subway car, the commuter train. What remained in the aftermath of her gnashing was a chaos of serrated flesh. Inkblots of blood would appear on her clothes: evidence she'd gone too deep. When she saw others see the fallout of her demolitions, shame, that boiling mud, spread through her, but she couldn't stop. Half her fingers were wrapped in Band-Aids.

What sort of a man wants to hold hands with that. An old voice nagged.

But he'd been right. None did.

Mainly she stuffed her hands in her pockets, and lately she indulged her sickness only when alone, in the convent of her room. Finally, though, she'd decided to change. This couldn't go on—the nail biting, the drinking, the way her mind seemed to be, well, how else to put it, dispersing. I will no longer steward my havoc without objection! This she'd said in the bathroom mirror, forcing herself to face her face. An unfamiliar wraith. She thought her formulation quite lyrical—*havoc, stewarding*—and felt certain casting her decision as an epic journey might propel her toward real renewal. She'd transform herself, she'd said (and we must admit it, said while stinking fucking drunk), into a consummate disciplinarian, would become, as it were, her own impossibly cruel mistress.

Painfully she'd lifted her lips: a grimace in the skin of a smile.

She'd begin with the biting. She'd thought, at first, mantras would rewire her circuitry through repetition alone. Vision boards, manifestation rituals—she'd read *The Secret*. An astrologer she bartered with on Boylston for a ten-minute reading told her she was in an era of molting, but she would find she was her own best teacher. She was only in need of guardrails, a language with which to make meaning from nothingness. Still, she'd found that speech was not action, and then polish hadn't worked, nor had clipping her nails to the quick. Not even—by god, she'd tried it as a last resort—coating her fingers in the spray her mother used to keep their dogs from chewing the furniture. After a week, or perhaps two, Jamie began to enjoy its bitter flavor, and would pucker pleasurably at the chemical sting, its strange sobering effect.

Fifteen dollars down the drain.

It hadn't worked on the dogs either.

The drinking, of course, was every night since June, or she didn't sleep. Not that the sleep she got ever brought any rest. She tried cutting back—she *did* try. Took two nights off each week to start, but soon the sober days seemed years, and in bed those nights, she'd lie awake for hours, staring at a spot of mold on the ceiling, sure it was growing larger, sure it was infecting her, all while praying the Specter would fail to appear, that she wouldn't feel it hovering while she counted desperately back from a hundred, trying to bore herself into unconsciousness. In daylight the Specter no longer disturbed her—nothing but an enormous mote of dust, she'd say—but at night her mind fixed itself to the question of what the Specter wanted, why it wouldn't leave her be.

She saw it was somehow *of her*, they were made of the same stuff, which maybe meant only that it was borne from her, that it might be, as it were, an inheritor to her existence. A minor pleasure: thinking of the Specter as her baby. But she knew, too, there was a membrane connecting it to the dream, to the night in June, that black hole. The absence divided the universe of her mind in two: there was her life before it (a mess, but a mess nonetheless with a story), and then her life after. An explosion of particles. Nothing seemed any longer to connect.

She understood that until she remembered that night, the Specter would stick gummily to her. That she would never be free of it.

She returned to her body in the kitchen where it slouched against the sink. In her hand, a knife. 7:56. Thirty minutes had peeled apart from one another as she drifted.

The day of course unraveled. It was what days did.

A crash down the hall, but what? The Specter was customarily noiseless, and if it was a ghost, it seemed only to be the thin kind, atmospheric; never banging about or slamming drawers or doors shut; not seeming able to touch anything, really, not touching anything at all.

In August there'd been a broken window in the empty basement apartment. Human shit in the toilet, too. Jamie discovered both troubles while washing a load of whites. Probably the shit was some crusty repairman's, but Edie liked to frighten Jamie with tall tales of menacing transients. She'd unfurl a story of some cracked-out murderer, a real nut who'd escaped McLean, laughing maniacally while the color drained from Jamie's face. The door leading to the basement was flimsy, after all, and opened into Jamie's bedroom.

Surely she'd locked it that morning. No one had come into the house.

Hello?

Nothing.

Irritably, she clamped the hangnail between her teeth and tugged. A clean break, no fuss: only a hole in its place, and the satisfying flush of wet pink gathering in the gap left behind. It stilled her, that prick of pain. Something about it decided the shape of her day. She felt positioned, more solid somehow.

I think I'll buy the flowers myself, she announced, and it sent a thrill through her to utter the familiar sentence aloud, like she could be some fabulous hostess, a *giver of parties,* a rich old biddy who'd spent her youth in English manors, her middle years surfacing above the wreckage of wars. That, Jamie thought, would be a kind of life. A world historical one. You'd come to the end of this mess and find you'd lived, as it were, *importantly.* It was all well and good to fritter away your twenties explaining the novels of geniuses to entitled nineteen-year-olds, but what would it be to be your own genius, to have lived on the front lines, to navigate worlds that no longer seemed possible at all. Everything was phones now, and websites. Rate My Professors, Mark Zuckerberg's woman-hating media empire, dating apps. It was prestige dramas and four-year campaign cycles and bombs that always dropped somewhere *over there,* in countries where people became broadcast back to you in sepia. Like their lives were less real than yours was, and so it didn't matter if it was your tax dollars used to blow off their sad sepia-tinged limbs.

The whole world had gone flat. The I was thin as paper.

She pictured Woolf now at the lapping edge of the Ouse, stones in her coat pockets, fleeing doom: the promise that whistled behind the sound of air raids. Death. A looming ground invasion in London or at Rodmell, and the bubbling river before her, its water, oh god, frightfully cold. After *Three Guineas,* Virginia's and Leonard's names were scrawled on one of Hitler's lists, you know. Her fear, all said and done, was no miscalculation. The bell tolled for she.

What, meanwhile, had Jamie to show for all her suffering.

No *Mrs. Dalloway,* surely, no Bloomsbury, and no suicide. Or not yet. Mangled hands, yes, and a dissertation her committee despised. A long trail of ex-boyfriends who'd never loved her, an affair with a professor, not to mention the silk cushion of alcoholism she'd perched herself atop to soften the blow of all her dumb, dull desire. There was her childhood, yes, another evacuated vista, and the ghastly sketch drawing of one night in June—hovering, impenetrable veils. Was she damaged, was she ruined? She was alive, after all, and each morning rose from bed to inhale, to exhale. To pulse. So she swam through the roiling ocean of her days. A moment followed this one, and then others still.

But what was the procedural subsistence of time when held up to life?

Repetition.

Her hangover flared. She swallowed back a thrust of vomit.

Now she texted Foster: *bring adderall later? im dying* 😊

Three dots appeared on the left side of her screen and danced for ten seconds, then twenty, then vanished. She placed her phone face down on the counter. No use fixating, and so much to get done before evening, besides.

They were to have a party, she and Edie, a celebration, really: costumes, decorations, the whole lot. Twenty people coming—more if they were very unlucky. Jamie appraised the apartment, wondering how to smash all those bodies inside it. But then, when the night unraveled, the constriction would become its own inducement, would encourage people, oh, to draw near, to whisper to one another above the din, and awaken in them that ache toward privacy. Confinement, in short, prompted sex, and what good was a party that couldn't manage that.

The night before, the women had scoured the place, blast-ing Etta, Nina, Ella, and Dinah on the portable speaker, shout-singing old standards at each other between gulps of raspberry vodka fizzing over with tonic. They'd mixed each drink with numb fingers, chasing lime wedges where they swam between rounded jewels of ice.

On all fours they'd reckoned with each corner, interrogated every cabinet, fluffed pillows and tidied book stacks and polished already spotless surfaces until the rooms spun. In this labor they were meticulous and intent, with the monkish concentration of the very drunk. Edie cried twice. Lately booze left her weepy.

The opening quake was mild: a misting of the eyes and one astonishing tear. She'd been recounting a blind date from the week before, which was foul, first, she told Jamie, because his breath reeked, and later, because his dick curved so violently leftward that she'd not been sure, when they arrived at that determinative moment, how—in her words—to ram it in.

And how did you? asked Jamie.

I slid down, Edie laughed, very slowly onto him, you know . . . real incremental, sort of at an angle.

At which point she figured she might, with caution, begin to bounce. One stroke, two stroke, three, and he'd cum, with no warning or fanfare to speak of. It was all of thirty seconds!

Thank god I'm a condom girl, she said, but what a waste of an Irishman. Not—she hastened to add—some soggy Boston townie (for Edie hated those, being one herself), but the real McCoy, from Dublin . . . or was it Galway? (She'd had a lot of scotch.) The accent alone . . . She trailed off. God. Why don't we ever meet decent men?

Maybe there's none left, Jamie said.

Edie pursed her lips.

She was of course seeing him again the next week.

Disappointed in love, the women instead enumerated and

theatricalized the penile oddities of their hookups. A dick, they agreed—this, the first confession sealing their friendship—could be a staggering thing, eminently holy. To kneel before a truly beautiful one was a joy forever; its loveliness only increasing. It would never pass into nothingness. But Edie seemed always to stumble on penises of the unusual, and the rather usually small, variety. She reported on these in the way you might describe the lumpish gray stuff that could be found pickled in jars at old freak shows.

Jamie had the opposite burden, if burden it could be called. Nearly every man she went home with was enormously hung, and if she recognized the prize of a huge cock—like any respectable slut—there was, nonetheless, a sort of limit point. To feel you'd been cleaved at the root wasn't, in itself, much pleasure, and it seemed, after a fashion, a bit uncivilized to lead an afternoon lecture limping around the front of the classroom with so obvious an injury.

You stingy bitch, hissed Edie.

So these men would recede, then, to be replaced in story by the phantom monoliths of their strange or massive members. Curveball, Hack-job, Noodle, The Destroyer. In recollection, these cocks accrued an experiential density. They came to have their own sovereign histories, as though separable from the men who wielded them. At times, Jamie would imagine them gathering in a library or a beer hall, where they, too, would tally notes on Jamie's and Edie's sexual performances, cheerful and chummy, a flash mob of severed shafts. But Jamie was celibate five months now. Neither woman had orgasmed with a man for the better part of a year.

They never dreamed, or not really, of demanding better, for they knew to set a higher standard would mean, rather than go on a dozen awful dates a year, they'd go on none. And perhaps the better pleasure lay in this performance of disappointment;

perhaps it allowed them to feel romantically superior to their martyrish singledom, making it so they might suppose they were big fish, after all, dropped in a pond too minor or dried up for any meaningful estimation of their intellect, their desirability, their charm. She fought to resist cynicism, but femininity seemed to Jamie inextricable from a curtailment of experience. Like the fabric of beauty, womanhood was lately measured in yard lengths of pain.

Both she and Edie witnessed this affliction in the plot of their mothers' lives—working-class girls of the '70s who'd been animated by women's lib but found, as the years passed, nothing reflected back from it but a sharper image of their own subordination. One day you cried over a photo of Gloria Steinem in front of a crowd of shouting women; the next you were a zombie, two kids, two jobs, night school, and no support checks coming. Was it any wonder the state sided with the deadbeat dads of the world? Was it any wonder all the muckety-mucks in ill-fitting suits took everything you had and called you a Welfare Queen when you asked for it back? When she looked at it, *really looked,* Jamie thought how the state was sort of a deadbeat itself, one more bum who shoved you into an awful circumstance and sat there laughing in your gray zombie face. Like it was your fault, like you had any choice!

Not that they hailed their mothers' struggles. To do so would have been, in some slantwise fashion, to admit defeat, to acknowledge the revolution that was promised had never come. And they required utopia to stay where it sat: just around the bend. Their petty chatter, in turn, concerning these men granted them the continuing possibility that something better was hidden out there, almost within reach, and that all their sorrow was leading up to something, a summit at the top of which fluttered a bright flag in the clear light of a gleaming sun. Happiness.

Yes, there were times Jamie thought all this endless talk of men and sex cheapened her friendship with Edie in an obvious way, like they'd allowed themselves to be lumped into some dreadful club: the Beneath the Botox Tax Bracket Society, say, or the Coalition of Career Girls Who Talk Like *Cathy* Comics. Had they, in turn, given their complexity over to the smoothening god of categorical thinking? Did they repudiate a truer, stranger sort of womanhood by allowing themselves to be reduced to their heterosexual functionality? Had they become two more sad women who saw themselves only in the mirrors men held up to them?

Jamie longed to believe there was something grander between them than cocks and cum, and that, moreover, it was psychologically useful, not to mention emotionally rewarding, to disentangle their resentment of the male race in harmony—men remained, in this way, a problem to be solved. The women acted, then, as their own consciousness-raising dyad, and perhaps it kept them from being anchored in the muck, sedimented in erotic bitterness. So much of life, besides, was just a trouble of timing, and that so great a portion of the day was taken up now with labor meant all your freedom, at least if you were a woman, was oriented around the friction of sex, the psychic real estate required to cultivate one's sexual personae.

But this was what women nearing thirty were meant to do with their time: find someone to love them. Jamie's and Edie's failure of discovery didn't negate the covenant, and they alone could not be held responsible for the proliferation through culture of misogyny, internalized or otherwise. They hadn't invented the marriage contract, had they? Anyhow, it was only with Edie that Jamie allowed herself to be vulnerable, and only with Edie that she sidestepped the droning conversational rhythm of the academy. The women met each other through feeling, and for Jamie this was a radical thing, she who had been divided from that

zone of interest, she who'd been compelled all her life toward
the narrowing horizon of the cerebral.

In Edie's second fit of weeping, the women were discussing
Jamie's likely leave-taking that summer. By May her stipend
would dry up, and she saw no use fighting to stay. She hated
Boston, after all, and by any observable measure the animosity
was mutual.

Lately, she told Edie, she had felt sort of funny. In need of
escape. The city, she said, was closing in on her somehow; its
borders had grown tight. She couldn't seem to breathe properly.

What for? Edie poured another round.

I'm unhappy, I guess—though it's hard for me to tell. She
didn't, she confessed, have much to compare the feeling to. She
didn't remember happiness.

People, Edie considered, frowning, talk a lot of shit. It's not
easy here for you, I know that.

But it's more intense now, said Jamie. Like I'm being
hunted—or, no, that sounds crazy. I have a kind of target on my
back. Like I'm being watched. Is that totally paranoid?

Edie shrugged, then narrowed her eyes.

If she'd told Edie about the night in June, Edie never mentioned it. Sensibly, Jamie kept the Specter secret. The last thing
she needed was to end up in McLean herself.

Maybe, Jamie backpedaled, it's just bad luck. Everything's
been a mess, all of it—the program, my friends, the men, money.

Moving, Edie said, won't fix that. She gulped greedily at her
drink.

Jamie nodded, looping a loose curl around her finger. Yes, she
replied, but it might change me.

For a time she'd thought of expatriating—she liked this
fancy word rich people used to name their own immigration
techniques—having stolen the idea from a college friend. He

taught English now in Shanghai and was dating a sexy, "independently" wealthy New Zealander—a fellow expat. They seemed to be positively surrounded by them. It was all very Lost Generation, thought Jamie. Now she'd decided she could run to London, or Paris (her French was bad but not awful)—maybe even Berlin, though every German she knew was dour and neutered. But when she came down from this high, she remembered she didn't have the cash for an international flight, let alone an entire transatlantic transplantation. It was another castle in the sky: something to turn your eyes up toward while you wrangled your corpse from bed each morning. Instead she dreamed of New York. The rents were comparable, it's just she'd live with more people, and in a smaller place. But who could put a price on proximity to the center of the world? She'd be surrounded by artists and writers, fashion legends, hot men. Here the whole city shut down at midnight. Imagine: real nightlife.

And I'll be able to work, she told Edie, on books I actually give a shit about—to really *work*. I haven't written a poem in four years!

You can't eat a poem, hiccuped Edie. I mean, fuck, you can't even sell one.

Jamie said she'd patch things together, that she could bartend again, and tutor on the side, this time privately—there were so many rich kids in the city. On top of that she'd been scanning sugar daddy sites. Now there'd be no worry over the department finding her out, because even if they did, there was no money coming. Nothing to be rescinded; nothing held above her head. In New York the market was larger, and the men more amenable to a girl of her *type*. Bostonians were bigots, far too conservative. She'd put the sex money away, and if she loathed New York, she would keep running. She was bound to no one, beholden to nothing. She was light as air.

You'll be safe though, right? Edie started, then, to weep, and leaned in to grasp at her.

Jamie said she would.

Near midnight they stumbled to their beds: twin planets, unhooked from orbit.

In light of day, the apartment gleamed too clinically, as if untenanted: the couch too unimprinted on; the cleaning scents too chemical; the dining table overlong, looking, she thought now, like a sort of coffin lid. As she stood there and surrendered to the sluggish tempo of her migraine, Jamie saw how, bare of mess, the place looked scrubbed and shorn as a prepared body. It wouldn't do; no, it wouldn't do at all. There was needed a flash of color, of life. Flowers were the thing, though not white—surely not lilies.

From the fridge she pulled the sisterless half of the previous day's grapefruit. From the bedlam of the silver drawer a knife. From her buzzing skull she summoned the day: there was the meeting with C at noon, and then class, which would be followed by a dreary procession of student conferences. She could grade between each of these, so as to begin drinking the moment she landed back home. She should, she thought, ask the flower vendor—if he was parked with his cart and his blossoms in the twilight of the Square that evening—after the hardiness of the week's dahlias. These would be, she knew—if in his possession at all—at the end of their season. And with the night's cold snap, well. The bouquet would survive the party, yes, but how lovely should it last the long weekend.

A decadence, she told herself, to keep fresh-cut flowers in the house. She'd have to forfeit lunch. But this too was a tidiness. A sea calm settled over her.

The Specter materialized then in the kitchen. It clotted quietly in front of the pantry door.

Are you pleased with yourself? she asked it. If you must know, you scared the shit out of me last night.

Really, it had been a nuisance all week, paying visits nearly every day. In the month after the Specter first appeared, each arrival dropped like a bomb, causing her to scream out in fear, at which point Edie would shout back to ask what had happened, and Jamie would, in turn, be forced to invent the abject flash of a mouse or spider. As time passed, however, the Specter silently assimilated itself into the tedious regime of her dailiness, morphing into a kind of background actor. She became accustomed to its odd heft. It seemed almost companionable, except at night, when she thought it rather rude of the Specter to watch her while she slept.

She knew it was madness, this talking at it like it was a person, and that, surely, seeing the Specter at all was proof positive her mind was dissolving, but here she was.

It never said anything back, though how would it. It had no face, and no limbs, nor any body to speak of. It was a dishwater-colored cloud. But she seemed to think it understood what happened around it and could feel it listening to her while she spoke, which was more than she could say for most of the people she dealt with on a given day. Because of this, she extended some little generosity toward it, but that it never answered her nonetheless nagged.

I decided on dahlias, she said now, but what of peonies? Or maybe orchids?

She'd taken to asking direct questions, thinking this might prompt it to respond. It hovered.

I guess it doesn't matter—the species. It's only a need of contrast I feel. Nothing's fragrant now, besides. If I were more practical—here, another slamming sound down the hall: something fallen, something dropped?—I'd make do with daisies, as they're so much cheaper, but what grown woman sets daisies out for a party? Cute, yes, but not womanly. For the wrists of young girls.

The Specter seemed to shift positions.

Yes, yes, I *know* I'm down to thirty dollars, and I *know* my next paycheck is five days off. I'm not stupid, OK?

The Specter seemed to vibrate behind her. She sighed and turned toward it.

I'm sorry; I'm a bit tense. The dream again . . . but I guess you knew that.

The air around the Specter whirred.

Daisies are no calamity, it's just I love dahlias. The Empress Josephine kept them at Malmaison, you know. They were dangerously rare in Europe then: she swore her gardeners to secrecy on their existence in her gardens. On pain of death. Imagine! I was reading Jamaica Kincaid on them the other night. I couldn't sleep, no thanks to you. Sorry. Anyhow it was the "naturalist" Francisco Hernandez—one of the colonialist "marauders," as Kincaid might call him—who "discovered" them among the Aztecs. Some say Montezuma favored them above all others—

The Specter inched nearer.

—but so much of the dahlia's origin is tangled in myth, really. That the Toltecs and Aztecs used them medicinally seems to have been disproven. Probably they were just weeds.

The Specter deflated slightly.

I know. It's all sort of boring, isn't it? Or maybe not boring, but I don't guess you're into flowers . . .

Her left hand steadied the ruby half-moon of the grapefruit. In her right, the blade was poised above its pulpy flesh. A murderous tableau. Another bang down the hall, a thudding sound, loud but dull.

So's this your doing? Or one of your ghost friends?

Silence.

Her grip on the knife tightened. She was too aimless, she knew, too unnoticing. She'd left herself imperiled, and for what reason but that she was talking with an apparition no one else seemed to see. Again.

Hello? No reply.

In a horror movie this cry would be no better than a calling card for the killer, her death warrant: signed, sealed, delivered.

Stupid, she whispered, stupid, stupid, stupid.

She inhaled deeply . . . counting four and holding her breath at the top, two, three, four. And exhale, slow, three, four—meditatively: box breathing. The Specter synced to her rhythm. Probably the noises were nothing. She'd named her little hallucination, for Christ's sake! Too jittery lately, she was, in body and mind. A nervous nelly, her mother said.

And no help from you, she sighed.

The Specter solidified through what she thought of as its middle.

If it *must* hang around now, though, she had a duty to be honest with it. Not cruel, of course, no use in that—but honest. It *had* been keeping her awake nights. It *did* frighten her at times. The fact that the Specter was surely no more than a psychological knot didn't require her to prostrate herself before it. She was no supplicant. Paralyzed by recent history, perhaps, but not totally gone, and *not,* she insisted, some dumb stooge in her own life.

She pushed the knife against the fruit's softness. The blade slid in. Pink juices swelled: obscene. She saw she'd pulled a plate out already. Atop it sat one boiled egg, beside which was a dollop of mayo, cracked peppercorn spackling its viscous whiteness. In the French press, black coffee, still steaming.

When had she done this? Now it was 8:28. She'd lost more time.

Her hands went on separating citrus segments, flesh from rind. The juice stung where it spilled over her fingers, pooling and sucking at the battered shore of her cuticles. Where the hangnail had been, the sharpest ache. The acid odor flooded her sinuses, clarifying something in her headache's shape. Such stark reminders, hangovers, of the awful mess—this being a body. Held there between the ill edges of form and made to face it: decay. No escape.

Now, her hand stilled itself. The cutting board was gone slick.

Another slam. The world cracked. Behind her she felt the Specter searching. Attuned to hers, its fear rose.

Edie?

She peered down the hall, finding nothing there; the bathroom too was empty. She checked behind the curtain, throwing it open, as though speed would guard her from what she felt sure was waiting there. In her room five faces stared back at her. Postcards pinned above the desk. Plath, Woolf, and Sexton. Morrison and Nin.

Your carousel of suicide girls, said Edie.

Toni and Anaïs didn't kill themselves!

But I bet they thought about it, Edie countered.

The basement door remained locked. Nothing under the bed, and no one stuffed in the closet. In the kitchen the Specter had vanished, and just when they'd locked into a rhythm, just when its presence began to cheer her.

She took up the knife. Perhaps she *was* going a bit batty, she thought, perhaps what had happened in June was a mental disjointment, a fall, maybe what it was was something being knocked out of place. How absurd to be in thrall to the past! Then, of course, the past was not dead. Any border between it and the present was a fiction, a fable conjured to cover the shame of where we came from. The humiliation of having been in process, having been, as it were, a person. Each history is an account of having won, of the self having come to this particular moment, where it was full, and discrete, and utterly unbridled. Here or there the past, like a boa, would surface, and heave its wriggling weight across your time-reddened body, clutching at your fragile throat. Choking the words out. We were only tenuously tethered to the now: time's most pitiable vessels, Jamie thought, chipped at by every minute, every second, then eventually the years would lay themselves like marble slabs on your chest. Possibility leaked and ebbed until there was nothing but the minor kernel of what you'd always been. Something small. Something bound.

An energy surrounded her now, a force, and it was not, she knew, the bland mass of the Specter. Her breath hooked in her neck, becoming labored, dragging around inside her as though nettled. The hairs on her arms were cilia, darting anxiously to attention.

Again, a thud.

She did not cry out. She was petrified, as in gone to stone, and while she coiled motionlessly into herself, the atmosphere of the kitchen shifted—a barometric disturbance, like the pressure dropping in the center of a cyclone. She tried to swallow her fear but could not, and a trembling seized her; the moments seemed to launch themselves past her body in slow motion, syrupy rockets.

With a great effort she looked down. The blade was angled in such a way that she was forced to meet her reflection in its surface. A mask of a face stared back, a dead thing, with its gaping mouth and emptied eyes. Behind its head the kitchen ceiling hovered, with cracking paint and yellowed plaster behind that. Then a sort of shimmer: some fog of motion. Like heat above the hood of a car. Her whole body contracted. She was trapped. And cold. She tasted bile.

There it was. The grinning mouth, with its flash of teeth, that white gleam of bone. The smile from the dream. Which was from the night in June, she saw now. Attached to something, or rather someone; this had happened, she murmured, the infiltration. I remember it. And laughter. Then force.

WHAT?

A shout from the living room; a violence.

The knife slipped. A slash of wet red split the tip of her left thumb. The shriek that flung itself from her was instinctive only. She felt nothing.

Oh god! Edie was on the threshold, her makeup half done.

Jamie watched blood slip from the wound like a comet's tail. Indecently, her life slid around the basin of the sink. She admired her own downpour.

Edie's face was ash pale.

Honey, what happened?

She turned on the tap, letting the water run cold before shoving Jamie's hand beneath the faucet. Edie's touch brought Jamie back to her body. She coughed suddenly, as if chucking up something lodged.

I don't know, she said. I . . . must have lost my grip. What are you still doing here? Didn't you hear me calling?

Edie smirked. I was too hungover for the gym. Puked all night! I had my earbuds in until just now. Who were you talking to out here?

Jamie looked out the window.

Oh . . . I was on the phone. With Foster. We need Adderall later.

That shit'll kill you, Edie laughed. She was all action now, wadding, with one hand, a mass of paper towels to stanch the flow.

It's nothing, Edie, really. A little cut.

Jamie began to drift from the scene, watching her roommate attend to the department store dummy of her body. She saw her arm go limp. Edie swatted her back to attention. The wound was deep, she told Jamie, she might have lost her thumb.

Jamie nodded.

Suck on it a second. I'll get a Band-Aid.

Jamie slid the thumb between her lips, letting her tongue linger on the bloody opening. Searching. Lustful. A blush of copper, like rolling a penny in your mouth. When they were girls, she and her sister flattened coins on the train tracks beside their mother's house. How they'd cackled at the melting outline of Lincoln's face, like it was his fault, and not theirs, he'd gone all wobbly—that it was *he* who'd somehow permitted the borders of his body to fail. How embarrassing.

Jamie thought now what a fright he must have looked when the shot rang out. A mess of brain matter all over, splat! Like a Pollock. And his wife beside him, wondering where the rest of her husband's head had gone. Maybe it had just *done that.*

In her mouth, blood slicked her teeth, pooling between her gums and underneath her thick tongue. The sensation wasn't displeasing. It seemed a proof of something—that she was a body, after all, and even if she *was* losing her mind, she was anchored, still, to form. This imposed its immovable limit. What happened next was unanticipatable, but her life, as yet, was still subject to certain laws of physics.

Edie wrapped her thumb back together and glanced suspiciously at the assemblage of wrappings on Jamie's other fingers.

You've got almost a whole set, she said.

When she finished, she shoved two twenties into Jamie's intact hand discreetly, like there were others in the apartment with them: tiny bankers logging their transactions. Edie said to take the money and not protest—put it toward the party, she told Jamie, or whatever. Flowers, maybe, or some tonic? More limes for sure. I'll grab vodka and beer. Don't worry about anything. Tonight, she went on, is supposed to be fun!

Jamie smiled then at Edie, meaning it, or wanting to, and the light from the window latched on her face, drawing some peculiarity from its outline.

A touch of the bird about you, Edie said once, some other drunken night. A bit sparrowish. Like you have hollow bones. A weightless quality . . . continuous motion.

Jamie's eyes darted now to the stove clock. Edie was late.

I'm late, said Edie, and vanished.

C urtis was a mess of fallen acorns, battered shells scattered garishly on the sidewalk, the curb, the cracked ugly tar of the street. They crunched delightfully underfoot. Above her the sky remained unblemished. As she looked, three gulls broke its cloudless monotony. Past them, the sun, bulging and smug. She could feel it looking.

Every other house had a cop car in the drive. She didn't see how this was possible, but felt it was dodgy to investigate further. The leftover vehicles were branded by loud, antagonizing bumper stickers: HOME OF THE FREE <u>BECAUSE</u> OF THE BRAVE, and WARNING! POLITICALLY INCORRECT ZONE, and, most common, BACK THE BLUE, superimposed over an American flag cast in shades of turquoise, slate, cerulean, and navy. At the edge of a yard on Fairmount a sign informed her she was NO LONGER TRESPASSING: YOU ARE A TARGET. The words were stacked above an image of crosshairs.

She wondered who such pronouncements were meant to hail, who these homeowners thought they were accusing, and of what. The idea that Davis Square, of all places, was a cradle of chaos, or soon would be, was a reactionary wet dream: total fantasy. The interlopers in the area were bookish Tufts kids and cyclists in freaky toe shoes. Anyhow, everyone knew the cops ran this town. It was never a question, nor the fact that said cops were rank with corruption, Mafia ties, the 1919 strike, John Mulligan, and all that. Boston's reputation was as an intellectual capital, because it was stuffed to bursting with universities, but its bedrock was townies all the way down, and the inhabitants the city wanted to claim for its face—the financiers and students, the Brahmins—were only passing through, or preferred the city part-time.

SMILE, she was instructed, YOUR ON CAMERA. A grinning yellow orb—one apparently inclined to homophonic confusion—stared through her.

In her pocket her phone pinged. No need to look; she knew it was the Professor. Another ping. He'd started early today. The thought of seeing him or looking at his messages exhausted her. Occasionally she would go to block his number and find her hands trembling when she opened his contact. They'd go numb. She would travel elsewhere.

The phone waited in her jeans, an unlit fuse.

She turned onto Holland. The bus stop was a ways away still. She walked with purpose, jogging nearly, as crunchy goth music rushed into her ears. She should make the bus in good time, she told herself. No—she *would* make it in time, and the ride would be uncomplicated, and she'd disembark in the Square, smilingly, just in front of the old theater, with perhaps twenty minutes to spare, minutes she would use to grab a coffee at the lesbian café. She could sit in back, reading, or perhaps people watching, quietly hollowing herself. This small window would be the only unplanned sequence of her day. She could become an urn of time, but voluntarily, and time would pass through her, opening her, summoning a universe entirely apart from her dead, bland, cramped life.

Ping.

A third text landed. A fourth. She hadn't let the Professor fuck her in over a year.

Officially speaking the café wasn't *for* lesbians, but it was owned and staffed by a ropy crew of self-proclaimed Dykes to

Watch Out For, who all had consonant, wonderfully genderless names: Rock, Oak, River, Coal. She thought this quite beautiful, as if the shop were constructed and animated by a reassuringly intractable collective of natural phenomena. They sported butchy Mia Farrows and militaristic buzz cuts, going about their business loose gestured and slouchy in men's workwear: Dickies, Carhartt, Patagonia. Though Jamie rarely went in for other women, she found it all rather sexy, especially how their very presence acted as a middle finger held up to the homophobic logic of Boston, its hatred of any spectacle of difference.

Four long blocks ahead stood the bus stop. People milled and bobbed around it, a kit of pigeons.

Something behind her cracked and boomed, sounding like the shot of a pistol.

Once at the café, she thought, trying now to run—for it was the bus, she saw when looking back, only the sound of its engine—she would invite the dream to reenter her. Twenty minutes seemed time enough to solve the trouble of her life. She saw she hadn't properly sat with it, this perilous fact of her being-ness, for any length in the months since the dream began, for she feared what she'd find, but needed (she knew now) to rid herself of the Specter, to exorcise it. At moments she liked thinking she was no longer wading through the waves of her life alone, that it accompanied her as a sort of guide, but in her heart she understood it wasn't right, the Specter's being there, it wasn't sanitary somehow.

It signaled a disintegration of the border between her mind and its outside, and she didn't wish to go mad, really she didn't, and there was an anarchic energy surrounding the Specter, some dark matter of disorder creeping around its edges and reaching toward her.

She longed again to feel things, to sleep—to truly sleep!—and be in her sensual body, to love and fuck, but as it was, she lived in a stricken frigidity. She knew it was something to do with these gaps, the infirmity of her memory, her refusal of looking. An analyst would have a field day.

The bus overtook her. She waved frantically at it, shouting at the driver to PLEASE STOP, and she saw passengers near the front begin to gesture to him and point back at her. There seemed to be an argument going on, and she was certain salvation had fled her, but then the bus tires screeched, and the vehicle sat there resentfully rumbling, so she scurried to the entrance and up the stairs, showing her pass to the driver and smiling, first, at him, and then at the crowd hunched in the walkway between the seats. *Thank you*, she mouthed, thinking meanwhile how horribly nihilistic she'd been lately about the city, how low she'd allowed her estimation of its denizens to sink. Look what they'd just done for her, how they'd halted the very wheels of urban transit for her benefit! Saints, really, they were, possibly even making themselves late to wherever *they* were going, all to ease the arduous journey of a fellow wanderer.

Gathered now as a mass, they sallied forth.

Time stuttered and slowed: the bus crawled up Holland, trapped in traffic. Through the window she watched the deli and hair salon—the one run by the gossipy Greek sisters who'd recently cut Jamie's hair into a chic bob—bleed behind her, then the slice joint, the credit union, the mystifying "wellness" "center." Finches darted between bushes while the scenery smudged past. As they edged closer to the Square, Obama signs slipped in among the others. FORWARD 2012. The ambiguousness of this messaging seemed ominous. Where was it they were meant to get to, and what waited there? A cardinal alit on a dingy mailbox. They were the same shade of red. In the bus the sour smell of morning breath drifted among the bodies. Beneath this, cheap perfume, the sort you'd swipe at CVS. A thin metallic gardenia.

Ping.

She felt a shift in the air behind her. Like the electrical charge earlier.

Ping.

The bus stopped in a swath of shadow; the window became a mirror. In it a woman stared back at her. Jamie met the woman's gaze and held it, daring her to keep looking. She felt a spark of fury and nearly decided to say something before realizing, with a dumb clanging, that the face, again, was her own. She'd looked at herself so little in these months her image had become alien—like looking at an old photograph, from a time when you were another person. Maybe it was her new hair. Maybe she'd not made peace with her own transformation. Her anger fell away: dead skin.

Something pressed against her ass then, hot and fleshy, a hand cupping and grasping, two fingers spreading and searching. She screamed, dropping her bag. Its contents splashed across the rubber mats lining the bus floor. But when she turned, whoever had been there was gone. Had she imagined her assailant, or was it like the Specter, something only she could sense? Anything seemed possible. But no—her skin throbbed where it had been touched. Invaded. Probably a pickpocket.

Now no one bent to help her. Across the aisle an old woman dozed, Coke-bottle glasses dangling from her neck on a chain. A young mother eyed Jamie warily, bouncing a baby on one knee. How loudly had Jamie shrieked? A few paces down a group of teens snickered. If before she had been their kin, she'd become the worst a city offered: a screamer, someone capable of entirely unpredictable acts. As she gathered what had fallen, shame settled on her, an oily film. She felt sticky and clotted, and her face was red—she could feel the heat. There seemed a thousand eyes on her, sucking and tugging at her surfaces, little tentacles. She floated above the scene, thinking to evaporate along the ceiling of the bus.

Ping.

By the time they reached the Square she was back in her body, but the traffic had held them longer than she'd thought. 9:30—no time for coffee. She ran for the commuter rail.

Allan found Jamie marking papers on the train.

AH! he yelled.

He was in the habit of identifying others in the program by surname alone, like they'd been deployed together and were in active battle, which, in a sense, they were. Each day the lines of one's intellectual territory were redrawn, and every claim made—particularly if uttered on campus—was material evidence, an indication you were a rightful tenant in the life of the mind, or else weren't, and were a fraud, a fissure in the system. Thus were you exposed, an insidious contaminant requiring expulsion.

Allan wasn't much older than Jamie but walked bent into himself, as if guarding something precious at his center. She and Jean (R!), the other woman in their cohort, teased him for this, pointing out that he and Professor Bradshaw—who'd taught in the department forty-three years now—might be twins. Allan had a voice that sounded like a put-on, a kind of cosmic, sonic joke humming somewhere in the space between the dulcet tones of Gilbert Gottfried and the gravelly texture of the oldest man outside the deli catcalling you.

Nominally, Allan was a scholar of Shakespeare (whom he called "Willie"), but his fixations, in the main, were with matters of bodily disturbance: plagues, the humors, scatological comedy. He seemed to like Shakespeare mostly because Shakespeare was a pervert, but Allan sought the grotesque in all things. In their modernism seminar he was drawn to Joyce, not because of the Irish question or Molly Bloom's oracular sensuality or the mythological revisionism of the text's relation to Homer, but because Joyce, too, was a degenerate, a true savant of excrescences, particularly those oozing from his wife, Nora.

For reasons unknown, Allan was always trying to get Jamie to read Philip Roth's 1972 novella *The Breast,* in which a neurotic professor wakes to find he's become one enormous boob. Thus far she'd demurred. Allan goaded every woman he encountered, which didn't help him when it came to sorting sex, something he did not have and seemed to never have had. But unlike many of their male colleagues, he took what women said on the subject of literature seriously. He wouldn't read women novelists unless forced—smart skirts, he called them—but nonetheless he believed in an analytical duty to listen to women when they spoke in his presence.

I've got grading, Jamie told him, not looking up.

She gestured at her papers, the red pen, the seat beside her—filled already by her bursting tote bag. With him it was best to be friendly but firm. Out-and-out animus he took as a challenge.

C'moooon . . . what gives!

She glanced back. Allan was grinning and wagging his eyebrows like a cartoon pest.

She pinched the bridge of her nose and massaged upward, fanning her fingers toward her temples.

Fine, he shouted, I'll sit over here.

Allan's only volume was LOUD.

Jamie rolled her eyes as he planted himself opposite her. Outside, the city fell away from them. She liked Allan, though, she did—maybe because nearly no one else seemed to, and knowing this brought on a melancholic feeling, it made her root for him. He was an underdog in an ecosystem of climbers, and yet he wasn't there to schmooze or impress, only ever to learn. This was crucial. He loved his studies with a fierceness, despite being always behind in the work that was also hers, that was also all of theirs. He was a slow, cautious reader, and what he knew he knew without doubt, while what he hated was worse than trash, it was dumpster scum, an affront to the hallowed groves of academe.

The others loathed Allan because he lacked their primness, the hemming accoutrements of cultural class, which was to say he proved even a man who intellectualized poop jokes could rise without too much trouble into their ranks. In this he reminded Jamie of herself, for they were both usurpers, even if Allan's trouble was not economic, as hers was, for he'd grown up alongside Los Angeles royalty, had studied *Hamlet* with the pampered enfants terribles of A-list actors, and had partied only a few months back with a recently famous alt-pop diva whose songs Jamie sang in the shower almost every day.

Nothing going on up here, he'd said of her, crooking a dry finger to his skull.

Jean approached.

Can I sit?

Jamie saw she'd get no more work done.

Please, she said. Allan was about to game his *Ulysses* talk. I can't bear it alone.

Allan wanted, he told the women, to lead the class in a group recitation of Joyce's letters to his wife—notoriously filthy letters, he reminded them, brimming with *fuck*s and *cunt*s and *arse*s, letters where Joyce named Nora his "dirty little fuckbird" and insisted he'd "know Nora's fart anywhere." They were funny, Jamie thought, but what they had to do with the "Aeolus" sequence of Joyce's book she hadn't a clue.

Hugh won't mind, Allan said then, pushing his glasses up, he's like any man: he has a dirty mind.

It's a risk.

This was Jean, a pragmatist at base, a Pre-Raphaelite beauty and post-colonialist scholar with an utterly unbending manner. Jamie found her dazzling.

It could backfire, Jean said presently. It might make Hugh think you don't respect his authority. It could piss him off, and you've done that with the rest of the faculty. Is it worth provoking the last one in your corner?

Jamie wondered if this was a dig by Jean at Jamie's recent decision not to ask the department's sole confessionalist to stand on her dissertation committee. Jamie had been the woman's research assistant three years earlier, and had found the process tiresome and emotionally thorny. She'd become privy to all manner of interdepartmental gossip she'd wanted no part of. There was a sense, with this scholar, that what Jamie did in her work was or should be secondary to the psychodrama of cocktail parties, conferences, and affairs. Of course it was entirely possible Jamie just hadn't wanted the woman to discover Jamie's own ongoing affair, but in any case, she hadn't liked the way other people's lives seemed to dribble from the confessionalist's mouth like oil, viscous and irrevocable.

Not all men, said Jamie, think the way you do, Allan. Not everyone wants to talk buboes and clit dicks all the time.

Think again, Allan said. You don't hear these boys when you two aren't around. It's cum all the way down, baby.

He cackled. Jamie narrowed her eyes. She and Jean had, over time, become inadvertent wardens of Allan, guiding him, in their sidewise fashion, through the social modulations of the program. They were his defenders when the assaults felt unfair; they the instructors who pushed him to read work by writers who weren't dead and white and men. They, too, his cheerleaders—encouraging him to date again, for he seemed so awfully lonely. But in the process he came to feel like their enormous child, a wailing, gnashing creature they'd woken one day to find in the spare bedroom of their lives, and at times like this, the burden was heavy, his prodding would dig beneath their skin.

What's the point? Jamie asked then. You think we haven't said "fuck" before? Is it some revelation; does the exercise illuminate something about *Ulysses* by us acknowledging Joyce enjoyed eating his wife's shit?

Farts, shouted Allan. It was her farts, not shit!

Whatever. It's how you want to disrupt things for the purpose of disruption, which feels—to me anyhow—like a time suck. And if that's all it is, I'd rather be elsewhere, getting my work done.

But it's not that, Allan protested, because it lifts the veil. It proves we're just the same if you boil it: we're meat. Animals. Acting on instinct while pretending there's a prevailing logic. We're vessels for these disgusting processes—mastication, digestion, expulsion of gases, ejaculation—but we cover them in perfume, in words like "epistemology" and "abjection." We're gooey, nasty, sex-starved freaks. We're ineluctably violent, we kill and rape, we beat other human bodies to pulp. We eat the creatures we dominate, knowing we're no better than them. Just leopards in cheap suits. We destroy the world because we aren't satisfied with our own arrogance. Homer knew it. Joyce knew it. Your dear dead Woolf? Maybe less so. Here—he indicated the campus, which appeared outside the train window—we split ourselves from it, fake like we're floating brains, but there's nothing separating us from the maggots. Nothing but silly little words we set out in rows and raze whole forests to print and toss. We're right down in the grime. Worse, really, because we've made it unnatural, we've used a greater power to conceal our depravity. The obscene nature of human life.

Jean's eyes had glazed over, and rather than answer, Jamie unlocked her phone—an endless series of messages lurked there, tiny, maddening flares bursting across the screen's glassy surface, all courtesy, of course, of the Professor. He no longer beguiled her, though, and she didn't want him, and besides had felt nothing near desire for months. There was a smallness in his desperation, an effeminacy; she couldn't see him, any longer, as the man he purported to be. The Professor, as it happened, was no iron-fisted daddy. He was a groveler, needful and leaky, and she saw now how his theater of domination was just that, play-acting, and his begging a diminishment. She deleted his texts without reading them.

Listen, H, you've *got* to read *The Breast*.

I know. Jamie returned with her red scalpel to the paper at hand.

It's Roth doing Kafka. Kepesh is this neurotic Everyman, see, like I am—Allan laughed—and in a way, he's a proxy for the flailing American intellectual class, but as usual, Roth is in on the joke. It's a takedown of the headshrinkers for one thing . . .

Now Jamie wished the Specter would interrupt the moment, that it would deign to fill her ears with cotton wool, or wrap Allan's face in its fog, silencing him until they'd come to their stop. His voice went on droning for what seemed hours while the words on the page before her swam viciously through their surrounding whiteness. Piranhas in foam. Suddenly, the three were stood in a semicircle outside the library, but how had they gotten there? Jamie watched herself saying goodbye, and Allan again made her promise to read the Roth, which she acquiesced to, smiling.

We'll see you tonight, Jean called back.

What for?

The party, said Jean, studying her face. Oh . . . you're kidding. Ha.

Right.

As Jean and Allan staggered toward the slate cube at the end of the path, Jamie felt the separation like the release of a valve.

Allan's battery of words bubbled from the place they'd gathered in her and started to seep, almost imperceptibly, back out. She floated there a moment, wan and nunnish, then set out to trudge the rest of the way up the long hill toward the department.

It was Friday, a holiday weekend, and the students were costumed already for the evening, many with faces hidden, some with perilous expanses of bare flesh exposed to the cold. Here, a Roman senator with a headpiece doubling as a beer bong; there, a sort of bunny woman in fishnets and a little fluffy bunny tail. She was reapplying lipstick far too dark for ten in the morning. The contrast between their adornments and Jamie's pilling, cheap blazer and sensible pumps cast the scene in surreality: the campus seemed poised on the edge of some orgiastic expectancy; all the world around her had the animating quality of a gasp. Already, empty beer bottles littered the green, and Jamie understood this to mean her class would be chaos, there would be no end to the no-shows during her afternoon conferences. She should have canceled them; perhaps she still would.

Academic life lately seemed to Jamie largely a technique of fleeing the first person. Or persuading yourself you had. Then when people *ooh*ed and *aah*ed at your torturous disarticulations of *The Waste Land* or *Ulysses* or *Mrs. Dalloway,* you delighted at the opportunity to act like it was in The Text all along, and you were but a scientist of words who had dissected the brilliance already there, and which was quite evident to the truly refined observer.

She thought she heard laughter behind her, but found, on turning back, no one there. Still, she had a sense of being watched. She looked up into the trees and saw, with a shudder, that the wild turkeys had returned and were tracking her movements below them with black button eyes. Their bodies were a lesson in shapes: a series of variations on the oval, rounded all over except where scaly legs poked out from a forest of feathers, the scrotal extrusions of their rosy wattles. Since she'd arrived in the city they had frightened her, and rightly so, for when first she came here she hadn't known how massive they were, or how violent. She was shocked, too, to find they could fly. In flocks they invaded the campus each fall, terrorizing unsuspecting freshmen, who were, as yet, too trusting—who didn't know not to approach the gabbing beasts without fear.

As Jamie reached the English building she saw one pacing in front of the sliding glass of the entrance. It seemed to be trying to break in. Despite its girth, the turkey wasn't heavy enough to trigger the automatic doors. Behind their mirrory panels stood a gaggle of wide-eyed undergraduates, mouths gaped, one or two laughing nervously.

At least, Jamie thought, these knew better than to plunge into its path straight on.

Get! she screamed, coming up on the turkey and throwing her heaviest book beside it. Get!

The text landed on the concrete like a slap, and the bird peered back at her, its gaze a senseless abyss. She hadn't expected to erupt like this; hadn't known this sort of feeling lived in her. But the creature was a bully, and she didn't have time for its antics today. She yelled again and waved her arms, making herself large, intimating she too might be able to fly.

The turkey clucked and fussed at her, bobbing its head, squaring up. The students took advantage of the distraction and darted out from behind it. There was a look of indecision in its glance, like it thought it might unearth more pleasure chasing them, but it stopped instead in front of Jamie, staring with escalating concentration into her face. It seemed then almost to smile, and in its expression was something uncanny and familiar. It sent a shock through her body; she felt herself split up. Its eyes glowed, and though she knew it was only an angle of light she felt disoriented, and lost her nerve, and the creature reared back as if to charge at her, as if to come flailing toward her, aiming for her eyes and all her available skin.

Ivan appeared. He stomped on the concrete behind it, and rather than advance, the bird began to fly. It soared above her head and went on, settling somewhere ten or twelve yards off among a few others in a beech tree. With a little wave, Ivan smiled and walked away. She exhaled. The turkeys, in their roosts, eyed her coldly. She stepped through the open doors.

C had arranged two seats in front of his desk. He lounged in one, and with a stubby finger, indicated the other, as if Jamie couldn't solve this riddle of placement, as if she might perch in some other, more insurrectionary position. There were two south-facing windows in back of the desk, but heavy damask shut out the light, and with this and the dark mahogany of the furniture and the thick damp Turkish rugs sheeting the marble floors of the room, the space had a sort of bordello feeling.

Come in, he said, and how are you?

Like they were in the middle of a conversation already; as if he were continuing a line of questioning that began without her present.

Fine, she lied. Busy. You know.

I do, said C, and the chaos only increasing near the end of things. Time passing. So on . . .

Mm.

He was ruddy and imposing, thick through the middle with decades of high-functioning alcoholism, but handsome enough if you'd stomach a snob. As she watched his mouth move, last night's vodka swished in her gut. C's liquid present seemed an ill omen of her possible future. He was American, Omaha-bred, but spoke with a peculiar British lilt, like maybe he'd studied at Cambridge or spent a few years teaching in London. He had a nomadic air. He wore small round glasses like the sort you'd see on an academic in a movie, the kind you never really called "glasses," but rather "spectacles," and as he edged his chair closer, he removed them and rubbed a palm against his eyes. An unchaste gesture, the way it left his face nude before her. At last she saw his eyes, as in actually *saw* them, and found there an impossible blue, so pale they were nearly colorless, like God forgot to finish shading him in.

As I'm sure you've gathered, said C presently, you're here to discuss . . .

His face began to open and shut like a Pez dispenser, plastic, stuttering, but only the occasional phrase surfaced. Jamie saw herself dig in her bag and pull out a pen, a notebook: like watching a TV on mute. Her hands uncapped the pen. She wrote. At a distance, the words were loops and scratches; they seemed to have no meaning in them at all. C clasped his palms behind his head and leaned back. His legs were splayed. A lumpy swelling stuffed the crotch of his pants. Not much to crow about there. Meanwhile her legs crossed themselves daintily at the ankle. She saw her mouth bite at one of her last unbandaged fingers. C stared blankly at her hands and asked if she'd considered hypnosis.

Jamie could hear Edie's laughter now. Hypnosis, she'd shriek, what a scam! I mean honestly . . . What you need is to figure out what you really want, she'd say, and if you *really* want to stop doing something, you stop! Without giving money to some con artist—who's probably a sex pest to boot. The nerve of that man . . . he barely knows you! How much fucking money does he rake in every year at that place anyway?

The university was always *that place* to Edie, who thought the whole program ridiculous, too high stress, and interested mainly in making smart people less employable. For what?

Jamie herself admitted there were no tenure-track jobs. Lots of highfalutin words to say: "book good." Or "book bad." It didn't warrant the respect of its proper name, *that place*.

What Jamie wouldn't admit to C was that she *had* considered hypnosis, and after some deliberation found the thought of surrendering her body—her silent, absolutely inert body—to the hands of some quack disorienting, disturbing even. C of course was a strict Freudian. Naturally he believed any hitch might be solved by laying a woman on a couch. Or was it a chaise longue? Jamie found it silly you weren't meant to look at the analyst during, like he was a priest in the confessional box, or like you were so ashamed of your life that eye contact was unthinkable. It was all rather ham-fisted.

I hadn't thought of it, she said.

C, she reminded herself, had married a barely former undergraduate after Jamie's first year in the program. When the wedding was announced, Jamie and the office administrators clucked over the girl's good fortune. How mousy they thought her, how intellectually unexceptional—Jamie had been the girl's teaching assistant, in a class called "Psychoanalysis and the Sedimentation of Modern Subjectivity," led, of course, by C. That he'd sniffed out such an uninspiring specimen from a horde of ninety-six Jamie never understood, but something in her admired the girl's audacity, the feat of such a plain creature securing a chic MRS degree scant months after graduation. What luck.

There were whispers among the faculty and the graduate students, but as far as anyone could see, there'd been no evidence to suggest C had transgressed sexual or other boundaries during the time the girl—who was by that point not The Girl but The Fiancée—was his student. By all appearances they'd come together in the summer after her senior year, when she was not only not a student any longer, but also a twenty-two-year-old woman. She was grown, and the engagement, anyhow, wasn't announced until the fall. If the timing of their union carried an odor of wickedness, there was nothing to prove what they'd done had been wrong. And what condemnation could Jamie have laid over them? At the time of the announcement, she was still fucking the Professor. She was only twenty-three.

C leaned forward conspiratorially.

She's had troubles, you know—my Mary. She sees hers every Monday. I could refer you . . .

Oh, said Jamie through tight lips, taking care to sound incurious, wishing to avoid any arduous elaborations. She ran a hand through her hair.

She's highly symptomatic, C continued, you have to understand this . . . she's always hiccuping and coughing, then add to this the nail biting—well, I see you know all about that.

He edged closer. Jamie was in her body again, feeling the heat of him: his animal mass. His knees brushed hers. She suppressed a queasy sharp feeling in the hollow of her belly, but behind this, a wordless pulse of desire. C's magnetism at last laid itself bare, and she saw it was not his intelligence or cosmopolitanism, or even the milky certainty he could promise an economic security she'd never come near to. It was the brute fact of his beastliness, the way you had no trouble picturing how he'd fuck you, silent and hard, against a classroom wall. That he was disgusting, and hairy, that he was a lush and bound only to infidelity were signal flares inextricable from this allure, for his eroticism repudiated the cerebral, it bucked against his cultivated surface, acting, instead, as a reminder of the primal orientation of life toward more life.

Between sucking on her hands, he said—tracing two burning fingers across Jamie's thigh—and the esophageal tics, Mary's mouth is always full of something! (Laughter.) She didn't speak a word for weeks! *Aphonia,* he offered in a maudlin whisper, like

Freud's Dora. But the doctor fixed that . . . eradicated all sorts of nasty quirks.

Thick with scotch, his breath drifted toward her.

He was the Professor all over again, and her capacity for seduction—this tedious possibility of allowing herself to be seduced by him—left her hot with humiliation. She hated him. She hated him, and when she shoved her chair back, its feet screeched desperately off the rug and against the floor with a kind of wounded sound—a hare in a trap.

C screwed his mouth up, like he'd tasted something bitter. Then he chuckled, in his fey way, as if pleased with himself, or like he'd let her in on an especially wanton secret, as, after all, he had. She was not above idle gossip, but the thought of being wed to a man who relayed to his subordinates the rhythm of your darkest hours caused something essential in her to shrivel. How could someone who'd sworn to honor and protect you make your suffering so small? Another violence: that the one man meant, on occasion, to hold your pain for you would witness it and feel a sort of smugness, like your experience of that pain was somehow beneath his station, below the regard of his evidently quite superior psyche.

She wondered whether His Mary had chosen silence, if perhaps she decided on it each morning, like choosing which shoes to wear for the weather. Perhaps every day to Mary looked like rain. Or maybe, just maybe, she had nothing left to say to this sneering man, seeing how full of words he seemed always to be, how stuffed and bursting their house must be with all his words.

Then Jamie understood he'd told her this to convince himself they were in cahoots, that, by making her notary to His Mary's "disturbances," he felt they'd together settled something about the fatuous customs of wives, or the constitutional fluidity of the wifely mind. As if the very fact of the matrimonial bond rendered a woman more porous—a devoted but capricious sponge.

And as he went on, in his bragging manner, with his paisley scarf and gleaming oxfords and hot dense breath stinking the office up, Jamie pressed her lips painfully together, inclining her head, in the hopes he'd see from her gestures that she'd heard what he'd said, without in turn believing she agreed with any of it.

Behind him the Specter appeared, gathering mass, humming in its strange cloud like a live wire. She flinched. She'd never seen it out in this manner, mixed up in the usual world. A minor house-guest, she'd thought: bound, as in a ghost story, between the walls of her apartment. She couldn't let on that she was seeing it now, hovering over C's shoulder. This was easy—C was high on his own supply—but she was frozen. She kept her eyes trained on his. In her lap, her right hand pinched the skin above the tendons on her left. Little crescent indentations rose redly there. She couldn't hear C above the buzzing. Like walking through a cloud of gnats in summer.

What was it doing here? Why had it followed. At home it had begun, almost, to feel like a pet, but she was at work. This was her job. Its presence now seemed to indicate an expansion of its powers, or a diminishment of her own; a furtherance of her psychic deterioration. A spot of blood pooled on her hand while C continued nattering. This went on a long time, and it began to seem the Specter would blot out all the light in the room until she couldn't take it any longer, until she shot up from her seat, until at last she fled, shouting behind her that she was late for another meeting.

The Specter watched as she ran from the room.

Outside she scanned the landscape, but there was nothing there, and no one. She was alone.

That evening in the Square—for absently, she must have taught her class, eaten lunch, held court across a dozen conferences . . . but where had the remainder of the day gone to?—she was relieved to see the flower vendor still at his post. Later than seemed usual, she thought, though how would she know, really. Maybe it was a slow week.

Hello, she said, nice to see you.

He nodded.

The other day, she went on—waving a hand over his now quite empty cart—I noticed your dahlias. They were so lovely, I thought I might bring them home. We're having a party, you know, some friends over. A costume party. The house looked so sad without flowers.

He stayed silent.

She smiled again, but inertly. Her dull chatter thickened the air between them. He was unswayed; he was, she felt, being deliberately inscrutable. Her shoulders slackened and rounded. She was failing, again, to be the right sort of person. But seeing she hadn't particularized these others who made up the "we" giving the party, she thought how she must sound—like she'd invented a collective in which she was embraced, or was speaking of herself in some rigidly formal way.

My roommate and I, she offered. A thin heat spread across her cheeks.

Ah, said the vendor, pointing to two bunches of sagging blooms in the back of the cart. He shrugged. There were more this morning.

Hmm.

Her smile sputtered as she recalled the Technicolor explosions that had stopped her dead the other day: Babylon Purples and April Dawns, Evelines, Doris Days, Que Seras. My god, how dazzling were the Autumn Sunbursts . . . enormous, fluttering anemones. All in a flock they'd put the simpler blooms to shame, towering above and flowering out from them, imperious. Left behind now: two bouquets of White Onestas, perfectly serviceable, yes, with their creamy petals and lemon custard centers, but she'd desired something rather less mannered. On their own, they were unmistakably bridal; had a virginal aura, really, which—it must be said—set a terrible tone for a bacchanal.

The sun started, frailly, to fall from the sky; now shadows waltzed in the streets. The Specter, surely, would be waiting in them.

They're lovely, she said then, smiling more warmly but feeling panicked. Just lovely. She fumbled in her pockets for the cash Edie'd shoved on her. How much for the pair?

At this—because she would buy these last limp flowers, or because of her obdurate cheer—their shared atmosphere shifted its clarities. The flower vendor warmed to her, or seemed to, and surrendered a bashful, slanting grin. At the limit of her vision, Jamie saw the sun break below the horizon. Between two buildings it was cleaved, and began, there, to quickly vanish. Its last light hooked in the man's eyes, beatifying him. The moment passed. Night stood up and commenced its preening. Night gathered her shawls.

We'll say ten, he told Jamie, for it's been a long day and now I am free.

He wrapped the bouquets carefully and handed them, swaddled, to her with her change. She bade him good night. He turned from her.

She set out toward home.

The light drained from the Square like dishwater from a sink. It seemed to suck at the scene's edges. She was cushioned by the tittering of dusk birds, which ebbed and quieted, a symphony of lullabies. In her arms the dahlias rested, pale newborns; fragile, nearly weightless. She pressed her nose to their ruffled petals and inhaled. They smelled of nothing. As she knew they would.

They make me think of death, her ex had said once. Charlie, the poet—her first mistake. Another was asking why he'd never given her flowers.

No one but my mother, she told him, has ever given me flowers.

And after so many years, and so many lovers, the fact of this grew dense and tumorous, intimating not an omission or absence but a coordinated act of dishonor, as if—due to some unseen but irrevocable lack—she was singularly undeserving of flowers, or else (she'd said to Charlie) like she wasn't—how, then, to name this asymmetry?—in the same *class* as the other women her boyfriends dated, those manicured belles who seemed always to be receiving affectionate trinkets from the men they stooped to companion, and so maybe, Jamie considered, it was just that in their minds she had no sustained reality, so when she wasn't with them she receded from consciousness like a dream, the thin vision of an ornament they'd admired, or an orifice that lived on in the subterranean memory of the body, which wasn't to say they had no fondness for her when she was immediately present, but that the very idea of her drifted beyond the borders of their collective imagination otherwise. Exiled in the hinterlands. And what use paying tribute to a trace?

Still, though, it hurts. (This, yes, she'd confessed to him.) It festers in me.

You overthink shit, said Charlie, you fidget with each insignificant slight and rub until the surface wears off, where underneath, you find another crisis and become even *more* fixated, like the blemish you've "uncovered"—which wasn't a blemish until you made it one—becomes the definitive attribute of any given situation. It's obvious—he threw his hand up dismissively— there's nothing you love more than feeling you've been exploited.

Of course in those last months, their relationship had been animated almost entirely by a relentless parrying of resentments, routine heterosexual variations on his neglect or her nagging. She hadn't understood before how effectively hatred could sustain the connection between people. Then the end of things manifested in the body. She began to dread the taste of his cum; it unsettled her stomach; she'd suffer cramps hours after swallowing. A far cry from first infatuation—then, she'd been insatiable, she'd begged for his loads, wanting him to cum on and in her mouth, in all her holes, a half-dozen times each day. Until one night she looked in his eyes while he fucked her and no longer found his love or her face in them. He was lost to another world; she saw he'd met someone else, or wanted to, and knew they were through.

They fought things out awhile longer, an impractical deferral, since they'd never done conflict well—a bad omen in any relationship. No matter how exacting her effort, she couldn't keep her composure when they went at it. Her neck would go hot and her voice quavered. With no foreplay at all, tears welled and she was compelled to turn from him, hoping, discreetly, to brush them from sight, to hide her porousness, her *dysregulation,* as he called it, all while knowing he would know—by her failure to maintain eye contact—that she'd dissolved into weepy disorder.

Charlie loathed her crying. Disingenuous, he'd sneer, just crocodile tears, one more chance to play the victim.

Later Jamie thought this a rather convenient method of wedging distance between his behavior and her response to it. She and he, as he saw things, journeyed through their shared world in proximate but ultimately nonintersecting lines, like what he said and did had no texture, no materiality, like it was all—even when addressed directly to her—only vapor scattering, untouched and unobservable, to the farthest reaches of the universe. It made her want to shake him, to demand he reckon with his impact on her life and see how his tempests tore through her. How could she show him his incapacity to ask about her days or passions made it seem her life didn't matter to him? *Seem*— another concession.

But when she said such things she felt her energy grow frantic, and knew, then, what would come next. He'd keep himself entirely even; his speech curse laden but affectless. He knew to draw his complaints out meticulously, like matters of public record. He was the type of man who supposed coldness indicated an argumentative superiority to the other's tumult, particularly if the other in question was a woman. His rationalism was a tyrannical machine, his logic a heartless technique deployed against her indeterminacy, her pitiful sentimentalism.

When she'd raised the trouble of the flowers, she said to him it wasn't like she needed them every week—or even every month—only that, now and again, this minor demonstration might soothe her of some half-remembered pain, or affirm something about her goodness in his estimation, her lovability, might make evident his belief that she deserved his care. But she saw, as she said this, that she'd insinuated—somewhere in the understory of her submission to him—that there was something lacking in his love. Fury disturbed his brow, if just for a moment. He smoothed it away but not, she was certain, before having decided her desire had nothing to do with her, that it was, rather, a not merely misguided but deliberate and defamatory accusation against his moral character.

She watched the muscles in his jaw tighten. In the gray glassy pool of his eyes she saw his reason's shape recalibrate.

Shouldn't you, he asked quietly, esteem yourself? I'm with *you*. I chose *you*. I've got nothing to prove. The better question is what your craven need for legitimation says about you . . . it's sad, really, maybe even a sign I've—how had he phrased this? his speech by that point was so tiresomely baubled—misjudged the solidity of your ego. You can't, he continued, depend on other people to make you worthwhile, and this whole (here, he'd gesticulated broadly at her bedroom) capitalist longing for putrefying objects to confirm your value should be seen for what it is: a victory of consumerist propaganda! Another defeat of the working class.

She saw, yes, she was just a symbol for him, an aborted fantasy, but of what? Did it matter? To him she was no longer Jamie H, no, she wasn't a single self at all, but a million selves, atomized and infinitely changeable, entirely available for discursive repurposing whenever he felt the need to score a point. She'd become a vessel, an extractable resource with which to fuel his suspicions of the sexed class he understood vaguely to be women.

Anyhow, he went on, it's decay, through and through. I can't endure the smell.

He'd suffered too much death, buried seven grandparents—this number seemed always to be shifting—and, when appraising the sordid history of his life, childhood looked to him like nothing so much as a sea of funereal bouquets. He'd been awash in blossoms, rolling, insurmountable waves of them. For years, he said, his feet never seemed to touch the bottom of things—he'd nearly drowned! Why couldn't she offer a little sympathy?

Why couldn't she just fucking drop it? But then why would she. Her whole family was living. She'd had no true loss to grapple with.

All this he said in the dry cold manner of a doctor, as though diagnosing her with an unsightly but finally curable condition, like her being unbrushed by death was itself the disease: an unwieldy growth on the ethical organ of her personhood. Her whole existence, in this way, seemed to him to thumb its nose at the seriousness of life. It confirmed her time on earth was more artificial, flatter, really, because to this point it had subsisted just this far above the merciless bottom of animal reality, the way we all ended up in the same brute spot—flesh, rot, dirt.

By then, though, Jamie felt far from their fighting. It was slippery and directionless, a babel of barbed sidebars. She no longer had the energy to protest his proclamations concerning her defectiveness, which came hard and fast and continuously, and which Charlie seemed always to be nailing into the door of their relationship like he was Martin Luther at the church in Wittenberg. A decent day together would be followed by three cloudy, horrible weeks. None of this to say she'd been a nonparticipant. She pouted and shut down, she let cruelties congeal thickly in her—a grim grammar. In her custom of leveraging silence, she grew sick with what she wouldn't speak. Inside her, grief was a diamond—glittering and compacted.

If, in the moment of rupture, she was unable to pinpoint the genesis of their disassembly, she found in his intractability on the subject of the flowers an effortless truth: he would never know her, not really, and didn't care to. He refused to measure her pain or desire as equal, not to say braided with, his own. Her faults made up the whole sky. There was nowhere left to go. The day she left him—some insipid Sunday at the end of an interminable winter—she arranged thirty peach tulips in a vase at her writing desk's center. For four days they reached toward the thin high light of the afternoon sun, looking, in their grace, like a bevy of blushing ballet dancers.

For the first time in years she'd felt the promise of renewal ushered in by spring. When the tulips' petals began, however, to curl into themselves and to flutter, suicidal, down onto the flat, dreary plain of her desk, Jamie wept, not for her lost love—if such a word described the flu she and Charlie passed for a time between them—but for how he'd proven to her, in some awful, ineluctable fashion, that men demanded perpetual darning. You could fret and fret at the holes mottling their lives until there was no time left for the repair of your or anyone else's woes. And then you'd be stuck there, strung up all filled with your own emptiness, flapping feebly in the breeze. And the whole of life would pass through you, cold and unnoticing. She had never felt so deflated.

Severance was simple. They didn't live together, so once the screaming phone calls at last died out, she put his toiletries and the three faded pairs of boxers he'd forgotten in a cardboard box and set it out on the porch. She texted him to say so and went out drinking. By next day, remembering little of her night, the box was gone. She never saw Charlie again. Thirteen months later, a mutual friend told her he'd moved to the West Coast, Portland maybe, or Seattle, and had married a very blond, very vegan nutritionist named Ashley, or perhaps Lauren. In the baby shower photos Jamie dug from the dregs of a stranger's Facebook profile, Ashley-Lauren beamed back at her, her belly an enormous watermelon. She was barely distinguishable from the horizon of blond blow-outs.

Jamie saw from the balloons that the child was to be a girl. What a pity, she'd thought.

A voice on the street yanked her from this memory.

Hey, it called, throaty and curious. Got a name?

A black coupe was stopped in the middle of the street. Two men in the front she could make out, townie types, Bruins hats on the both of them, and—she reminded herself to breathe—two or three shapes bobbing in the back seat. The man at the wheel was the one who'd spoken. The front passenger stared expressionlessly forward. Both gripped beers. The blue and red print of a Sam Adams label peered smugly back.

That's all right, the driver continued, we like shy girls.

Beneath the glow of the streetlamp she saw his teeth, yellow and sort of crooked, and his skin, milk pale, jagged with old acne. He smiled then, a smile that stalled in the lower half of his face. How obvious the look was, how fabular: his grotesquerie, that wolf's grin.

C'mere.

This wasn't a question.

In the car's dark rear, two cigarettes blinked on like the lights of a camera.

Her phone pinged.

Your man? The driver chuckled. His crew joined.

Motionless, Jamie scanned the street for other people—for witnesses. No one, and no cars coming, which was unusual for the hour but not impossible. She saw then that in her absent-mindedness she'd wandered off the main road. She was on a side street she took sometimes, a bit wayward, but one she liked walking down, because of an amiable black lab who roamed a fenced yard along it. He'd stretch his lanky dog body up against the aluminum separating him from freedom and wag there, awaiting attention, overjoyed by her caress. She missed her dogs so terribly here. In a way, he'd come to feel like one of them.

She'd never seen the dog collared, and realized now she hadn't learned his name.

Don't be scared, said the driver.

Yeah, echoed his passenger, no need.

We're just looking to have a little fun. My buddy says you look like a fun girl.

What a fucking line, she thought—cartoonish, really. He revved the engine. The noise bolted through her, but she shoved her fright back. What was worse: she felt herself beginning to split up, atom by divisible atom. Soon she'd drift above the scene like smoke, leaving her body, and if this happened, the men in the car would be able to do whatever they wanted. She bucked against the urge. Stay sharp. Stay present.

The driver was studying her more intently now. She was a flank steak; she was a head mounted on a wall. The passenger turned to face her, squinting his eyes, like he'd seen some mystery in her, an equation needing solving. He muttered something to the driver. Laughter rocked their silhouettes.

Her legs were stiff. In the secret space of her shoes, a place they couldn't see, she flexed the muscles of her feet, testing them, readying herself. They were leaden and tingling at once.

You, the driver shouted, snapping his fingers, what are you, mute?

Jamie shook her head, which seemed only to rile him further.

The passenger leaned over the driver, impatient. Don't you talk, bitch? We're fucking talking to you.

He tossed his bottle into the road. Slowly it rolled toward her, before stopping on the curb a foot ahead. She looked down at it, then shifted her stone gaze back on the men.

In the shadows of the car their bodies congealed, melting into one another, as if they could form a single, throbbing mass. Their laughter became a roar. Her ears rang. It was difficult to separate their words through the din, to make sense of what they went on shouting. To the right of the car, Jamie watched a porch light snuff out. She didn't seem to be breathing. Awful and automatic, her heart went on pumping inside her chest.

I'm good, she felt herself try to say, but the words cracked and burst in her throat. Her hands clenched, the shredded nails dug into the soft flesh of her palms. She felt a sticky wetness.

You're what?

I said I'm good, she managed now, more forcefully, or at least perceptibly—but some unanticipated angle in the shape of her voice snagged their attention, something they heard there pulled them nearer, shifting the density of the scene. Everything went viscous and edgy. The men regarded her in unison then, and again the passenger leaned over the wolf for a better look. A sick sneer broke his face open like a door. He said something to the driver.

The fuck? the driver yelled. His eyes journeyed over her: across her jaw and down her throat, past her nose, her mouth, the expanse of her hands, searching and pulling at her exposed skin like little hooks. Fucking faggot, he spat.

And again revved the engine. In the drawling languor of his speech—the way "faggot" seemed somehow three syllabled—she recognized the driver was very drunk, and if the driver was very drunk, the others must be beyond him, blitzed, turned up from a pub brawl or a rejection from some unfortunate woman there. Probably they were heading back to Medford, Melrose, maybe Malden, coming from the Irish spot just off the Square, hunting Tufts girls or punk chicks who lived in Porter, Teele, Central.

I'm talking to you, faggot, the driver repeated, and started to pound his fist on the side of the door, drumming now an ancient beat, the selfsame song that must have pulsed through the ears of Cain. He bared his wolf teeth. He revved the other men, also—we're gonna fuck you up, freak, she heard them hooting—and their words fell apart from her, and she wanted to lie down, to let go of all of it and let them dictate what came next. How simple to submit, for she was in the dream now, crawling around in that place of force. She was so tired. These men, after all, were her fate; they hollered and thumped and threatened, and she felt the moment become abstracted, a kind of mute action scene, as in a silent film. Above the chaos it ascended toward climax. Time turned its back to her. She'd need to decide: to stay, or else to go.

Unthinking, she darted forward, grabbing the beer bottle from the curb. She took aim and launched it at the car, watching, rapturous, as it smashed beside the driver's face and shattered against the immaculate paint of the door, spraying glass that seemed, in that moment, to freeze midair and catch the light beaming down from the streetlamp. It was gleaming and iridescent, a cloud of black opals.

She didn't wait to see if the driver was injured. She began to run. She raced from the car and down another side street, thinking how if the men were drunk, they were slow, and stupid, and she was all motion now, weightless and electric as a shadow. She could again hear them yelling but the sound grew distant, like a record played in a far room. A quarter mile from the scene she stopped to crouch behind a parked car, breathless and damp. Instinctively, she rolled beneath it—ears perked and expectant—and flattened herself into the floor of the earth like roadkill.

Beneath her aluminum coffin her lungs expanded with the thin

October air. It ballooned through her middle, slithering around her diaphragm. She found she was grinning. She felt a strange prick of desire, elliptical: relief's thundering illogic. Her body warmed to itself, puddling against the asphalt. Her legs shook uncontrollably while she waited, no longer hearing the roar of the coupe's engine, or the shouts, the violence of the men. At last she rolled out and began, again, to walk home. Above her the moon lifted its veil of clouds. It was a night flower, white jasmine. There was the bubbling quiet, a lone bird's curious call. The sound darted through the thickening dark, and after, there was nothing. An astounding silence, cosmic and impassive as God.

B ehind her, the bolt clicked in its lock. Force fled; she trembled on the steps, feeling, then, she might collapse but didn't, and so staggered up the stairs into the hall.

Edie?

Nothing.

She hung her coat. She set her keys in the seashell dish on the living room end table. She dropped her bag to the floor with a muffled thud and sighed, feeling, for one blessed instant, absolutely unobserved. Was the Specter waiting somewhere in the apartment? It didn't seem to matter. The day had been long, and they were to give a party. Let it join; let it reveal itself to the others; let her crack up. Each outcome was the same.

Two blocks off, the church's turret clock chimed: five, six, and, yes, half past. It was overloud and oddly clear, as if coming from within the house. She saw she'd forgotten to shut the kitchen window before leaving. She stifled a shudder. Below, the cars glided evenly up the boulevard without honking, their drivers unhurried now that the sharp needle of the day was consigned to the past.

She lowered the lights throughout the house. She set the speaker to charge. She lit candles and placed the cutting board out with a lime and a knife on the counter. She would need to change, to freshen her makeup. And to run out, again, for tonic, more limes. No time to shower, she saw, but she could blow out her hair, she could spritz more perfume. She wasn't ready, or not yet, to don her costume.

The wound in her thumb throbbed, remembering itself. The bandage had fallen off without her noticing. Her cut was exposed; her palms streaked with dried blood. Where had it gotten to? One more relic of the flesh. She imagined herself being slowly unwrapped like a mummy.

The flowers! She'd lost the flowers. Days spent dreaming of dahlias only for them to be forsaken, stomped on and savaged somewhere in the street. Perhaps, she thought, they were sacrificed so she might live. No one would miss them. Only she knew they were meant to be in attendance. She stepped over this annoyance as if over a puddle, and thought, then, of the pang that split her while she waited beneath the car, panting there—a shot doe. A shock of need: longing mixed with fear. This fusion was familiar. The men had struck in her a sense of materiality. In her terror she'd been repositioned in the body—*her* body.

She understood now how she would unfasten the condemned memory. How palpably this solution presented itself to her, now she'd been broken down to her rudimentary parts. She needed only to look at things from another angle; had only to submit, and flagellate the marionette of her self into its original knowledge. Determinedly she stalked to her room. She would force the fog of desire to coagulate, to settle like a shift over her; she would call it like a dead thing, command its presence. There was a small window before the arrival of the guests, and her attention must be guided, now, through the narrowest of tunnels. Her body sharpened to one imperturbable point. In the lowest hollow of her belly was an abrupt contraction—no cramp, but rather a pleasant, emptying feeling, a sense of her innards being scooped out. Like they were conceding an absence for the filling. The flesh of her thighs commenced its tingling, waking from the long hibernation. The nerves spidering her legs startled toward the surface of her skin. They were beginning to be freed. All over, her body hummed to readiness, a coiled snake. She lay back against the pillows.

The trouble was, she'd thought all that was behind her: the wet humiliation of yearning. After June, sex was no longer possible. Or, in any event, she hadn't wanted it, and saw now that this lack was key. In place of desire lived the dark matter of that night, entirely unknowable—a memory that had become substitutive, despite its self-effacement. How cliché this was; how conventional! And yet. That night sat glumly in the center of her, tugging the rest of her experience and her history into its silent O-gape, its illegible aperture.

In her diaries she'd searched for evidence of what happened, but the whole of June was a blank, only a blinding, awful whiteness. Even July was filled by pages and pages of scrawled dates and chicken scratch, with hardly any discernible words in them. She knew what the event had been, the detonation. It was idiotic to go on pretending otherwise, for she *knew,* but was unable to look on it directly, for it signaled a kind of cognitive eclipse, and she'd come, in fact, to persuade herself of the ineradicable impossibility of such reflexivity, insisting it was her eyes that failed her somehow, the firing of some neurons. This absence took on a biological facticity, it calcified in the very molecules of her ravaged, inarticulate body. Or maybe, she said to herself at moments, it was that the rupture might be said to exist beyond the universe of perceptibility altogether. That it blew out all possible utterance. She didn't know it because she couldn't: the event itself was unknowable.

But there was no truth in this. Silence had its opposite. And of course the dream was no dream, or not really, but a repetition; a representation; a dream, as it were, from life. It became the place where memory hid, the black hole that sucked at and seized the remainder of her world, a world it had broken into infinitesimal particles and held hostage somewhere, a thousand miles underground. She'd labored, yes, to stand straight before it, honestly to look at it—that fracturing June night—because this seemed the done thing: the rational act anyhow, for one must reckon after all with one's own life, even or especially the very worst of it, so that that life might go on. Neither as a matter of course, nor in a kind of rote continuance, but in a fashion that allowed a life to crouch more deeply into its significance. Without having been made—my god—reducible to its rock bottom.

When she'd attempted this, though, anytime she set herself up, say, before a mirror and muttered—*think, Jamie, think what it is that's happened*—she would slip apart from herself, rather like the Band-Aid perhaps, and become at once a horrible Not Jamie, an indeterminate, drifting other with no face or will to speak of. On some of these occasions, a hard kernel of her previous self seemed to solidify and stand atop her own shoulder like a homunculus, watchful and irreverent—although split from the activity of the lobotomized Not Jamie's dailiness. Was it observable to the others in her life, this fragmentation? No one had said anything of it; anyhow she went on cooking and tidying, gossiping, running, teaching and grading papers, drinking, mocking poor dull sweet young wives and laughing. All the while wafting just over the front lines, utterly empty.

And that the deeds of her corporeal life and this displaced consciousness of them seemed to play out on unjoinable planes meant nothing at all could any longer cohere: the narrative of her life had been spliced and was displayed, now, on multiple, discontinuous screens. The chronology of any given moment, when held beside the others, came always out of joint. Nothing synced to anything else anymore; none of it was connected; and the possibility that this bedlam was all that remained appeared awful beyond imagining. Time was not itself. And a story outside time had no harmony of experience, no proper subject—it was plotless, in short. And what then. The very notion of her self was discomposed. She was all broke up.

The erasure began with desire. Immediately she'd been severed from it. This was the first requisition. Just after the splintering, it seemed a sort of joke to her, a trouble, she thought, for the greasy philosophers, for what is a person divorced from self-presence, what use an "I" that can't know itself in a sensuous manner? Already she saw her colleagues lining their dead thinkers up in a row. How they'd love to pontificate on her—what would they name it?—mind-body problem. Heraclitus would be trotted out, and of course Descartes. Freud, Derrida, and then would come dissent, so Levinas could arrive on the scene, or Edith Stein, Butler, Beauvoir, Merleau-Ponty. All together they would pin her there, this creature known as Jamie H, and dissect her, examining their astonishing specimen of the fractured feminine, this split self.

But was it any matter, her not lately having sex? How trivial it felt, how obscene, with her dissertation around the bend, and her teaching load, her tutoring, the transcription work. Then her plot to flee the city, this program, her life, all of it. How simple to subordinate the sensual to her intellect, how tidy—this submerging the bodily fact of her experience, its bothersome female reality. Why, after all, be a body when I might be a mind? What had this mess, she thought, this catastrophe of being a woman done for her, besides. What could it prove to any of us, she wondered, except, in a game of two, one was always placed second, one must be the shadow above which proper person-hood was stood, all sunlit and superior. For herself, too, there was the dull certainty that anyone could saunter into her life at any moment at all and call her one word—"faggot"—and so strip her for parts, thinking nothing of it. It was no matter. She was no matter.

Would it not be better, then, to polish one's self as Emerson's transparent eyeball; becoming, in turn, relentlessly, disinterestedly, hopelessly absorbent? Of Eliot, Jamie also thought, supposing she could playact, as he did, that there existed such a thing as an "impersonal poetics." Even Woolf insisted in her *Room* that the discharge of feminine emotion in literature was woefully inartful, and so, if Jamie were to be fettered so regrettably to the resentments and violations of her sex—to her own, yes, stubbornly female complaint—how could she dream of producing work that sang, intelligibly and without interruption, over the murky dross of the world's inequities?

Sex, well, perhaps it only ever got in the way. Or maybe she'd gone frigid, had lost the ache of things, and should see this metamorphosis as a sort of victory. She still harbored, yes, her foolish crush on Ivan—that enclosed tenderness, her gleaming pearl of yearning. But even a nun would on occasion wake to find herself damp between the legs, having had glorious, heaving visions of Christ in the night, would need, yes, to clamp trembling thighs around her flat, pious pillow, grinding her wetness against it toward ecstasy, dreaming of the sweat-drenched cross, those punctured palms, his gaping mouth. Who wouldn't long for an annunciation? Desire exceeds us; is leaky; is opaque. Why should it follow that we be its wardens?

She knew Ivan didn't want her, had known it long before Mia's arrival in the program. Tonight, the pair would walk, hand clasped in hand, through the party, aglow with infatuation, and Jamie would spread open for them her apartment, this asylum, privately smiling: the perfect hostess. And Mia would become Ivan's perfectible helpmeet, would be his wife, unfurling the sail of her personhood in the current of his dreams, his work—would be divided, and in her splitting, would bear forth his enormous, corn-fed brood. What had Jamie to do with any of it? Being dishwater; being barren. She thought how the Professor had liked best to cum deep in her, grunting and yowling like a farm animal, and how after, he'd string up fantasies of her insemination. I'm sure, he'd say, that this time it took. I've knocked you up! And for his pleasure she would wait there with legs elevated, prone and wordless, a mannequinish elaboration of his desire, for she was the soil in which he tilled his virility, his authority, his inviolable continuity.

In his bathroom later she would laugh, pushing gobs of his spunk from her cunt into the toilet. It was hot and kinda funny, this odd idol of his erotic persistence. She was able to admit, yes, that an idea of being owned by him might rev her body into motion, that, yes, there was something in the slouch of this sexual orthodoxy that settled a chaos stirring in her. Now and then she longed for the anchor of a child she would never have, for a devotional life, a life lived for others, because a great potency would be required to snuff the flame of her ego. And so she participated in it, his impossible vision, and came, even, at times to enjoy it. In her bedroom after, she might recapitulate the memory so as to cum three or even four times consecutively, rolling around in the bright density of his need.

What the Professor couldn't see, however—in supposing she was a mere supplicant at the foot of his fantasy—was his own powerlessness within it, the fact that he'd arrived at his late age and discovered a loose thread. He was a being with a discrete ending after all, and now wanted—not even the reality of off-spring, but—the tableau of a child's promise, an expressionistic speculation on his immortality slashed across the canvas of her infertile form. How conventional, this desire, when held to the light. And how practiced his avoidance of its effectuation, for they both saw he could impregnate any number of twenty-three-year-old women if he wished . . . he was handsome, after all, and stable . . . women who could bear his children and would stand by him, women who would feel (at least for a time) fortunate to have been ensnared by him in some variation on perpetuity.

Suddenly it arrived: sensation. Thinking of him, Jamie's dizziness returned. She settled back on the bed, a timid bride. Now she submitted to form. The familiar heat spread over her, whirring and incremental, like a stovetop burner surrendering to its righteous function, giving itself over (apart from any question of will) to its neon orange glow. She was stiff at first; yes, and remote. Of course! It was five months since she'd felt anything, five hollow, bodiless months. Still. She remembered touch, encoded there. Pre-civilizational.

Automatically, she slid two fingers in her mouth, slicking them, and allowed the hand to wander liquidly beneath the waistband of her jeans, the drab cotton of a bland panty. A stifled gasp. The arrival of a stranger. What passed through her? The ghost of a man, just an outline, some composite of old lovers. There was hardness, yes, a heft, and gold chains dangling, groans of pleasure. A chest in its thicket of coarse dark hair like a pelt. For a moment the face was Charlie's—an awful boyfriend, but he knew, always, how to make her cum. Then the Professor, with his sweating, needful thrusts. His needling verbosity. The river guide she'd dated in spring appeared also, with his kind eyes and his gap-toothed smile, his surprising girth. All the men of her past danced before her as in a kaleidoscope, many colored and melding, ceaselessly mutating, becoming one another, then becoming something else altogether.

Her attention latched on this shifting image. She urged her mind to settle. Listen to the sound of your body, she reminded herself, thinking of the yoga class she'd taken just before things went haywire. Let—here, the instructor paused, establishing visual contact with each practitioner, as though to affirm that she, their leader, extended deep holiness; that she was a conduit for the inextinguishable spirit of the universe—let, the woman repeated, the body *speak through you*. At the time, Jamie found her ridiculous, another proselytizer for the Church of the Immaculate Woo Woo, but now the memory helped her loosen, she breathed deeply and unpeeled. Her hips thrust against her palm's pressure. She knew how far to carry herself: right up to the edge. For she must have her vision. The truth would appear, of this she was certain; it would reveal itself at last, and in looking at it, she would conquer it, would make of it a dead object. Her pace quickened.

The Specter appeared at the end of the bed. So what. Let it watch. Let it witness the revelation.

You, she said, channeling Yoga Woman, are your greatest teacher. All of you is sacred. Her hand continued its agitated rubbing. By habit or repetition, she would summon orgasm from her coldness—she had to. Pleasure bent there, yes, couched in gauzy awe. Time slowed. Then expanded. The seconds rose and stretched their arms lavishly. A voice came to her: Do you like that? it asked. Well do you? A labored inhalation. She thought she might, or could. I want, she whispered, voice cracking, I want, I want, I want. Another memory of the river guide surfaced from where she'd stored it, while her hand gathered energy . . . her hand, was it? Now his hand, or theirs, and now his cock, as she recalled its fatness, its imperturbability, the wide vein rivering from root to tip. From him drifted that astonishing odor, the earthy musk of balls, a salt-sweet bleach of pre-cum. He'd leaked a lot of that, which excited her, and she'd studied his face as a thick jewel of it spilled over his foreskin. Greedily, she caught this with a finger and lapped at it, looking directly into his eyes. She had done this to him. *She* had ushered him to this joy. In such wonder she adorned herself, plucking desire from him like a petal, until he'd begged to slide inside her. Yes, she said at last, yes, yes, yes.

Now his name escaped her. Rapidly he was blotted out by something else, a shadow figure. Where was it he'd gone in May, leaving her there, unprotected, condemning her to all that followed. No. She shucked self-pity from herself like a skin. She was getting close now. Her thighs tensed. Her toes clenched. Her body bucked toward the ceiling. She'd arrived at the cliff edge of annihilation. The light in the room sputtered; the air grew thick; a sort of humidity crammed itself around her, clogging her rasping throat. He was here with her now. The Diplomat: as solid and awful as he'd ever been. Enormous and grinning, he thrust himself in her. There was sharp pain, yes, and terror— immobilizing. But she would look at it, this history, for she had to, she would look at all of it and remember (she said to herself). Remember this.

Jamie saw she must yield the mantle of the third person. She would face the Diplomat stripped of distance. Such elisions, after all, were unsustainable. Inside them he'd never let her go. The bare fact of the "I" proved indispensable; so I looked into his eyes where they floated above me in the bedroom. And I was silent. And I was fearful. And time split.

Now it was June. I let my self go. I went back before the rupture, to when our lives intersected some hours earlier. On the dance floor my body vibrated against his, in rhythm with the thumping of indistinct club beats. A processional of pop divas: Rihanna, Carly Rae, Nicki, Rihanna again. A chemical stench of poppers rose above the sweat, sandaled feet, thick cologne. Beneath: a wreckage of smashed plastic cups, cocktail straws, and browning limes over a hazard of melting ice. The room reeked of cock, delirious. The Diplomat cupped my ass with both hands, pulling me nearer, snaking his tongue through my mouth. I wanted him. I won't deny it. I shoved my hand down his pants; he wore silk boxers, expensive seeming. I closed my fist around his length, gripping his hardness. He groaned. I had never been so powerful.

In my ear he whispered how he planned to fuck me—no, he said, "destroy" me; he said he'd stretch me out the way I needed. He asked if I liked being a slut. I said don't call me that. He said he'd still fuck me. I said we'll see, but I was drunk on his desire. I was also just drunk. Behind us my friend Serena was dancing with some other man. Did we want to join them at his place? I said if he had liquor. She laughed. We four left together, stumbling to an apartment in the South End, some bougie block, quiet-like. All the lights in the buildings were darkened. While the summer night gathered gummily around us the Diplomat said he was only here a few days. I'd seen a ring on his finger. I

asked about his wife. I have needs she can't fill, he said, I travel
often for work. We stay together for our daughter—she was
seven, or maybe he said eight. Blah blah blah. I asked if they
had an arrangement, his wife and him, and he replied: of a sort.

In the other man's apartment, club music went on blaring.
Deafening. By this time I was sat in the Diplomat's lap, perched
like a child, and he was holding me in place with big hands. I'd
been given something else to drink but hid it behind the sofa.
I saw I was too trashed to go anywhere with him: too drunk
surely, and too high. Anyway I was slurring my words. Humiliating. You see, it was a matter of changing my mind. I hadn't
known a woman could do this: change her mind about sex, but
I had; I couldn't go through with it. I never lied to myself about
this transformation. I understood how when we'd stumbled over
I planned to let him fuck me. In a way, really, I'd needed it. I felt
his dick throb against my belly while we danced close in the
club and shuddered with desire. There were reluctancies, yes,
mainly the wife and daughter, sleeping in familial immaculacy
five thousand miles over the Atlantic. But I had never been a
saint, and it was his life, his marriage. He was kissing all over
me in the apartment, my neck and tits, he bit my nipples too
rough, and I lost, for a moment, the current of my longing as
nausea crept through me. I was unsteady. I told Serena (slurring)
how I needed to get out of there. She was fixed on the other man
like a barnacle; she didn't hear me at all. Again I asked, did she
want to come with? She waved me off. Did she have any cash,
I said I needed to find a cab and had nothing left, my card was
overdrawn, but she went on kissing the other man. They were
someplace else. Maybe the Diplomat was in the bathroom then,
or making drinks in the kitchen. He'd gotten insistent in a way
I found unnerving. I thought to slip away unnoticed, as if anything about me in that moment was discreet. My body was over-
loose; the room hot and full of smoke; everything spun. I needed

air or I'd puke, so I fled to the stoop and gulped night in. The moon was high and clear, a waning gibbous. In Aquarius—my moon sign. Everything I'd brought I had on me. I thought of calling Felix but didn't, as we'd fought the week before. The Diplomat appeared and I said I needed to be put in a cab, that I was wasted, and I was sorry but could he please help me out. He laughed in my face. He put his hands on my hips, angling me against the heavy door of the apartment's vestibule. I apologized, I did, really, I said how sorry I was, and I'd go home with him some other night, and again he laughed. I'm so embarrassed, I told him, it's just I'm too drunk, I'm a mess, I need to go home please, but he was shoving me against the door then, he was grinding the weight of his body against mine. I said stop it, and for a while I kept saying *please,* because I thought I might reorient the scene, I thought there was some way to come back from this. I was stupid. In those days I had hope. Maybe, I told myself, it was just that he hadn't heard me. The whole world was dissolving, maybe I only needed to speak a little louder. Maybe the words had risen from me like smoke, maybe they'd been muffled by the wet June air. Stop it, I said again, and then his hand was clamped on my mouth and I couldn't breathe right, I began to panic, and he was pushing his chest against my upper body and face. With his free hand he undid his belt. I bit his palm, but without much force—it was hard to catch my teeth on anything substantial. He snatched the hand back. His face was filled with fury. I thought he'd punch me. That was when I got really scared. Back then I was a beanpole, six feet but a hundred and fifteen pounds, and he was enormous, a behemoth, six six I remember him saying. I said sorry, I began to placate, I don't remember all the things I said. I only wanted to go home, but I saw I was going nowhere until he'd finished. He shoved me on all fours, pulling my shorts down, tearing my panties. The steps dug into my knees. I said no a last time and then he was pushing my face into the top step so I shut up. When he gripped my waist with both hands I sort of bucked against him, I don't know what I was thinking, maybe I'd knock him off balance and run, but this, too, was thoughtless, just a pipe dream. I was a rabbit in a snare, I was cattle, just meat. My body gave up. I separated. It's much easier than you'd think. The cobblestone gashed my brow. While I submitted to him I watched the blood drip out of me. Where it pooled it caught the moonlight, becoming a kind of mirror. He ripped me open. This didn't last that long. Probably he worried the neighbors would see. I don't know how loud I'd screamed. Later I'd think it shouldn't have mattered. If he was who he said he was, wouldn't he have immunity? I've never known how those things work, but maybe that's why he did it. Most people will do anything if they believe they can get away with it. I was rocked by his rhythm until it was over, watching blood pour from my face. It was gore on a movie screen. After he came in me he stood up and fixed his pants. I lay still. Maybe I was playing dead. Slut, he said, and spat on my back. It oozed on my bare skin while I waited. I didn't get up until his footsteps vanished.

I banged on the apartment door awhile, and then the window. I could hear the music still, I knew Serena and the man were there and tuning me out. It wasn't that I planned to tell them what happened, only (again) that I needed money for a cab. After ten or fifteen minutes I dug around in my pockets, my socks, everything I had. I found a ten between the back of my phone and its case and set off again into the night. It was three in the morning. The city'd been dead a couple hours by then. No cars passed. I must have walked a mile before a yellow cab pulled over. I'd been staggering in the road with my hand held up, all pitiful. I saw I was sobbing. I'd been smart enough to wipe the blood from my face, or probably the driver would have sped off. When I looked in the window I saw a woman behind the wheel.

Thank God. I said I only had ten dollars; I asked if she'd take me as far toward Davis as that would get me. I told her sorry. I said I didn't know what else to do. She was wary but nodded. The city flew by us. I hung my face out the window like a dog and kept sobbing. The moon above us was itself. She dropped me at my front door, having never turned on the meter. I gave her the ten and thanked her. I went in.

Part II

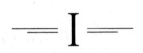

Boston, February 2013

Two months before the bombing of the Boston Marathon I was raped again. It was eight months after the Diplomat, seventeen following a 2011 triple murder in the suburb surrounding my university, seven before I fled my life there, and eighteen before I'd be brutalized in New York once more. As I write this, I choke back an ache toward causality; these events, I know, were discontinuous, and—beyond my flight between cities—were happenings outside my control. Anyhow, I didn't connect them at the time, or if I did, no such link was recorded in the diaries I kept then, which were compulsive, meticulous, and tediously recursive. What I find in those writings, rather, is a woman absented from time, unmoored from reality. I often wrote of floating above myself, a "paper doll person." There's nothing radical in this self-description. Dissociation, we'd call it now, though the term, I think, was less common then. I was a vacancy. A room without any people in it.

This seems an elemental texture of unanticipated violence: the sense that, for most people, such shocks are not just divided from but utterly unassimilable to the recognizable order of everyday life. But I'm here to tell a story; I must make meaning from mess. And as that decade hardened in my mind, my rapes, those murders, and the bombing formed an unnerving affinity with one another. Through that time, they've leaked and thickened, have spread like a strange film over the rest of it. I remember the horror of these eruptions with disorienting clarity. Past the particulars, though, my days then seem abstract, washed out and unreachable now, submerged beneath a sludge of seconds, minutes, hours, years.

The marathon occurred on April 15, six days before my birthday. Dzhokhar and Tamerlan Tsarnaev were brothers who'd become bombers, born to Anzor—a Chechen man, handsome, like his sons, a mechanic described by relatives as a "traditional Muslim" opposed to ideological extremism—and Zubeidat, an Avar who worked intermittently as a cosmetologist, like (I remember thinking) my mother and sister had. The family text of the Tsarnaevs is a story of Soviet-era tumult and ongoing geopolitical displacement. Having first been forcibly relocated from Chechnya to Kyrgyzstan, the family moved often, living briefly in Dagestan before applying for asylum in the United States.

Here they settled in Cambridge, on Norfolk Street, where they'd remain for the next decade in the third-floor unit of a caramel-colored, wood-frame triple-decker. From where I was living on Powderhouse Boulevard, I could have walked three blocks up Curtis, hung a left on Elm, and been there in forty minutes.

While looming a history of my time in that city, I've often thought of those boys—men, I suppose—and that attack, particularly after evidence surfaced to suggest the older of the two may have been involved in the 2011 murders. Those killings and the bombing seemed, later, to bookend my rapes in some slant way, to signal something about the unexceptional quality of the violence I endured. I seemed, rather, to be living in a general ecosystem of rot.

For the four years I was in the area, I lived in Somerville, just outside Davis Square—where the old theater played five-dollar matinees, the café was run by stone butches, and klezmer bands had regular nights in small wine bars. The rowdier pubs were

affiliated with an Irish Mafia no natives would confirm for me
had ever existed. I hated the city and could not flee it. My education was my sole capital; I'd never held a straight job, and had
no training for one, so it was service work or intellectual. Nothing else was possible.

I refused to actually live where the school was, on a hill in the
southwest part of Waltham, a nowheresville where nothing ever
happened and no one smiled. The rents, yes, were cheap, but
further isolation in the already-isolationist life of a PhD student seemed to me breathtakingly unsurvivable. Suicide wasn't
something I'd attempted in seriousness, but the fog of it began
to accumulate somewhere inside me, and an image of the act
itself would materialize now and then, a little light bobbing at
the top of a buoy. Every apartment I saw in Waltham looked like
the sort of place you'd gas yourself, and it seemed silly to have
learned nothing from Sylvia Plath in the exact moment I found
myself writing a book about her.

Because of its dullness, or because—according to local
police, anyhow—nothing like this had ever happened there, the
murders, this unimaginable flare of brutality, seemed to be all
anyone spoke of for months, though perhaps I'm inventing this
collective fixation in hindsight. Possibly I was one of an obses-
sive few. In the week immediately after the news broke, though,
you might have thought Charlie Manson had come to town, and
behind our macabre nervousness lived a longing to have been
invited to the Tate house that night, and to have said no at the
last possible minute.

We'd been brushed by the wings of death and passed over.
Proximity to annihilation confers its sort of glamor.

The crime scene where the men were found felt plucked from
a horror film. The three had had their throats slit with such force
they'd been nearly decapitated, which seemed an odd detail to
hear on the local news, sandwiched, as it was, between reports

of a coming cold front and a small fire at a pizza parlor. Its grue-someness was hypersaturated and banal at once. I remember thinking how awful it would be to have your death made equal to an eyewitness account of a wild turkey blocking a gas pump, both items read out by the same stiff suit with bleached teeth. The description of the bodies evoked for me the story of Nicole Brown Simpson, whose killing hung oracularly over my child-hood. My mother had been horrified, and then outraged, and then had railed against OJ, who she said everyone knew was guilty—even those who claimed to believe otherwise.

(Only later did I understand how transportive that story was for my mother, why it haunted her, a woman who—first at the hands of her ████████, and then, at the hands of my ████████—barely escaped Nicole's fate. "When I get home, I'll fucking kill you," my ████████ said. It isn't your fault and you've got to know when to leave: both statements hold true. The batterer "will not stop himself," as Andrea Dworkin wrote in memory of Nicole, he "has to be stopped . . . or she has to escape.")

The Waltham murders, like Brown Simpson's, remain un-solved. According to neighbors, the victim whose apartment the men were found in was either a quiet "welcome change of pace" from the hard partiers they'd grown accustomed to, or a strange bird who rarely left his house, but who, nonetheless, hosted a steady stream of disquieting guests. Another of the three was, in an old friend's recollection, a "nice Jewish marijuana dealer," someone she no longer hung around with (having quit weed), but the sort of pot gourmand who'd be running a dispensary, not the type to be snuffed out by a drug lord.

The Middlesex district attorney drew a straight line between the marijuana and the murders and insisted the killer or killers were known to the victims, as there'd been no forced entry. They were let in. Or it was a robbery gone wrong. Or, no . . . maybe it *was* the work of a cartel, meted out by skilled assassins, assassins who'd want nothing to do with the rest of us—we, the innocents. They'd acted, I suppose, on the orders of some shadowy kingpin. This was a message scrawled in the blood of a small-time dealer and his unfortunate friends. Sunday-night football played meaninglessly on a TV in the background.

Even then, people saw that the center of the official story didn't hold. Why leave such an exorbitant quantity of cash and weed at the scene? Five thousand dollars and a pound and a half of pot were dumped on the heads and bodies of the decedents. Was this a brag?

Two years later, and just over a month after the marathon, an FBI agent shot a man he and state troopers were interrogating in Orlando about his relationship with Tamerlan, supposedly in connection with the Waltham crime. The reports out of Orlando were conflicting: Ibragim Todashev owned up to the crime, it was said. He'd conceded, in any case, that he and Tamerlan were involved, or did it. They were obscurely aware of it, certainly, or was it that Todashev admitted to knowing who was responsible? Perhaps it was that he'd said *Tamerlan* had done it, and he, he as in Todashev, wasn't there at all, he'd only heard uncorroborated gossip. Didn't that prove, really, that Tamerlan had orchestrated the bombing also?

According to his wife, Todashev's debit card purchases placed him elsewhere than Waltham on the night of the murders, but text messages between the homicide team assigned to him alleged he was penning a written confession when things went south. The FBI agent had *had* to shoot Todashev during questioning, because he'd grabbed a metal broom, or was it a samurai sword, a bowie knife? Maybe it was that he'd flipped a table and bolted. Or he'd made to grab one of the troopers' guns. Had he had a gun of his own, had he pulled it suddenly? At any rate he charged at them, they said, even when they started to shoot, and just kept coming. A preternatural energy must have animated his bullet-riddled body.

All told, Todashev was shot seven times.

Another link in the plot's chain broken.

In 2011, I recall the media and police tapering off the story after a week, maybe ten days. I wonder now how a case so high-profile, not to mention one positioned as totally unprecedented, dissolved from scrutiny so quickly. It seems funny now, minding the long historical arc of the "War on Terror," that less was made of the fact that the killings went down on the ten-year anniversary of the events that incited it. If allusions to an invisible cartel presence in the suburbs were meant to assure us there was nothing to worry about, they had the opposite effect. Now we found Waltham had an underbelly, and its dullness, as it happened, was a scaffold erected to conceal something darker.

In my circle, we convinced ourselves it had nothing to do with us. I hadn't known those men, nor had any of my friends. It was possible our students bought shit off them, or got weed from an intermediary who bought shit off them, but we were beyond that particular pale. We didn't live in town, and god knows we never partied there. We fled campus as soon as our responsibilities for a given day had ceased. Mainly we gathered twice a month in the same tacky pub outside Porter Square. The fries were good. The beer was cheap.

Besides, what we numbed ourselves with was drink, not weed. Or, on the rare occasions we went dancing or to the karaoke bar, we'd snort a little Adderall, because Foster had a scrip but didn't like to take it regularly. It made him feel cracked-out. I said to him that's the fun part, I said downers were for people who had time to kill, and we were racing time—deadlines, the commuter rail, the demands of the faculty, our students, comp lists, one another. We wanted out of there, and fast. No speed was too great for me.

But our bravery in the wake of the murders was a bluff. Who wouldn't have been shocked by such baroque annihilation? It was an act of cinematic grandeur, not merely a life's terminus, or the end of three, but total death.

Nineteen months separated the murders and the marathon. My life, meanwhile, disintegrated. In a customarily grim diary entry from the end of February, shortly after my 2013 rape, I wrote that my life was "entirely superfluous, my existence an exercise in enduring an endless sequence of horrible minutes." In April, after the marathon, I wrote that the bombing was not reducible to its matter of time—the seconds it took for two homemade pressure cooker bombs to explode, wounding 281 people and killing three others, one an eight-year-old boy.

(My diary again: "Historical events displace the individual sense. And yet these people were individuals; all had particular lives.")

Tamerlan and his younger brother, Dzhokhar ("jewel" in Chechen, though his friends called him Jahar), were photographed placing the bombs on the scene. After the detonations, Dzhokhar tweeted, "Stay safe," before going to the gym. He napped then, and partied later with friends, who said he seemed "relaxed."

The ensuing manhunt dragged on for four days. By Thursday—the bombs had burst on Monday—one of the men injured in the explosion photo-identified the brothers. In flight, they shot and killed Sean Collier, an MIT police officer, who'd tried and failed to free his gun from its holster as they approached. They carjacked a student of the institute, Dun "Danny" Meng, and took him hostage, trying to gaslight him into believing *he* was responsible for the bombings, *he* accountable for Collier's death. Spontaneously, they decided to drive to New York, where they hoped to plant additional bombs in Times Square. Meng, though, escaped at a gas station, alerting police to the brothers' whereabouts. In nearby Watertown, they were cornered. Tamerlan was injured in the shootout that followed; Dzhokhar ran over his brother's body with the stolen vehicle and went on driving, though he abandoned the car shortly after to flee on foot.

The next morning, a local man found the nineteen-year-old stowed in a boat he kept in dry dock in the yard. Dzhokhar was huddled there, wounded, and in a bullet-ridden notebook, had written in pencil that "the U.S. government is killing our innocent civilians but most of you already know that."

From Dagestan the boys' father pleaded with Dzhokhar to give himself up. He had "a bright future ahead of him" if he would only "come home" to Russia. Dzhokhar: his father's *jewel*.

Dzhokhar later told federal agents his and Tamerlan's actions were a direct response to war crimes committed by the U.S. military in Iraq and Afghanistan. In his notebook, he'd written that he couldn't bear to "see such evil go unpunished." American soldiers must be made to understand they "are fighting men who look into the barrel of your gun and see heaven," a turn of phrase I didn't recognize but found strangely beautiful.

In another world, I wrote, he might have been a poet. What was unsound in his claim about the atrocities being committed against the Iraqi and Afghani people? Of course for most Americans, no truth would rise above the foreignness of Dzhokhar's name. Nothing could withstand the blunt axe of that word: "terrorist." And in his speech, they'd hear only the deafening swarm of *Allah*s humming there.

In the weeks and months that followed, we were instructed to remember we were "one—Boston strong," but I wondered who among us might be left out of this "we." On April 17, two days after the bombing, a number of applicants—among them, a T-shirt company out of Woburn and a private individual in

Allston—tried and failed to trademark the phrase "Boston Strong," not, one said, to "police" it, but only to keep its profits within the borders of the city. By April 22, the retail arm of the T-shirt company was hawking branded merchandise from the web domain Chowdaheadz.com. If you looked the part, to live in the city at all was an act of allegiance, of solidarity, whether you wanted it or not. Clearly the Tsarnaev brothers hadn't. Intra-municipal nationalism became the machine through which to honor those who'd been "sacrificed."

We were meant to see that the American dream was under threat. Freedom, again, was on the line.

The clanging language of jingoism permeated everything. On the news everyone talked like Giuliani after 9/11. It was sick.

Of the end of the manhunt, the poet Fanny Howe writes that four days of collective trauma culminated in a "spectral image of an ordinary teen sprawled inside the pale outline of a boat." He'd lain there in the fetal position, awaiting salvation, waiting, in other words, for death. At the time I couldn't see any difference. As his story proliferated, Howe continues, a series of conflicting images were assigned to him: "Now a beautiful boy, now a zombie, a doper, a sweetheart, now a migrant washed up on the banks of the Charles River." I remember being bewildered by the fact that he was younger than me, that he was the age my students were, and how he looked, in some lights, even smaller, frailer, somehow more exposed than they did.

I felt incredibly aged.

I remember the last day of the manhunt clearly, April 19. In my diary I wrote that things were "largely routinized again" by Thursday, just before the release of the suspect photos. On Friday, though, Edie and I woke to the city in lockdown. Wordlessly, we walked to the corner store for liquor, cigarettes, junk food. A side street nearby was cordoned off by police tape. Reporters milled along its perimeter while the blue and red lights of cop cars revolved in their rooftop spaceships, electric eyes. Sean Collier, we learned, had lived a block away from us. Edie was horrified. She had family in the force, and before his retirement, her father was a firefighter. Boston Strong. I don't remember what I felt about Collier, if anything. Of his death I recorded only the facts. My emotions about the week's events seemed beyond the point, and most of the time then I felt nothing at all. Besides, I was leaving the city, lackadaisically looking at apartments, already, in Brooklyn. Shedding my dead selves.

Back at the house we chain-smoked on the awning we'd climb out to from my bedroom window. Four days had vanished into unreality. We'd fallen into a kind of cosmic stutter. Anxiously we joked about becoming embroiled in the chaos. If we weren't iced in the shootout we believed would end in our backyard, we'd probably find ourselves in the B-roll of a *Cops*-style reality show, frozen and monstrous in the gleaming gaze of a drone's camera, looking unsavory—like Depression-era hobos, Edie laughed, or Bigfoot in the forested distance, standing on the roof in our pajamas, clutching two p.m. vodka tonics with last night's mascara blacking out the blank space beneath our eyes.

Edie said it was like she'd come to in an uncanny valley version of the world we'd been living in. I nodded in agreement but was thinking, really, how *this* world at last reflected what I'd always known, that violence was everywhere, and all the time. It was the earth's very marrow. Chaos might boil over at any moment, for any reason or for no reason at all. I'd been slipping, since the Diplomat, into this surreality for nearly a year, and in the two months since the last rape, my disorder had become so irrepressible I suspected, some days, I was losing my mind.

In February I'd surfaced in a strange room. I was in darkness. On top of me was a man. He was inside me, too: my legs parted by his thick torso, knees over his shoulders. He didn't notice my stirring. He went on slamming his pelvis against me, shoving his cock in my ass. A heaving beast; grunting and slick—sweat dripped from his chest on my tummy and tits. When he came close his breath was hot and dense with whiskey, the stale stench of cigarettes. Nausea blew through me. I turned my head. On a side table to my left was a pack of Marlboros and a small square mass. His wallet, I figured. These objects rose from the shadows surrounding me. They remain among the few details I recall of the space itself. Meanwhile my eyes stalled and revved behind the holes of my skull.

It was true I'd been drunk the night before, but not like this. Where had he plucked me from? What was it I last remembered? My limbs were unfathomably heavy. I had an urge to vomit but quashed it, worrying, in my semi-paralysis, that I might puke in my mouth and begin to choke. Then what would happen. I thought to alert my penetrator of this fact—I wasn't able yet to call him "my rapist"—but seemed unable to speak. My tongue was thick in my mouth, a sick slug, stuck there, filling everything up, pushing all my words back down. It was revolting. I wondered then if I would die there, and would anyone find my body, would it be left bare, bloodied, what would my name be.

Each thrust shot a stabbing, awful sharpness through my

spine. If the man had used lube, there wasn't enough. From far away I felt the stickiness of blood. I smelled of copper. I didn't need to see it to know I was torn. My botched birth. I heard the voice of an old boyfriend calling me a messy bitch, a whore, and at the time I'd agreed with him, said, yes, you're right, said I'm sorry. Laboriously, I pushed this remembrance away; it didn't serve me here. How badly I was ripped I wouldn't confirm until morning, squatting in my bedroom above a hand mirror, investigating the slasher scene of my remains.

Even in the moment I was thinking of infection. Even then I was thinking: How will I grade papers tomorrow? These thoughts meant I was imagining a moment beyond this one. They meant I still believed I might have a future.

As the Man in the Gray Room punched mechanically in and out of me, I started to drift.

I thought how I'd been tested just weeks before this, and what a hassle it was. The free clinic was in Jamaica Plain, which meant schlepping ninety minutes there and another ninety back. The doctor who did my intake prodded me with leading questions on my sexual practices, frowning and fretting, insinuating, by his tone, that I was some common slut. Probably he saw a lot of us, though, so I couldn't make sense of this hostility. At last he said I'd probably gotten AIDS, which seemed to me the sort of thing a doctor shouldn't say to a patient unless they knew for certain, but this was a free clinic, and I was a dumb young woman who'd spread her legs a little too easily, so perhaps I'd earned it. My face went hot. I knew I was about to cry. I said to the doctor I'd been raped over the summer, and it was true I wasn't always smart about sex, but mostly I was worried about that particular event. The man hadn't used a condom, I told him, which really added insult to injury. Didn't he agree? I said this was my second round of panels: I needed to be sure. I'd read certain viruses take months to appear in bloodwork.

The tears poured out of me then, and I found myself apologizing, I said I didn't know why I was telling him this but maybe it was useful information. I said I tore easily during rough sex, and there was blood after he'd finished with me, which seemed a bad sign. I said the word "seroconversion," sobbing. I couldn't believe he was the first person I'd told about the rape. The doctor's sternness slipped a moment; his face went all dim and flat. I liked that. I liked seeing him realize how small and cruel he was. He began to stammer, to tell me, oh no, it's just we're not equipped for this, we're not the sort of clinic that handles people like you, we don't conduct rape kits, and was I sure, because really, he didn't have the expertise.

A violence bloomed in me then. I wanted to shut him up. I imagined slapping him across the face with his stupid notepad but didn't. Something in the suddenness of my fury stilled me. I grew calm. It seemed funny now *he* was the one babbling, behaving, as it were, in a hysterical manner, and I was sitting across from him, smooth as a tumbled stone.

No, I said, no need to worry. Thanks very much for your time.

I grabbed my purse from the hook where I'd hung it on the office door and walked with what I thought of as a quiet dignity out into the street. It was that I couldn't suffer a fucking lecture on begging a rapist to wear a condom. It was that I couldn't suck on the accusations implicit in his paternalistic haranguing. Anyway, I already believed what had happened to me was my fault. Why must he rub it in?

The tests came back negative.

While I lay there in the gray room, I thought how awful everything was, and how absurd the timing, how silly it would be to go through that frightful, debasing process—possibly with the very same doctor—all over again. I'd like to say I shouted no at the man on top of me, because to not have done so, and not to have fought, to not have left that place with his skin caught beneath my nails, to not have been beaten within an inch of my life, or (better still) to not have been killed in that room—which is to say, to not have left a corpse there, which would, if I were lucky, determinatively prove the story of my innocence—would mean I hadn't been raped at all. It occurs to me I might, in actuality, have said it, that crashing word ("no"), but my memory is clotted and hazy. We aren't supposed to admit this, that our recollections are fallible, as if my confessing I don't know what color the drapes were where I was assaulted discredits the testament all together. I've often heard rape skeptics and apologists claim that experiencing rape would be so totally unthinkable your mind would be forced to capture everything about the event, as in a photograph—that your capacity for recall in the moment of violation would be heightened somehow, or total, rather than diminished by the impact of trauma.

Perhaps it's true for others, but for me this didn't hold. I hope I dissented. Times I've dreamed I got a punch in but I can't know for sure. I was crying; I remember my cheeks were damp and my eyes ached; I remember the painful cleaving; I remember it being hard to breathe. We were underwater. The facts were far, everything a distant image, separate somehow—a scene witnessed through a camera obscura.

If there was a room, I wasn't in it. If a body was being fucked there, it was the meat sheath of some other luckless bitch. The thing on the bed beneath the man was nothing to do with me, it was a sex doll: me and not me at once, a sort of body double. The resemblance, yes, was uncanny. Curious, I watched their death dance. With one hand the man pinned hers above her head, as if to immobilize her, but there was no force left in her body, this was plain as day. Fight back, I shrieked, heave him off you; flee, little bird, flee! Useless. Of course. I had no thought of liberating myself. Whatever he'd slipped me had deadened something essential. My thoughts were cushioned by a kind of reverb; some painstaking delay came between them and the most microscopic of motions.

This wasn't the first time I'd been roofied. I knew if I got out from under him I'd make it no great distance. First I'd have to seize my limbs from the molasses tug of the drug, pull and lever those defamiliarized instruments to journey through an unknowable expanse outside the room. Each step would be through bog mud. Then: Where in the apartment was I, or was it a house, a complex, were there others inside it (allies or enemies?), and how would I find the front door? What floor was I on? I had no sense what neighborhood he'd hauled me to. We were partying in the South End again the night before, me and Felix, but there was no reason to believe that's where I'd been kept. Was there time to grab my clothes—would I have the strength to dress myself? I couldn't flee shoeless. It was February in Boston, savage in its own right, and a historic snowstorm was set to engulf the city at any minute.

These speculations supposed the Man in the Gray Room wasn't violent—rather, that he wasn't capable of violence further than the brutality of this rape—that he didn't mean to do away with me. But he could panic if I made a wrong move. I began convincing myself I might recover the layout of the space, that I needed only to summon one minute of intense, uninterrupted concentration. I felt certain the blueprint sat somewhere deep in my brain. What I needed was a plan, but I couldn't hear myself above the slapping sound of his flesh against mine, the recursive *suck* and *thwack* of his drilling into me. The tempo another inconvenience: an attack against my stubborn pragmatism.

I felt unable to stand, so I thought he must have carried me in. This increased the likelihood of witnesses; people, after all, are so irredeemably nosy. His moans, like bullhorns, bounced around my head. And if I hadn't been able to walk—*thwack*—I saw he must have had a car, or—*thwack*—we'd ridden in one, which meant we might not be—*thwack*—in the city at all.

The thought that I could be anywhere rose above me, a punishing sun.

He was near climax; his grunts had that anguished, bovine sound men get when they're about to cum. But the drug was dragging me back under. When I'd woken, I guessed he must have been fucking me—here, I correct myself: *raping* me—for some time. Besides the tearing, I sensed a pulsing soreness through my lower half that signaled ongoing endurance. Probably it wasn't his first go. *Thwack.* It was impossible to tell what hour it was; the room might have been at the bottom of the sea. Possibly he'd been raping me all night, ejaculating, napping, going at it again.

I remember saying one thing: *Please don't cum in me please.*

Of course he probably had already. Please don't cum in me please, I'd begged, how fatuous—my second "please" the true humiliation, a pathetic recapitulation, and me sniveling like a child asking for a hall pass. Please, please, please, I heard. *Thwack.* I floated. I imagined traveling back in time, before this night and that bar, before last summer and before all the men in my life, before my youth even, back to infancy, that brief gasp before the fall. Who might I have been?

Thwack.

No dreams remained. Sound carried me back to the moment, to the gray room. The man was busy, reminding me of what I was, just trash, and there he filled me with what I'd earned, his rot, which was and had always been mine. In that instant I realized he might actually kill me; the possibility revealed itself like relief. For a few seconds I thought of nothingness . . . silence . . . then shut myself against the abyss. It wasn't any use. His pace quickened and I felt the raw tunnel of my insides expand around him, his cock thickening before release. He groaned then, and shuddered, freezing midframe above me, then collapsed on my body, his torso slimy, his limbs slimy. A massive jellyfish. Bile rose in my throat.

I sank beneath.

Some minutes or hours later I woke to the silver light of winter illuminating the gray room. I sat slowly up. The sun stabbed my eyes. A few feet away, the man was tossing my clothes toward me from where, I saw now, they were heaped pitifully on the floor. Silently I dressed. I lifted my legs, tugging leggings on, then jeans. This took great effort. Above my right nipple was a purpling bruise, a thumbprint: I'd been marked. I shrugged my blouse on, my whole torso was aching, like I'd been clenched into myself a very long time. My sweater, my socks; two of them! I felt amazed both were there.

I asked (*please*) if I could use the bathroom. The man nodded at a door that materialized behind me. Inside it I wanted nothing less than to face myself. A sobbing feeling surfaced but collapse was no option. There could be no further break. Not while I was in his grasp. I splashed my face with cold water. The bathroom was oddly immaculate, but the hand towel looked ratty. It needed replacing. Roughly I patted my face with it, catching a glimpse of my death mask in the mirror. No one lived behind it. Oh well, I thought. I might as well go on. I gargled warm water and spat in the sink.

Steeling myself against what came next, I returned to the gray room. I looked past the man's shoulder, as he too avoided my face.

Ready?

He offered me a ride home. I accepted.

Later I imagined some ruthless attorney cross-examining me. An icy, hard-eyed blonde like the one on that TV show.

Why would you get into a car with the man who'd just raped you?

The eyes of the jurors would widen. A hush would fall over the courtroom.

I needed a ride, I'd say, and my eyes would go wet so everyone could tell I was a person. My hands would nervously pick at themselves in my lap. Perhaps I'd tremble. Maybe my voice would crack.

That accepting this from him would undercut the veracity of my victimization didn't matter, because nothing did. The decision was automatic, and marvelously practical. I'd no clue where I was, no money, and could barely walk. I knew already I wouldn't report, so there'd be no rape kit, no interrogation or lawyers, no judge, no testimony, no jury.

Were you scared to get in the car with him?

I don't recall.

Was it possible the Man in the Gray Room would drag me to a second location, some frigid warehouse in Dedham or Revere, string me up, carve me like a Christmas ham? Of course, but I didn't care. I'd live or I'd die but neither fate gave me pause, neither seemed so singular. My future stood before me, a flat painting drained of color. It was all a trap. Whatever happened was just more time to suffer.

Part of me figured if he wanted to kill me he'd have done it already. I'd outlived my use, for one thing, and it would have been easier to do the job while I was out, completely at his mercy. Awake I was a wild card—tensed with unknowable potential. He couldn't see I was already done for, that any fight I had left was dissolved. If I made it home, I'd grade the papers. If I didn't, this would all be over, and I could finally sleep.

What was he was doing while my mind buzzed about there?

Probably I only stood still a few seconds, but time was long, it was pulled taffy. Gathering his necessaries, maybe. Phone, keys, wallet.

Again: You ready?

Yes sir.

I couldn't look him in the eye, but I must have followed him out. Nothing about my inertia shocked me, for what is survival at base but thoughtless repetition? Temporal continuity. What seems strange are the things that remain particularized—his cigarettes, the terminal stench of his sweat, my amazement at both socks being there—and what is just an outline. I don't remember walking out of the Gray Room, for example, or the apartment. The things I'd thought I needed to know (what floor were we on, was it a single unit or several, where had the front door been) are no place in my mind. This absence seems somehow profound now: it introduces a possibility that I never really left, that, even if only in some bubble universe to the side of our own, I might still be there.

The outside was sunless, and the air heavy, pregnant with the coming storm. I should have felt cold but didn't. We were at the end of a cul-de-sac. Later I'd google the cross streets and see we'd been in some cozy corner of Jamaica Plain, which made me laugh. He could have dropped me at the free clinic, no problem. And the doctor could have told me what's what again, he could have pinned the tail of some other virus on me. Maybe he'd have figured out if I was dead or not.

While I searched my purse on the porch, the man started the engine of his car, a Toyota maybe, some bland sedan, I couldn't be bothered to check the make, model, or license plate. Anyway I don't know cars. I didn't then and never will. He let it run a minute, melting the patina of ice on the windshield. This was how I understood, finally, that it was freezing, but I remained numb. Behind the glass his face was blurred, overexposed somehow, as in aura photography. Through the cloud of condensation I saw his hand motion me over. I went to get in the back seat, reflexively—a child—but he said, what are you doing, and scoffed, then instructed me to ride beside him in the front.

I saw how dumb I was, my god, what was I thinking. I crouched into the passenger seat and let my body coil into itself. I was so tired.

The interior was a frenzy of trash, it stank of McDonald's. Beneath that, the stench of our bodies: mine as well as his. Having seen his nice clothes and clean bathroom, I felt surprised by how run-down the car was. Besides, this was a nice neighborhood, it was where all the young artists were living then, the tech queers and secretly wealthy folk musicians. The fancy cemetery was around the corner, where I'd visit Anne Sexton's grave sometimes.

But maybe his place was a beater too and I hadn't noticed. The drug still hummed through me. My head was a drum stuffed with wet cotton; my pulse pounded dully, ear to ear. Everything went on arriving in my consciousness on a delay. I felt thankful for this gap—a pleasant grace period.

Above us the sky was a mournful pigeon color. Flurries unhooked themselves from it, tumbling down atop multicolored beanies and storefront awnings, dotting the windows as I gazed out of them, feeling, then, irrevocably severed from the world of the living. *Us,* I said to myself, how odd I'd used that word—us, to make sense of the sky above the car, to imagine he and I together, a pair, traversing this landscape besieged already by the storm. Like we had somewhere to get to, a common place. Like this was normal. The snow wasn't sticking yet to the pavement.

I remember thinking how awful he'd ruined Jamaica Plain for me. It was a long subway ride but I liked trekking out on occasion, wandering past the vegan cafés and feeling so different from the other women there, who dressed like frugal hippies and reeked of patchouli. And what of Anne? Who would visit her now? I loved that graveyard, Forest Hills, the grounds were stunning, so well manicured and filled with flora. It was free, and quiet. Rare were the moments I was truly alone in the city. I'd smoke a few cigarettes—Anne managed three packs a day— and read her poems aloud, pretending she was listening. By now I know the dead don't hear a thing.

The man asked me some question about the radio, but the words fell from his mouth like anvils, too heavy to be arranged in a line. I wasn't able to speak at all. I thought of the other poet I was teaching that term, Sylvia Plath, and the line about her tongue sticking in her jaw, "a barb wire snare. / Ich, ich, ich, ich." My students didn't like her Holocaust images. A shitty marriage isn't a concentration camp, one said, and a cheating husband isn't Hitler. I realized I'd have to stand in front of a classroom again on Tuesday, but how.

My silence was taken by the man for an answer. He punched a dial in on the dash. NPR blared from the speakers, one of those exquisitely bloodless NPR-type voices leaked out, the sort that always seem to be apologizing for themselves. A kicked-dog kind of voice. The car progressed haltingly into Brookline. Across the road I saw we were passing a favorite bookstore, and I thought of jumping from the car, running over there and inside, mislaying myself among the books, waiting to be buried by them, waiting for sleep. The fingers of my right hand curled around the handle on the passenger door, plotting. But I was too slow. My reactions were still syrupy.

We curved eastward through Allston. He took North Harvard Street over the Charles. The river was still and sad looking, frozen over like a flat sheet of aluminum. I watched the path I jogged several times a week unfurl around us. I recall no further landmarks after that. The ride from this point was a horizon of dullness, just the sighing sound of the man on the radio, my rapist's unflagging chatter, the cold thud of my wordless torpor.

I couldn't bring myself to peer into the face of this minotaur. While the minutes dragged, his voice was an awful echo I couldn't stamp out. Surely that of an older man, I convinced myself, maybe he was in his fifties. I allowed a few sidewise glances: pale white skin, I saw, and his hair dark, threaded with strands of silver wire. Slack-jawed, going jowly. I sought a song in my head, something to anchor myself in the present tense, but only the sound of him slamming into me returned, the steady drip of his sweat on my tits. Drip, drip, drip.

His driving was even-keeled, absolutely unbothered. Two hands on the wheel, ten and two, not white-knuckled, hardly seeming to have a grip at all. His tone was flat: each sentence he uttered was an item on a list, indiscernible from every other, all equally important or unimportant. These rose above the road like stop signs, brief interruptions in the unfaltering flow of time. They were forgotten as soon as they were in the rearview. He seemed like the type of guy who knew nothing he said mattered—a background actor in his own life type of guy. He seemed to be talking a lot for a man who'd just raped a woman, but I guess I didn't know what the normal amount of talking would be. And then I thought how it was I who'd gotten into his car; I who ceded ground by embracing the courtesy.

I tried to tell myself his was an act of kindness. But I wonder lately if he interpreted my decision as absolution. If I got in his car—perhaps he'd said to himself later, on his own again in the gray room—it meant I'd forgiven him.

But I had no ethical relation to the scene, for I was not my rapist's angel of judgment. I was guided by practicality alone. His car was the simplest way of getting home. Violation, anyhow, was by this time unexceptional. Rape was a habitual event, the dense forest of my life, and I swatted at its darkness but could not break free from it. If I ran and kept running, I thought, and if I cried out, perhaps the gods would listen, maybe I'd become a star or a tree, I prayed I too could be transformed. But then I saw: the change had come already. I'd been crooked into place in my rape world, dried up, with knobby little branches and no threat of blossoms. I was scheduled for the clearing. Soon I'd be just a stump.

I shook this thought from the ends of my hair.

I was in a state of divided consciousness. I was only in a car with a man, biding time. Now I knew what I was, and what I was was a sort of vessel—an urn for male violence. It seemed entirely ordinary that the Man in the Gray Room had recognized this, had heard the whistle sounding somewhere inside me, calling him, as it had the others. My siren song. Could I blame him for answering?

I didn't see myself as a sexual agent, which didn't mean I'd never had sex of my own volition, but that sex had nothing to do with my authority or lack of it. The notion of consent was immaterial, for what was consent if I'd never been able to deny or revoke it? I said yes or I was taken. Sex happened to me or didn't. Sometimes I came out all right.

Rather than look at the man as he drove and droned, I looked out the window, watching bundled figures hunch into themselves while scuttling down perilous sidewalks. Thick gusts of snow swirled around us. I was a child peering into a snow globe, except it was I, and not the figures within that snowy world, who'd been made unimaginably small. The life I was cut off from expanded out and away from me—an impossible and perfect other place. The people past the window, in their wool coats and knit hats, were not the ones imprisoned inside it, but me, on the outside, exiled from their Eden. I hardened myself against them, those mindless, cheerful Bostonians, the smug hordes of the unraped.

The hearse that carried me glided into Somerville. I'd like to say I've kept up a sense of the city's geography, but I haven't been there in a decade and can't bring myself to return. I don't remember much of it anymore. While writing I scour maps, tracing routes from place to place, but the reality of my body in that time, in that place, buzzes illegibly as behind the bar of a censor.

That weekend, Winter Storm Nemo would dump nearly twenty-five inches of snow over Boston. On the morning of the encounter, a Friday, the governor announced a driving ban on nonemergency vehicles, effective after four p.m.—the first issuance of such an order since the blizzard of '78. Media coverage of the storm featured stills from the beloved children's movie about a fish and his missing son. I kept hearing Ellen DeGeneres's grating dialogue in my head. It was just after nine in the morning when the man began driving me home, a journey that would take, I realized later, nearly an hour. The thought of looking at him disturbed the tenuous détente I'd negotiated with my stomach, but I refused to vomit—another bodily humiliation.

He jabbered on, spiting my silence. His words were alive, squirming across the expanse of me like leeches, sucking up my blood, sucking up all the air in the car. Around us SUVs steered by harried-looking women assembled, trapping us in a spontaneous blockade. It seemed to me all the drivers that morning were women, though this was surely a distortion, some fantasy or need of mine to be ensconced in an undeclared sisterhood: my Amazonian battalion come to gather me to their ranks. Traffic stopped. It started. Again, it stopped. The yells and honks erupting from all directions in concert wove a cocoon around the car. The man didn't seem perturbed by the din, or I didn't notice him noticing—the more likely thing. I began counting the number of vehicles where I spied hoarded cases of bottled water, a doomsday prepper's paradise.

Scattered through the sea of metal were children, peering back from the safety of extravagant car seats—prisons, too, of a sort; inescapable plastic thrones. There they'd been perched and pinned beside stacked packages of Evian, Fiji, Dasani. I was one of their kind, just a girl again, terribly small, frightfully silent, endlessly manipulable. And the ride was a fever dream, one where I was being driven to school by a father whose power was total, whose temper unpredictable. He needn't mind my inattention, my desire. He could talk at me without limit, take me wherever he liked. My whole life passed by me in a havoc of fitful images, like I was watching a shitty documentary by a freshman who'd just learned about PTSD.

Thwack.

I wonder now whether his speech that day was manic, rather than amiable, a kind of uncontrollable excretion or expulsive disavowal of what I felt certain he knew he had done. Was he wrestling his shame? In that hour that lasted days, I had no interest in his emotional life, but as I look back, this seems to me the more beguiling question. I've often asked myself how these men assimilated their rapes of me into the history of their lives—what stories they told themselves of these events, happenings that had so obliterated the continuity, the integrity, the very principle of my reality.

Perhaps as the Man in the Gray Room sat beside me, chucking up all his terrible words, it was only a method of stamping out the gaps of our remaining time together, the hazardous spaces where he risked self-reflexivity or recognition. But maybe I grant him too much latitude. It's possible I'm overcorrecting for my own frozenness in the moment by awarding him this profundity. Probably he just liked hearing himself talk, and was emboldened to do so, with me struck dumb there, leaking his cum, forced to listen. A crash test dummy, really: saying nothing, feeling less.

The storm appears briefly in my diary of the period. I wrote of myself as a "space of blankness," like how the streets looked to me in the snow's aftermath. "I am only twenty-five," I went on, "and feel already my life is done for. No one will love me. I know this now. What sort of monster am I." There I noted too that Nemo was a contraction of the Old Latin, *ne hemo,* meaning "no man" or "no one," an etymology I'd learned not long before while studying Joyce's *Ulysses.* There I'd found a story I couldn't exile.

In a cave on the island of the "reckless" Cyclopes, Odysseus and twelve men from his crew are captured by Polyphemus, who begins to devour them, two by two. After getting the creature drunk, Odysseus ("the lord of lies") tricks Polyphemus by claiming his name to be Outis, Greek for "no man" or "no one"—the lexical progenitor of *Nemo*. When Odysseus gouges out the cyclops's lone eye, Polyphemus fails to summon help, for what he shouts to the others is that Outis attacked him, and if it was Outis who'd done it, no one had—"Noman is killing me by tricks, not force." And so none come to his rescue.

On the floor of the man's car was a pen, a cheap red and white clicker, branded by the name and phone number of some drab enterprise. Probably he'd seized it from a mug of identical instruments on a desk at the front of a featureless storefront, some rental company or law office in Roxbury or maybe Revere. I was overcome by a vision: I watched myself lean forward, as if to tie my shoelaces. Then I grasped the pen in my fist to swing it back around and into his eye. I thought how funny it would be to enter him like that, to feel the jelly of him surrendering to the flat force of my weapon: an asymmetrical penetration, a shock of perfectly justifiable violence, for who would blame me but everyone. Would he howl and swerve, would we crash, would I—inert there, with no seat belt on—be flung through the windshield and so face death, all while knowing I'd exacted my minor vengeance.

I made no such move. I lay my forehead against the window and waited for the cold glass to shock me into clarity. It did. The dream fell from my mind, another limp petal, the prophecy of some discredited oracle. Anyway I was no Odysseus. I was not the clever trickster. I was a great stupid body, sweetened by wine and trucked from place to place by this thief in the night. And the man was a piercing ache, a gray room in shadow, the anonymous pen from a shabby office. To me, he had no name. And no one was coming to help.

Ages passed. At last four of his words entered me.

You should get tested.

Still I would not look at him. I didn't speak, or perhaps I nodded, *of course*-ed, *mm-hmm*-ed. I was stricken. I felt if I saw his face I'd begin to scream, and if I began to scream, I might never stop.

No, he said, you need to get checked out. I'm positive. HIV, I mean. Undetectable, but you know—just in case. They have that PEP shit now. In case.

The clipped cadence of his speech threw me, that bland absence of emotion. Even this point of note couldn't intervene in his rolling monotone. The information settled on me like ash, or more aptly like snow, as in any case it melted quickly. Knowledge without weight; for I was out of body. What happened to that body no longer wore the shroud of materiality.

I must have confirmed I'd heard what he said. He'd done his due diligence. Finally I felt cold.

Somehow we'd arrived. I was ten thousand years old. I harbored, still, some defensive instinct, because the corner I asked him to drop me at was several blocks from my apartment. I knew better than to let him in on my exact address.

You're sure it's here?

Yes, I heard myself saying, well, no, sort of—I need some air. I think I'll walk a bit.

I said I wasn't feeling well, and this was true, I was nauseous, and the chill had given way to a racing fever, my whole body throbbed, my head ached. Each molecule of light that landed on my face sent shock waves through my eyes.

He asked, again, was I sure.

Yes. Yes. I thanked him for the ride. Slowly I lifted myself from the car. I felt his gaze sucking at my back beneath the ugly winter coat that covered it. Then I shut the door quietly, with a kind of strange solemnity, as if wanting not to break anything, though what I would break I didn't know. I didn't think I'd provoke him; it just seemed the done thing.

I walked in a direction opposite my apartment for what seemed a long while, but probably lasted only seconds. When I looked behind me, I saw his car turn left on Curtis and stood another minute, or perhaps an hour, waiting until I was certain he couldn't see me any longer. I doubled back. I staggered toward my building, not walking straight, legs shaky, as the cold and wind rocked me. Any composure I'd held on the ride evaporated. Pain radiated now from where I was torn; pain possessed me. I began, suddenly, to sob. The feeling, though, wasn't grief. Really, it wasn't an emotion at all, only an involuntary reaction to the relief of pressure—a temporary buoyancy given me by the man's vanishing.

I passed a young mother pushing a stroller. Its wheels caught in the snow where it had begun to collect. The baby reached fat hands out, its face red and round, a perfect apple. I thought how precious it would be to live through one uncontaminated morning, and how awful that they'd been forced to witness me, a monstrous Medusa, my frizzing hair rising from my head like smoke. I felt infectious. I felt badness leaking from me. The baby's mother frowned. I thought of apologizing but didn't; I had interrupted their day enough already.

Another time I might have been awed by the storm. It never snowed where I grew up, a tacky beach town in Virginia where city officials panicked and shut down schools in advance of even a thin flurry, a rarity in itself. Any dusting was a ritual purification, "the first clean thing in a dirty year," as a character in a Mavis Gallant story says: snow covers everything awful, all in your life that's gone badly. But I couldn't see a thing of the world around me, or not really, and nothing clean, I felt certain, could touch me any longer.

In my diary later, I mocked the tiredness of my self-hatred: that mawkish elegy for sexual ruination, the punishing, pathetic sense I'd been somehow *soiled*. Would I have said these things about any other woman in my life? I knew I wouldn't, but for myself I needed to feel something more than evacuation; I needed to stamp and writhe in my pain; to perform my own lurid dishonor. In actuality, I didn't feel ruined at all, for to have been ruined would have meant I'd started from an originary place of cleanness. That I had been like the snow—and I knew this wasn't true.

In the apartment I found Edie staggeringly hungover. We both looked like hell, and she must have figured we were sailing along in the same awful, alcohol-poisoned boat. She groaned and smirked and shut herself in her room.

At last I vomited in the toilet, but there was nothing left in my stomach, just neon bile. My throat was dry and shredded, as if I'd smoked a whole pack of cigarettes. I knelt like a penitent at the bowl, resting my cheek against its cold porcelain, not caring what mess was on it, not caring what bacteria crawled onto my face. Exhaustion tunneled through me. After a while, Edie knocked to ask if I was all right, but I couldn't answer. I flushed and flushed again. I ran the water in the sink until it was near boiling, then held my face beneath it. I couldn't feel a thing. Several times I brushed my teeth, but I couldn't get the taste of him out, couldn't scrape that film off. I swished and gargled and spat and spat until, finally, I gave up.

From the kitchen I took an enormous jug of water and lurched to my room.

I didn't eat for three days, or maybe I had an orange on the third, but in any case it didn't stay down. Not so different from the usual order of things, I thought: the eight hundred calories I granted myself each day; the puking; my merciless, ceremonial emptiness.

In my bedroom I shut and locked the windows, then tried to force them open, testing their strength, testing mine. My hands trembled, my arms were unfathomably frail. My body was a sparrow's, hollow seeming, like all my organs and bones had been sucked out with an enormous vacuum. I unlocked the windows, then raised, closed, and locked them again.

My room had two doors: the one that opened out on the rest of the apartment, and another with a knob lock and frame bolt that led to the basement three flights down. Once it'd been an apartment in its own right, but now it was a scary movie set, filled with dingy furniture, oily housewares, and ancient magazines stacked all over, yellowing and silent—a frozen tableau of sloughed-off domesticity. Most of the ceiling bulbs were blown out, and the interior doors connecting the rooms had all been unscrewed from their hinges and removed. They stood beside the barren frames like coffins. The place had become a kind of labyrinth.

There must have been a renovation planned once. Work gear and a toolbox crouched in a vacant corner but had been sitting so long they, too, were coated in thick dust. On every surface was gathered the shit of vermin and other interlopers, squirrels mainly, raccoons, maybe possums. The smell of mouse piss hung heavy—that peculiar odor of ammonia and something else. An inexpressible abjection.

Edie and I discovered the tomb in our early tenancy. Together we'd crept down to test the washer and dryer, which sat in a little room off the bottom of the stairwell. Above the machine were old posters: *The Texas Chainsaw Massacre, Halloween, A Nightmare on Elm Street,* and *The Rocky Horror Picture Show,* which, set against the more conventional slashers, appeared somehow seedier. The light was a bare bulb connected to a pull chain. When you arrived there, you'd be submerged in total darkness while grabbing at where you thought it might be swinging, and you'd finger and clench the metal, tugging desperately down on it, seeking the flimsy security of overhead illumination.

Each time I expected to find I was not alone; always I felt certain a face waited there for me, smiling blankly back.

For a while we'd known there were ancient ruins just past the laundry room but were too scared to enter them, or, at any rate, to go it alone, but one day we crept inward with our phones held aloft, both flashlights blazing. Naturally we understood there would be no axe murderers inside, but we egged each other on with eerie noises, fake screams; we were like teen girls at a sleepover.

In what would have been the living room we found piles of vintage *Playboy*s circling a bare mattress on the floor, lousy with unclassifiable stains. We guessed at the sort of man who must have collected them—was he contemporaneous with their publication, or had he alit on their pleasures later, scouring Goodwill or eBay, slowly compiling his Rolodex of tits and ass, entire acres of 1970s bush. Maybe he fancied himself a connoisseur, an archivist of soft-core spank-bank Victoriana. Some of the issues were less decrepit than others, less caked with grit. We elevated our skittishness by pretending the mattress still suffered its occasional guests, drifters or madmen passing through, keen in their newfound leisure to luxuriate in a little rub and tug with all this hoarded material.

We were too disgusted to flip through with bare hands, so I knocked a tower down with a timid foot. Rats had feasted on some of the pages. A dozen women stared back from the floor at us, overexposed, women of all varieties, some with teased shags, some with sculpted 'fros, women arrayed in fluorescent bikinis or wearing nothing but blue eyeshadow and hoop earrings. These centerfolds spread themselves open for us smilingly, but there was something sexless about all those genitals splayed in a row, like how staring at the same word typed again and again unmoors it from its customary meaning.

This was all rather distressing. It wasn't that I had a problem with porn or sex work, but that these women's banishment to our basement seemed such a singular disgrace. That their beauty, their electric sensuality, had been shed here and left to rot was awful. Better, I thought, to be shredded, pulped, burned. Beauty is meant to live in the light, I felt.

But after Nemo, I couldn't descend there alone. Our tall tales about monsters in the basement felt too near. My fear had become total.

In my room the morning of the storm I unlocked the basement door as I had the windows, and again locked it, turning the bolt, testing it, pulling forcefully at the knob, ensuring it was an effective barricade. None of it mattered, of course, it was just a habit, a ritual, like drawing an evil eye on my palm, a trick I'd tried before, telling anyone who asked it was another passing fancy, one of my ridiculous quirks. I'd have surrendered myself to any talisman that promised to ward off further damage. I couldn't pray, but on the sill of my window I charged crystals in salt water beneath the moonlight—clear quartz, amethyst, black tourmaline, obsidian. I pulled a tarot card each morning. I slept with lavender beneath my pillow.

I tucked a butcher knife there too.

I told Edie it must have been lost, or maybe someone stole it during the party we'd had in October—perhaps they'd grabbed it as a prop and took it home by mistake. But what would I do with it anyway? Stupid girl. In the movies there were always beautiful women with huge tits sliding massive knives from wooden holders, knives that always seemed to end up back in the women anyhow, slammed into their guts, their breasts, opening up their milk-white throats. I watched these scenes as if solving a sphinx's riddle, looking for some foolproof plan of attack, a way of being that would usher me beyond the end credits and into the sequel. Everywhere I went I noted exits, hiding places, I counted each possible weapon. More runes. I saw how useless this was.

By now I knew that if a man wanted to do something to me, he'd do it. I was no final girl. For one thing I'd been a slut, and in the moral universe of the horror flicks I watched obsessively, death was my righteous fate. I didn't feel safe in our apartment, but then, I didn't feel safe anywhere. I guess in a way I never had. It's not like I worried the Diplomat or the Man in the Gray Room would scale three stories of bare brick to reach me while I slept, but my paranoia had become broader in scope. It was a kind of general paralysis. If not them, then something else, or someone. I'd been marked, and every man could see it, the biblical smudge across my forehead.

I crawled into bed and refused to climb out. I abdicated myself: I was a void in the shape of a woman. For three days I kept the curtains drawn and my laptop plugged in, its screen an awful eye staring back at me, with some crime procedural whirring through it on a loop. *Bum bum.* I couldn't situate the images in an arc. Words fell from the actors' mouths and curdled. I watched their heads open and shut, but it was all nonsense—giddily I pictured empty bubbles rising from their lips and floating across the Manhattan skyline. Story disassembled itself—no scene had anything to do with any of the others—but I couldn't turn the show off because silence would obliterate me. I was utterly untethered. I too would float away.

Numbers, though, remained recognizable. Minutes passed

through me like the ticking of a bomb. I remembered what my newest rapist told me: *They have that PEP shit now.* I thought how a friend had said these drugs were effective for only the first thirty-six hours, and after, the virus would have fastened already to your system, an immunological corset. But the city was shut down, and I couldn't move an inch. I didn't know if I'd been infected, but I had no future either way. I pulled cards. Five of Cups. Ten of Swords. The Tower. I watched seconds melt into one another with astonishing ease. I thought of Dalí's clocks, their liquid uncertainty. I thought of Saint Clare, seeing alien images on the walls of her sickroom.

My mother's number materialized on my phone screen, but I couldn't answer. My movements were too sluggish, my speech nonexistent. The first day she called over and over again, intuiting something, but I silenced the calls, exiling her worry to the backwater of the voicemail inbox I never checked. Then I turned the phone over because its light offended me. For a day, maybe two, it buzzed every hour until, at last, it died. Relief.

I couldn't fathom seeing or speaking to anyone, I couldn't play at ordinary life or self-presence. I had no energy to reassure anyone of a single thing. All of it was unendurable—just another type of violence. The trauma of perceptibility; the infestation of witness. I longed only to lie there and stew in my filth. I thought perhaps I'd die, if I could just wait myself out, allow my body to shed itself from itself. "My" body, what a joke! While my mind drifted my self-hatred bloomed. Stripped of my adornments I knew I was a *rape girl,* and I began to imagine being raped as a kind of vocation: the one thing I was good at, my sole function. Knowing this made me stronger; it was a reminder of my purpose on this earth. It dispelled all my moronic hope.

I told myself I needn't worry those men would return, not because I'd escaped them, but because they wouldn't want me again anyway. I was used up, and their disposal of me was a brute proof of something, the fact of my categorical defilement. "Know what you are," I wrote in my diary, scratching the words into the paper until the ink bled and the page tore: "a nothing, disgusting—you make people sick. Probably they puked after." *They* as in my rapists. I thought how pathetic I must have looked to them, with my posable nature, all my rote *please*s, my pitiably weak *stop*s. Please don't cum in me please. Might I use your restroom, sir.

What a waste.

Who was this person, I'd wonder at times—this withering thing with no fire left. I, who'd withstood so much, lay three days as though dead, bent into myself, all pruned and stupid, a rotting, awful remnant. I longed for the end. I saw I'd never know peace. I couldn't sleep. I couldn't rest. You're not supposed to confess there's a limit to what a person can recover from, but now I knew the bottom. I knew there are things past which you can't go back. I'd like to say, while writing this, that I've come out of darkness, I've healed, but trauma is mercurial, an acrimonious angel. She's crouching in me even still: my steadfast companion, my throbbing tumor, my tiny double.

Time slowed. I thought of Woolf, and Septimus Smith imagining the word "time" splitting its husk, pouring its riches over him. He loses meaning but language goes on falling out of him, words like shells drop from the sky. Three days in my bed became a year, two, five years. Every rupture hummed in my brain, endlessly repeating. The Diplomat, the Man in the Gray Room, my ███████, my ███████. All their voices merged; this drone washed through me. It came to seem almost comic, the inconceivable repetition of that violence in my life. Slapstick almost. Farce followed tragedy, but what came next? The crack-up.

I hiked the volume on my crime procedural. *Bum bum*. I didn't want my laughter to worry Edie.

For three days I didn't shower. Perhaps some buried part of me thought of preserving evidence, but in hindsight I don't really think so. On the show I was watching this was a crucial point. The statuesque ADA was often hobbled by a lack of semen, hair, carpet fibers. At times the perp had been meticulous, others it was that the "vic" washed it all away. *Bum bum*. I wasn't stinking up my duvet with the thought of retaining anything. I knew if I lay down in that tub I'd wait until the water ran in my nose and down my throat, carrying me off. The irrevocable plunge.

All the same I felt too weak to end things. The integrity of my body was beyond my authority; it was for men to use up. It wasn't mine to do anything with at all, so to kill myself would be a sort of theft, a seizure of someone else's property. I couldn't steal my death.

By Tuesday I was unknown to myself. My god, I couldn't bear to look, but did. In the mirror I was radically aged, a feral thing. I hadn't slept, or if I lost consciousness, it was nothing near sleep. I was a gray span of static—a mist of atoms. Though I'd never slept well, this was the beginning of My Insomnia. Of his own sleeplessness, Proust said he was "living in a sort of death, punctuated by brief awakenings." In the early days, I never dreamed.

Edie and I hadn't lost power that weekend, as many houses nearby did. I had to teach that afternoon, so I rose, finally, and forced my body into the tub. I scrubbed and washed my hair, my body, rough when I might have been gentle. The water stung where I was ripped, but I didn't care; at last a sharp sense broke through the smog. I saw the bruise on my tit had gone a sickly green yellow. I scraped a bar of soap across my tongue and gargled with the suds. What all this was meant to achieve I didn't know, for I felt just the same afterward. I was a dirty cunt, a word I began often lobbing at myself, alongside the habitual guests: slut, bitch, whore, cow. The last was for days I exceeded my allotted calories. I'd squeeze the loose skin at my waist, pinching with serrated nails until I bled.

It was "cunt," though, that I luxuriated in: the blunt Germanic monstrousness of that word. Eighteenth-century writers called it "the monosyllable." The Wife of Bath preferred *queynte*. I carved all this in my diary, where I also christened myself Rape Girl, the title totemic and maudlin.

Already though the violence of Friday morning was far off, it was disconnected film reels: spliced and sutured strangely together, and projected occasionally on the blank wall of my mind. An image, a smell, a sound would stab suddenly into me but no story held. I understood what had happened was real, but the sequence of events, like on my TV show, failed to cohere. I tried to give myself over to disbelief, to pretend it was all a dream, but evidence clung to me: his thumbprint, the persistent pain inside, the dank odor of him on the clothes I'd worn that night. The morning after, I'd wiped myself over the toilet and pulled a wad of paper back to find a mess of blood, the gluey liquid of his cum—an awful mélange. I stared at the square awhile, seeking some sign in the entrails of this sacrifice. Was it anything to do with me at all?

"Dissociation" appears once, to my knowledge, in my diary of the period, and describes, there, a more general bodilessness. I avoided the language of pathology. I was resistant to diagnosis, because to have been diagnosed might have forced me to act, and I needed my hollowness; I required absence. It's clear, though, that I saw I was separating from myself, stepping, as it were, to the side of my form. In March I wrote of being "terrified of the flattening," but putting a name to what these men had done was as yet impossible. When I wrote of it I wrote of a series of bad affects and involuntary severances. By late summer the word "rape" appears a few times—first, in front of a question mark; then, with surety—but in the immediate aftermath, self-knowledge was miles away. The events were only "what I'd earned."

I returned to campus.

On the commuter rail I graded, or tried to, but kept losing the thread. My bag burst with library books I'd gathered for my dissertation. I opened some fusty tome on the Romantics and found there totally untranslatable symbols, they weren't even letters, just curves and slashes of black ink swimming across the page and into my eyes like an affront. For a week, then two, I was unable to read. I fell behind in my class planning, my grading, the impenetrable tangle of my first two chapters, which I'd promised my committee in less than a month. This term was the last I'd be expected to remain regularly available on campus. This should have been a relief but wasn't.

What was I to do with myself, with all that time? Would I lie in bed all day dispersing? Would I collapse in on myself, flutter into nothingness? The summer months stretched catastrophically out in front of me.

Three weeks after the storm I met with Frank, my gentlest advisor. His field was far from mine, but his vast experience in queer theory and belles lettres situated our interests on the same horizon line. He was in his late fifties, handsome and trim, with heretically emerald eyes. They bored into you as you spoke, not in an unnerving way, only so you knew you commanded his full attention. His office was cramped and sad, but then the department building was dreary in general; this was no fault of his. As I walked in I was panicked, for I'd come no farther in my project than the last time we spoke, some six weeks before.

I wanted, I'd told my committee, to write on women's projects of self-making in the postwar period, but wanted to do it slant—I thought "unliterary" art should slip in, so I'd begin with Plath and Sexton and open outward, thinking through the talk-show era, '90s women's rock, the contemporary memoir and the personal essay boom, autofiction, Lena Dunham's *Girls*. If the lyric had lost steam, I said, in the back half of the century, where had the confessional impulse gone to, how was it invoked in other structures, other media? What if writing from life, this giving an account of oneself, was, in fact, the technique by which one *composed* a self?

When we'd arrived in the program, we were told to explore multi- and interdisciplinary approaches to scholarship. This was the department's self-perpetuating utopia, a future where we could keep the humanities afloat by stringing all our fields together in a Frankensteinian intellectual raft. Strict lit crit was anachronistic, it was for the fogies, and job fairs weren't looking for the next Harold Bloom. What was sexy about Harold Bloom? Nothing. The market was primed for innovators. This was all fine for me. I hated Bloom, and the structuralists bored me. I wanted the career Eve Sedgwick had, or Beauvoir, Kathy Acker, Hélène Cixous.

What I found was that they wanted hybridity, but only to a point. Experimentalism, but not too much. Interdisciplinarity mainly seemed to mean you could bring continental philosophy or radical psychoanalysis into your work, or maybe an occasional anthropologist if you were truly in the vanguard. Not music, not television, surely not Ricki Lake. So my project was at a standstill. I'd have been better served by my committee telling me on day one they'd only accept the dissertation if it was all about Plath, and even this, I saw, would have been a begrudging concession. My fascination with Sylvia was condescended to—she was a read poet, but not a major one, was the common thought, and really, what was there left to say?

But I didn't care anymore. I didn't want to teach, and in my mind I watched myself being slowly sucked into a bureaucratic whirlpool—that was if I got a job at all. Most of us wouldn't. Oversight meetings seemed mainly to be about grading on a curve, cutting our readings in half, challenging undergraduates less. They had rich parents who'd specialized in speaking to the manager, and anyhow, books weren't these kids' futures; they'd become important people, lawyers, maybe, or they were premed. I couldn't give a C minus without approval from the head of the pedagogy program.

None of this had to do with *the life of the mind*. Actually, the program seemed to be making us all obscurely denser, and my work was utterly divorced from the writing I wished I was doing, writing that might move people, rather than just edify them. I saw I was naïve, but what could I do but leave? I couldn't bear the thought of being trapped in faculty meetings until I was dead. Only one student in my cohort went on to a tenured position. The rest of us dissolved into other paths and other lives. We lost touch—as the years passed, I kept up with only Jean.

In Frank's office we said hello, and I guess I smiled at him a bit too widely. I could feel the muscles in my cheeks twitch, like my face had stuttered. I put my bag down and sat in a chair across from him. His expression was cloudy, for he was a natural worrier, sort of maternal in his way. Some of the graduates liked to speculate on his early years, how he would have been in his prime at the height of the AIDS crisis, how he probably lost much of his life to it, but all this was idle gossip, just a way of making him more proximate to us, like we were on a level playing field. It was necessary to imagine ourselves in shoes like his, we told ourselves, anyhow if we planned to actually live this life, to chain ourselves to institutions that would erase the people we thought we were, the people we might otherwise have become.

Bathed in the tenderness of his concern, I thought of confessing everything there and then. I reckoned if any of the faculty could conjure sympathy for me, it would be him. I wouldn't need to tell him why I was in crisis—the thought of saying what had happened out loud turned my tongue to stone—but I could allude to my "mental health" or make vague reference to a convergence of negative events in my life, which resulted in this evacuation of time, I could say I worried I wouldn't finish the proposal. That I was thinking of leaving—planning to, I see now. But I thought if I told him any of this I wouldn't be able to stop telling him things, and I'd say I didn't want to go on with the project at all, go on with any of this, academic life, the way the building we were in seemed to choke all my words out, to efface my very capacity to witness beauty.

Instead I trained myself to meet his gaze straight on, because I knew the meeting was a test, and probably the committee had decided among themselves I was failing it, so if I wanted additional funding, I had to prove I was safe, stable, and sane—that I was, in short, a sound investment, because that was what we were, wasn't it, vessels through which the university funneled money, in the hope we'd perpetuate its system, parrot its politics, bring in future donors, and call attention, by our work, to its use value in stewarding that work into the world. I needed to prove I was a person, in short, or rather a mind, the selfsame mind that had been so diligent and vocal, so confident in her work these four years.

Beneath my seat my right foot twitched and tapped. I felt sure if I went still, the smooth surface of me would commence its dissolution.

You seem overwhelmed, said Frank.

No shit, I thought.

His brows furrowed and he leaned forward, a gesture I saw he meant good-naturedly, but that raised my hackles nonetheless. Not that he frightened me, but because I didn't want his pity, his or anyone's, and my instinct to ask for help recoiled as quickly as it had sprouted. I calcified. I drew up my curtain of ice. This was a betrayal of course, for Frank was so generous to me in my time there; among the faculty, he was one of the few who seemed, actually, to have any real faith in my work at all.

Sometimes we ran into each other at the lesbian café—we lived, we'd found, in the same neighborhood—and he was warm and kind, a good storyteller. He didn't keep grad students at arm's length, as his colleagues did. He treated us as people, and peers—he thought of us as having lives that were as vital and complex outside the academy as within it. I knew he'd hear what I said, if I said it, but anything or anyone who might ring the alarm about my wellness needed managing. He wasn't my enemy, but his concern could prove a problem.

I'd need to pivot. I said I was fine: stressed, yes, but making do.

He sucked in air; he was skeptical. He said he thought I would have sent more of my work by now. He said he knew I didn't like the changes the committee demanded. He sensed it was a difficult time, but "we"—with this framing I saw the meeting was called by the collective—needed to be sure the work would be completed successfully, and in a timely manner.

I sighed. I straightened my back. I held his eyes with mine, as words began to pour from me. I said it was only that I was trying to get it *right*. I couldn't hand them half-assed dreck; I needed to find the true voice of the project. Yes, I felt pressure— it's a dissertation, for fuck's sake, I'd be concerned about anyone who didn't wear it like an albatross, but anyhow I was constitutionally high-strung. The curse I'd inherited from my mother, and I'd told him all about that, her constant fretting, her tightrope walk above the experiential free fall of economic precarity. Didn't this stress prove my investment in the project? Anxiety is love's strange shadow, after all. Desire, aching toward its object.

My voice rivered from my lips evenly, seeming to have all the uncanny distance from me of a ventriloquist dummy's.

This was the most urgent writing I'd done to date, I continued presently, my feminist manifesta, an indictment, really, of the heterosexist literary machine—an impassioned apologia for the confessional, a bombastic ordination of my own *écriture féminine*! I'd been readying this work for years, it was what I'd dreamed of while biding time in the killing swamps of Virginia, the project I felt certain would heave me from under the awful smallness of my life. Yes, I was daunted at times. My scope was ambitious, but ambition was the lifeblood of the work, was it not, and hadn't they told us to exceed disciplinary borders? Was this not the very radicalism they'd said would make us more competitive on the job market? My work mattered, I said, it mattered in a way another close reading of the *Ariel* poems never would, it was stranger than Ivan's work on DeLillo, or Foster's on Pynchon, but that was the animating force behind it, not a death knell. It was taking longer, yes, than they'd predicted, but maybe this signaled that my experiment required more time, and wanted for a little extra support, not that I'd relinquished myself to despair or incompetence.

I stopped then, inhaling sharply, and held my breath. I quieted my body.

Frank sat back in his seat, disarmed. The words had fallen from me like perfectly rounded pearls, landing and bouncing on the tiled floor in a clatter. It was a kind of possession, I thought later, like I was seized by some dybbuk, an enigmatical other woman who knew what needed saying in ways I couldn't fathom. I watched Frank gather my pearls and string them back together—the perfect gentleman. He paused. He was trying to make sense of me.

You're all right otherwise?

Fabulous, I said, I'm just waiting for spring. I've been thinking of finishing in New York.

This was a gamble, as I hadn't mentioned remote work to anyone on the committee. Frank's bearing glitched; his mouth reset itself. I could see him plotting his reaction. I thought how he'd be an awful poker player.

It would be . . . unconventional. We've had several students go elsewhere in their dissertation year and falter. These things pile up, you see, big projects accumulate, and you'd lose library access, you'd lose ease of access to the committee. I just wonder . . . has something happened?

For a moment I let myself slip.

I hate this city, I said, and I have to get out. I told him a change of pace was needed, maybe I'd finish more quickly, and I could petition for library access at Columbia, besides. Boston was killing me. It would kill my project. In New York I would live and write; everything there was possible! It was the only answer.

Frank saw through my circus act now, but his confusion meant I had the upper hand, so long as I ceded no further ground. So long as I remained unbending.

Lying to him felt like what it was, an act of treachery, but it no longer mattered. I convinced myself I was lifting a burden from him and everyone: the burden of my self, and all my dumb suffering, my chaotic scholarship, my disintegrating life. For others now I was a time suck, a waste of goodwill, and really, a kind of grade-A cunt who'd managed to sneak into their intellectual paradise, a mongoose in the lapwing's nest—sucking on all the eggs, thieving what wasn't mine.

I didn't need Frank to believe me. He just had to indulge my little fiction awhile.

I lied to everyone I knew that year. It was easy. I was the program's resident party girl, always down to barhop or get high. On campus I'd be found chain-smoking on the stone bench in front of the department building like a French teenager. In my diary I wrote of feeling vacant whenever I wasn't performing for others. Beyond spectacle, my self extinguished, which isn't to say I liked attention, only that it forced me to pretend I was something resembling a person. Nothing frightened me more than the idea of facing my friends' questioning, their pity, or worse, their disbelief. My faith in my recollections wavered. I'd come to see the immensity of my violation as statistically improbable; I told myself my trauma stretched credulity. I must be a liar, or else what had happened wasn't all that serious. Really, I said, I was a wicked narcissist, centering my suffering in a world full of it.

Some nights I'd come to in darkness to find my laptop's blue flare illuminating my sunken face. I'd be sitting somewhere adjacent to my body, while that body scoured the internet for studies on multiple victimization, rates of revictimization, some first-person account that seemed in any way kin to my own. I needed to know it was possible other women had survived similar horrors and gone on to live normal lives. I'd guessed my experience was unusual, yes, and surely underreported, but the thought of being absolutely singular was immobilizing—I didn't know if I'd be able to go on. Later I met other women who disclosed similarly repeating, but ultimately discontinuous, incidents of sexual trauma, but at that time I felt like an alien marooned on a hostile planet. No one I knew ever talked about these things. Outside the movies I thought I was alone.

The percentages and graphs embedded in the digitized papers my body read blurred and bled into one another. I learned how survivors of childhood sexual abuse were more vulnerable to rape as adults, and that this history correlated with higher rates of substance abuse and domestic violence. I hadn't thought before to connect my childhood to what was happening to me now. I'd blotted out my youth altogether. I reminded myself, though, that the numbers were only estimates, and self-reporting lowballed things, especially if what was being reported existed behind a shroud of shame. And of course I'd never reported. I hadn't told anyone, anyone besides that awful doctor, which meant, if nothing else, that the studies I pored over in my insomniac hours hadn't accounted for me.

I was physically exhausted. Sleep was only a shutting out of the light awhile, a perilous in-betweenness, some half-conscious sputtering through the hours of night. In every shadow I saw strange faces, grinning faces, and when eventually I began, again, to dream, I dreamed of being gutted by hulking figures, cut open and chopped up, having my torso dragged over jagged walls of broken glass. Everything inside me would pour out then: wet slop. I suffered apocalyptic dioramas. In one, I sat before an easel on the summit of a mountain. Above me a comet careered toward earth. I was painting the scene on a canvas, awaiting extinction. Only booze knocked me out. Even still, I'd wake in the witching hour despite it, couched in the dark and the silence of other people's sleep, the oppressive atmosphere of a peace I was forbidden from, feeling I hadn't nodded off at all.

For years this went on: cratered nights and days without end, drab gray days filled by what the French writer Marie Darrieussecq has called the insomniac's "nothing time"—time that "consumes you nonetheless." I was a zombie, ambling senselessly through my life, entirely emptied of personhood.

I was convinced I'd be raped again, and that this rape might happen at any moment, in any place, at the hands of any man. I knew rape would go on happening to me for as long as I lived in that city, as long as I remained in the program, haunting the same spaces, the same circles, stupidly drinking at the same dreary, dicey bars. I suppose I could have changed my behavior, or at least have stopped getting so wasted, but drunkenness was the only act that subdued my mind, and nothing I did ever rendered me less assailable, besides. I was helpless. There was no hope of keeping my raving suitors from the garden gate. Rape was my destiny, and I became plagued by vague delusions of grandeur, telling myself I had to go on getting raped so the ordinary lives of others might continue apace. I was sure men could smell it on me, like my woundedness had a pheromonal discharge.

I saw that these notions were perverse, that they were crazy—and I was crazy—but I couldn't stop thinking them. I was dissociated, yes, even if I didn't have that language to hand, but my mind went on racing through every possible outcome, and all the time. I no longer believed it mattered what happened to me, but needed, still, to predict all of it. I needed to cobble a story together.

When I walked home alone in the dark I was consigned to my fate. That term I took a night class on women's life writing through a consortium at MIT. From six to nine every Wednesday I was entranced by Alice James and Maxine Hong Kingston, Audre Lorde and May Sarton. I admired these women and raged against their suffering, and as the days angled toward spring I read Kate Zambreno's landmark HAGiography *Heroines*, remembering all the erased women, the silenced women, the madwomen, while I thought how badly I wanted it all to be over. I thought the best thing would be if the next man who raped me finished the job, seeing as I couldn't do it on my own. I was so pathetic. I was so weak. At the time I didn't understand this as ideation, or not exactly, because of how passive my urge was. I thought there was nothing so radical about giving up.

My fixation with survival lifted from me, a ratty veil. That a man might murder me wasn't so different from what had occurred already; it was a matter of gradation, not extremity. What was my life that year? A grieving blankness. I was a woman destroyed and repossessed, an automaton. I was a mirror through which time passed.

I recall little of that last spring and summer. In the movies, they make it seem like your whole life stops when you get raped, but I kept arriving at the awful truth that nothing about it would stop, and I still had to wake up each day and do the same stupid, boring shit I did every other day, and would have to go on doing until the end. In a way I envied the girls in the Lifetime programs, who were stopped dead inside their little trauma cocoons, while everyone around them was forced to accommodate their sorrow. They were newborn babies, shucked of all the awful trappings of womanhood, deposited back into their lives anew.

Meanwhile I became an ugly diamond, setting all my pain to the side, teaching my little classes, pretending to write my dissertation, working as a transcriptionist in the off-hours—just a mindless echoer of other people's words. If I stayed any longer, I thought, I would just let go. Already I was destroying myself. After the Diplomat, time had decelerated to immovability; now whole weeks evaporated, with days gone in the dense smog of hangovers, and nights submerged in Burnett's vodka, frantic chain-smoking—"chugging butts," Edie called this new relentlessness animating my habit.

I distanced myself from my friends in the department, mainly the men, who I'd decided were jerks, they didn't respect me, they couldn't fathom what had happened to me or what I was going through, though of course I hadn't told them. They didn't even read women writers, I reminded myself, who they viewed (or so I suspected) as artless hysterics. My work was a joke to them, *I* was a joke to them. But then I was a joke to myself, some callous god's joke concerning the abjection of certain kinds of women. Poor little rape girl.

I guess I'd held them to a different standard. We'd spent four years together, after all, terrorizing Porter Square, Kendall Square, Brookline, Allston. Our particular pleasure was crashing Harvard house parties. If there was a man guarding the entrance I'd tell him it was fine—*of course* I went there, *of course* I knew someone inside! I was Hanna's friend or Lauren's friend, and I'd come to help get her home. It's just, you know, she's fighting with her boyfriend upstairs. That's why I brought the muscle. Then I'd indicate the boys waiting behind me, a ragamuffin assemblage of skinny poets, and the man and I would laugh and laugh. We'll only be a minute, I'd tell him, and usually we'd be let in. Inside, Foster raided the kitchen, stowing liquor, beers, twenty-dollar bottles of half-decent wine in his backpack, while Victor tried to get a number off some luckless rich girl with an immaculate manicure and Prada pumps on, enshrouded in clouds of Chanel No. 5 or Le Labo. Sometimes Allan pissed on the soap and shower products in the bathroom, which seemed even to us a bridge too far.

I see now I resented the men in my life because they hadn't protected me, which was neither their job nor their prerogative. Part of me had the awful thought that if I'd been romantically bound to one of them I never would have gotten raped, because I'd have been already owned, I would have been under the aegis of a man, loved by him, fucked by him, I wouldn't have been so obviously damaged, so desirous of the legitimation permitted by a man's attention. I was too proud to talk about any of this, even with my girlfriends, except Edie, sometimes, when we were on the verge of blacking out. I clung to Edie and also to Jean, whose sense of her self appeared to me entirely uninterruptible, she seemed to need nothing, certainly not from any man.

For them I twisted my earlier rapes into tales of revolutionary sluttishness, stories of a party girl getting just this side of out of hand, but this time was different. I couldn't transform the Man in the Gray Room into a wacky anecdote, because there was too great an accumulation of suffering by then. All of it together had become unintelligible: it was the absence of speech. Still, in the mirror—when I could stand to look at my face—I called myself disgusting and unlovable, used up, ruined. My hatred was exquisitely corrosive. It was what I deserved.

In the spring my Professor returned. He sent pleading texts once or twice a week, desperate messages, I had no notion what for. I was nothing. In the two years since I ended things, he'd gotten married, information I stumbled over in the paper. A wedding ring wouldn't keep him from me, he said, because our sex for him was shattering, indispensable, it was "like TNT," and he refused to imagine a future bereft of my body, a confession I gathered around myself like a glamorous shawl. It was silly but I wondered if he understood, as in *really* understood, what TNT would do to a body. Nonetheless, his comment rendered me substantial; I was once again a woman of consideration.

What he said impressed on me a possibility that I had the power to obliterate a man, a notion so beyond the pale, so profoundly implausible, I found myself perfectly seduced by it. *I* was meant to be the destroyed one: *I,* the abject. I'd never fathomed I could orchestrate the Professor's annihilation. I luxuriated in and feared this at once. But I begged off, conjuring excuses. I told him I didn't have the time or energy to be an other woman again. I said I had a boyfriend now, and I was happy with him, I said he worked as a river guide and we were moving in together soon. Lies, of course. Really I couldn't fathom being touched. To the extent I was able to enjoy sex at all, mine with the Professor had been, in its way, good, but the thought of being with him or anyone made my skin shrink and go red with hives. I'd have panic attacks, instant and debilitating, great black holes of cavernous affect.

The Professor, though, was immune to my reasoning. Like most men, he was sure there was a "yes" encased in the cold amber of my refusal. It's just he had to rub it down, wear my "no" out, cleave it open. Rather than bow to him I dyed my hair blond. I longed to look like the type of woman who cared for nothing: a woman as frozen and blank as a snowbank. He must have been stalking my social media, because a week after, he texted to demand an explanation for why I'd "done that" to myself. He said how disappointed he was in me—I'd spoiled my looks. I was so sexy before, he continued, my dark curls so sensuous. He said I seemed to him a kind of "gypsy." I didn't have the strength to argue with him over his political incorrectness. I didn't feel like speaking to him at all.

I thought then of Assia Wevill, the other woman in the chaos of Plath's separation from Ted Hughes, and how both poets exoticized Wevill in their accounts as a mystical Jewess. "She would quite like to kill me," Plath wrote. All this conferred on me a further force. I didn't look like me, the Professor protested, petulant and childlike, missing—of course—that this was the whole fucking point. I said to him a bartender downtown liked to call me Veronica Lake now whenever I walked in. Never mind that Veronica ended her life as a drunk. Never mind how they found some of her ashes in a Catskills antique store. I said to the Professor that this other man's assignation made me feel beautiful.

The Professor asked why I wouldn't allow *him* to make me feel beautiful, but I was growing sick with his whining. I didn't feel threatened by his goading, or his obvious sense that he had an irrevocable dispensation to fuck me, no, mostly I was annoyed, so I suggested he try fucking his partner, I said I'd seen the announcement, and I wasn't some fucking mark, a two-bit bimbo who'd spread her legs anytime he got bored. Isn't it a bit soon, I asked, smelling blood in the water, to be suffering marital bed death?

I was cruel but felt he'd earned it. I was learning to whet the edges of my lexicon, to render men as diminutive and debased as they'd made me. Now I would cast on them the awful loathing I spewed all over myself each morning. Finally, yes, I felt a sharp spark of feeling—pleasure!—the delight of being showered in his need, but more, the thrill of having come, at last, to master the power of squashing him beneath the boulder of my words.

I spoke with the Professor a last time late in the spring season; end of May, it must have been. He was at the marathon that morning in April, a fact I learned in one of countless messages I'd previously ignored. Not at the finish line, he amended, but ten blocks from it. I realize how ephemeral it all is, he told me, our connection here. The tether holding us to this life. When I read this I rolled my eyes, but he'd been on my mind in the aftermath, too. I could admit as much. Something about his pickup artistry reassured me, even at a distance. Really, it was his eagerness that first beguiled me, his shameless articulations of desire. He was the sort of man who knew what he wanted, and what he wanted was me. I'd been bewildered. I was never chosen, or not in that way, as if I were singular, as if I had value. Now I remembered the taste of Camel Lights on his breath, his cats slinking through his quaint apartment, both of us smoking in his queen-sized bed mornings. Breakfast, even. The way he cooked for me like we were a couple. Maybe we were.

Edie's sister Andie was getting married. This would have been the night of her bachelorette party. Edie rented a party bus for the occasion, and we hosted the pregame at our apartment, to keep the driver from needing to collect bridesmaids like Easter eggs all over the city. The weekend was eerily hot, the streets airless and empty feeling, like how it is in August, when everyone's on the Cape. I'd never liked Andie's friends, partly because I was a bitch, and partly because they all were. In my own home they ordered me around like a bar wench or live-in, like they were superior, like these weren't my polished floors they were clopping scuffed Payless pumps all over. I was annoyed but apart, as usual, drunk early, as usual, and I kept sneaking onto the roof to smoke and hide from them, to flee their gossipy nattering, to secret myself against their tiresome neediness.

It wasn't that I didn't understand their type. Their lives, like mine, were Sisyphean labors toward a class security they'd never achieve except in marriage. Mainly they were nurses, Dorchester girls, Quincy girls, the eldest daughters of working-class natives who made vile reference to the "A-Rabs" running the delis, which they called a slur not fit for repeating. Their fathers were firefighters or cops, mechanics or worked construction. Twice or five or a dozen times a year their beer-drenched brothers would be thrown in the drunk tank after starting or taking part in bar brawls with other surly, stinking men who'd made the fatal error of rooting for the wrong baseball or basketball or football or hockey team. Once I saw a van flipped over by a group of such men in the middle of a Bruins parade. I don't remember if it was because the Bruins won or because the Bruins lost. None of it mattered and it was life or death to them, a whole philosophy of being, Boston Strong, real chowdahead hours. I guess it wasn't surprising that the bombing sharpened the city's razor-thin racial lines. Everyone was on edge.

In my kitchen the wide vowels of a seaboard dialect stretched the corners of these women's mouths. They wore lipstick too dark for their skin tone, and flushed a brilliant crimson after two drinks, but marched ever onward, good Catholic soldiers. Their accent told the lie of where they'd been. In a way, too, it determined precisely how far they would go. They dreamed of decorating like Jackie and dazzling like Audrey. But they were of sturdier stock, and could fight as hard as their brothers when it came down to brass tacks. I knew their kind of trash because I *was* them. I too tried to peel the poverty from my language like bark in thick sheets. At the end of each day I'd tally the number of times I'd said "y'all" and would chide myself, thinking how fucking stupid I sounded in front of the other grad students and faculty, or teaching our well-heeled, accentless undergraduates. I longed for severance from the redneck rhythms of my youth, and after the year I'd had, prayed for nothing so much as the unconditional eradication of my past altogether.

In lieu of this I cowered in the thorny bower of cultivated contempt. Over free wine at department parties I mocked the Virginia women I'd grown up with, women whose sentences were infested with stray r's—who threw their "warsh" in the "warter," who had one brat too many and too many goddamn car engines on the lawn. I made them ugly so I might be clean. Dramatizing the disorder of their lives made the anarchy gnawing at the rim of my own seem less total. Andie's friends condescended to me for the exact reason I loathed them: our lives were too close. We exposed each other somehow.

When the party that night was in full swing, I crept into my bedroom and locked the door. I felt a foamy bursting in my chest, though it was probably just the Adderall I'd snorted in the bathroom ten minutes before. Purses and coats were thrown over my bed, and I lay across them, deciding without thinking to text the Professor. What I needed in that moment was to be alchemized by my own fuckability. I thought to feel yearned for would confer a kind of animal reality on me, a tactility—I believed it might reposition me inside my body.

The prospect of a stranger was too frightening, but with the Professor, every outcome was anticipatable. I knew what he liked and what he'd do to get it, that he'd take charge and I would feel something, anything, even if not purely pleasure. He wouldn't hurt me, I told myself, because he had too much to lose, and besides I knew where he lived, as did Edie, who knew about us, a knowledge of hers he too had been made aware of. I on the other hand had nothing, and so had nothing anymore to fear.

He replied almost instantly. He said he'd been thinking of me so I asked if he was already hard.

Rock, he texted back, like a fucking rock.

He asked, as I knew he would, if he could see me that night. I sent a winking emoji and nothing else, unsure now if I could go through with it. Already I was hovering above myself. Whore, I thought, you stupid slut.

Come on, he wrote, you know you miss it.

Miss what, I asked?

This cock.

Lmao, mmmmmm, I typed, recalling how he liked to be reminded of the distance between our ages, that it turned him on to see my youth made legible in text speak, vernacular, my cultural reference points. Baby have you heard the new Beyoncé, the new Gaga, are you reading Donna Tartt, Rachel Kushner, Marie Calloway. I told him about the shitty dance parties I went to, the rare club in the city, I bragged about seeing Beach House tour *Teen Dream* before the record release in a tiny venue in Central Square. Grimes opened the show—*Geidi Primes* had just come out, or was about to. Ten people watched her perform. How could I have known then she'd be one of the horsewomen of the apocalypse?

It wasn't, the Professor'd told me, that he didn't enjoy nearing fifty; he wasn't panicked about age or atrophy. I have the same sex drive I did in high school, he said, and this to me seemed true—his stamina astounded me; he liked to fuck slow and hard all night. But desire, he continued, blooms in difference, and he liked a shine on his apple, wanted to watch his coarse hands map the expanse of a supple, an unblemished, a perfectibly pliant body. His partner, I knew from the announcement, was age appropriate; this was why, he argued, their erotic flame had been so swiftly snuffed out. They were too alike, he whined, their experiences too parallel. He wanted, when he woke, to open his eyes on a world unlike his own.

But why me, I wondered. Beyond his pay grade and his title, our academic day-to-days were functionally indistinct. We spent all our hours in classrooms or libraries. All effort went to grading shitty student work. There was nothing all that magnificent about me. I was a nobody, and no one wanted me besides a handful of violent monsters and him, but then, it was easy to trick myself into thinking his infatuation with me meant I was headed toward larger things, that one day I would flower, if I were only able to endure all this a little longer. I felt bad for his partner, but not enough to stop. That night I was high and aching, and the resurrection of my lust seemed somehow celestial: it was Jesus on the third day. That I wanted to fuck at all seemed such an unexpected victory I was certain it trumped whatever ethics I might have had about his soured marriage. Or maybe I felt vindictive. Maybe I wanted to win once, needed to be the hot bitch for a night, the girl calling all the shots.

He sent a picture, then, with his cock in his hand. With his thumb he pushed it from his groin at the base, angling it toward the camera to embroider the intensity of his erection. I found this maneuvering sort of sad, his notion I was too stupid or else had forgotten the size of his dick, that I'd be bamboozled by a trick of the light, an unfamiliar positioning. Anyhow it wasn't called for. The Professor was enormously endowed, veiny and thick—illusion only got in the way. I felt annoyed then, waiting for my irritation to disperse, waiting for my body to respond to the idea of his. I considered touching myself but didn't. I was remote. I told him to wait up; I said he could take me to a hotel after the party. I said I'd do whatever he wanted. By now I felt I owed him.

From the purses on the bed I slipped a few twenties. Tips, I reckoned, for my being talked to by those women like the help. The party bus Edie rented was an indulgence, but her baby sister, she said, would be a bride just once. There was a stripper pole in its center. I swigged from a handle of Espolòn and swung around it awhile, losing myself. Back then tequila and I didn't countenance each other; it always made me sort of crazy. The bar crawl went on for hours; we schlepped all over the city. Somewhere downtown I surfaced from a brownout. I was dancing with a massively pregnant woman in some Irish dive. Patty, I told her my name was, Party Patty. Sweaty, we stumbled to the bar for shots. She paid for both.

In the bathroom I smashed another half pill on my driver's license and huffed it, cloaking the sound of my snorts with a flush of the toilet. I'm Stevie Nicks, I said to Edie later, and my septum must be obliterated! Isn't it glamorous? I was only having a little fun, and hadn't I earned that? It was good to have fun, because I *was* fun, and meant everyone to know. All night I danced like a dervish, inflating with strange mania. Meanwhile the Professor went on texting me. He said he had to have me; laboriously he narrated all the things he missed about fucking me, how it felt to be inside me, everywhere he planned to cum. I sent an ass photo from some other bar bathroom I ended up in—a grainy picture from a cramped, dingy stall. No illusions to be had. Do you want to own me, I asked him, will you destroy me? He said he already had. And he'd do it again and again and again. I watched myself from a great height. I wanted to shake this woman who'd sequestered my life, to beat her silly. She was my dark sister; my jailer; my lunacy. We both were biding time.

I called the Professor near midnight. I said he could take me now if he'd pick me up where I was, except I had no idea where I was and seemed to have lost track of Edie and the rest of our party. I saw I'd jumped a fence into a parking lot to pee; when I came to on the phone with the Professor I was crouched against a wall. On the other line his voice whispered back to me that his partner was still awake, reading in the bedroom. He couldn't sneak away just yet. Boo, I laughed, how boring! and hung up.

Back over the fence I went. Two blocks from the lot I spied the parked bus and raced toward it, a whirlwind. I could smell tequila seeping from my pores, it flooded my sweat. I'd be sick in the morning, on this I could depend. The driver watched me flounder up the steps. I'm OK, I said, as if he'd asked. Where is everyone? The bus was empty. Suddenly I woke, in my bed and fully dressed, with thirty-three missed calls. Four were from Edie, who'd at last left a voicemail. One of the bridesmaids had been hit by a car crossing the street. She was fine, or mostly, but Edie was at the hospital with Andie waiting for the woman to be patched up. She said the driver called to tell her he'd gotten me into the house. I didn't remember a thing. The other calls were all the Professor. He'd left a dozen voicemails, each from outside my apartment, where he'd waited for hours. He'd banged on the front door and my window and shouted for me until the neighbors called the police. He was furious. He'd risked everything to be there, he said, and it turned out I was just a fucking tease. He called me other names, too: cunt and whore, mainly. I felt I couldn't argue with this, so I blocked his number and slept for what seemed weeks.

In the middle of June, Jean convinced me to go on a girls' trip. We knew already we traveled well together. Three summers before, we'd ridden the Chinatown bus six long hours to New York, visiting Jean's boyfriend uptown. He was studying under one of my favorite poets, a woman who'd become famous writing on all manner of taboo topics: clitorises and papal cocks, divorce, alcoholism, abuse, and so on. Probably that trip had put the Brooklyn bug in me. I had a novel sense another life was possible. The city was rapt with music, people dancing, an utterly electric feeling. We walked everywhere—Harlem down to the park; Midtown into Union Square; the Village to the Lower East Side. One night we saw a performance of Plath's only play, *Three Women*. I was reminded that culture went on living outside academia; that poetry coursed through and between bodies. Poetry wasn't merely a puzzle of words demanding disassembly.

Now the two of us boarded a plane together. I'd flown just once before, when I was twelve, three hours down to Jupiter to meet my father. I was alone, an "unaccompanied minor." In Florida I spent a tense, surreal month with him in an enormous Spanish colonial he shared with a leathery-looking couple in their late fifties. I saw him one other time after that visit, on my sixteenth birthday, a dinner over which I had nothing to say to him. After I was older, my mother told me he was that leathery couple's houseboy, a revelation I found jarring but not unimaginable. He was handsome, my father, tall and tan and lean with surfing, and perhaps still is. This trip with Jean, though, was the first and only that took me farther west than the Mississippi. At the time this fact shocked Jean, as, to this day, it shocks anyone I tell. I've never had the money for travel. If I couldn't get someplace in a day's time by car, it was never worth the planning.

Five days we spent in Denver, crashing with Jean's mother, a radiant, warmhearted woman who put me immediately at ease. We ate great food, visited local galleries, and went to the only strip club I've been to where male dancers catered to audiences of mostly women. One of the performers asked to take me home, and he was kind and cute, but I was too fragile still. Besides I was trying something new—prioritizing my girlfriends over the attentions of men.

At the end of our time in Denver we drove to Cheyenne for a camping trip not far from where Jean had grown up. The only thing I knew about Wyoming was that it was the place where Matthew Shepard was beaten, tortured, and strung up on a fence to die. His murder was another of the stories that brutally curtained my youth, an abject omen adults flung in my direction to ward off my impending gender deviance. What happened to Matthew Shepard horrified me, of course, and I remember crying for him when I read what had happened, but there was nothing to do. I was a woman, and no violence ever put a stop to that. We stayed in a cabin with Jean's childhood best friend, a brilliant artist in the process of becoming an adult film star. As with Jean, everything about Maddox astonished me. I admired his keen eye, his campy irreverence, his radical repudiations of convention. He was a true artist. But his story isn't mine to tell.

The morning of our arrival we hiked ten miles. Despite the dry bright heat of a June day, snow was piled in places on the mountains. Many of the trails remained impassable. We stumbled on an ancient-looking outdoor church and hopped around the stone pews. We climbed the miniature bell tower and filmed one another performing stripteases while the *Twin Peaks* score played in the background. There was a mausoleum of sorts not far from the scene; a woman who'd died in the 1850s seemed to have been buried there. Her name (as I recall) was Hattie. The three of us conjured a life for her of soapy intrigue and betrayal; she was the town Jezebel, a real mischief-maker. We told ourselves she'd died of a broken heart, or some other savagery, though probably it was tuberculosis.

I'd never seen so much sky. Its blue was gleaming and pure, the saturated lapis of the Virgin's robes in old paintings. Wyoming did its best to put God in me. Maybe it worked. I saw chipmunks for the first time—scurrying through the brush as if on currents of air. There were deer, of course, and an eagle at one moment that circled above us. I breathed uncontaminated air for the first time. I found myself able to swim outside my throbbing trauma awhile and see things as they were, which was mostly not that bad. Nights we built fires and drank cheap wine, laughing and talking of all things forbidden. Although I'd have to ask Jean if I raised the issue of my rapes. Somehow I doubt it—I wouldn't have wanted to ruin the trip. Maddox's transparency about sex work relieved something stopped up in me. That week I made a profile on SeekingArrangement and set my location to New York. Five more days we stayed in those woods, wearing our bodies out beneath the sun, and by the time Jean and I flew back I saw that my life in Boston was over. This return was conditional on an almost immediate escape. I began to plan my new life.

Part III

YOU

New York, August 2013

In these years, you keep an exhaustive daily diary. Just before your move to Brooklyn, you scrawl a to-do list, which includes instructions to finish packing, to secure a lease guarantor, and to meet with your department chair. The matter of the meeting is omitted.[*] On Tuesday you run thirteen miles. Fifteen Thursday. Some days you write nothing of your interior life; there remains only a meticulous, punishing calorie log. You are reading *Infinite Jest*. You are reading *Our Lady of the Flowers*. You are listening to Fleetwood Mac's "Sara" on repeat. On the weekend, you go with Felix to the club, where he peels off from you to hook up with a cute couple. You write of feeling "humiliated" by this, "resentful, somehow, though it's not logical . . . I wept dryly in bed before falling asleep."

Felix was always peeling off with somebody or other. But your sadness to me seems petty—an unwarranted enviousness.

No matter, you tell yourself, you have "too great an accumulation of trauma and self-hatred" to let anyone in. The flat feeling is an "old tune, tired," you write, "and truly I begin to bore myself."

Brooklyn nonetheless is a lighthouse beacon:

I will remake myself. I will render life livable. I will write my dissertation, I will hold down a couple part-time jobs. One or

---

[*] Monday, August 12–Sunday, August 18, 2013

two nights a week I'll volunteer, and run, and find a yoga stu-
dio, I will eat better and drink less and keep plants and write
poetry again—maybe even a novel. There is time still.

I must learn, though, to live my life alone. I will never love.
Remember: exorcise desire.

The week of the departure your transcription work dries up. You panic about money. "I'd hoped," you write, "to work doubles every day, squirrel away an extra $500."* You have nine hundred to get to Brooklyn. Once, this sum would have seemed astronomical. Now it will barely stretch to the cost of the journey. You write of your thrill giving way to depression: you're leaving the people (Felix, Edie, Jean) who saved your life in these awful years behind. Serena is in Brooklyn, yes, and lives around the corner from where you're moving, but after the night with the Diplomat, you say, you don't feel you can trust her.

Solitude, of course, need not be loneliness. May Sarton writes of its value being that "there is nothing to *cushion* against attacks from within," that, in other words, you must meet yourself in solitude where you are: "The storm, painful as it is, might have had some truth in it."†

You decide to see uncertainty like a door. You must "come back to writing, you must make art—don't slide into the hole; don't dissolve again."

* Tuesday, August 20, 2013
† *Journal of a Solitude*

The trouble with archiving you in this period is the mercurial—or, rather, erratic—quality of your self-regard. One day you dream of metamorphosis, and this dream blows you open entirely. The next you write that "nothing is getting any better, nothing will improve. This will only be a change of place, and there, I'll have no friends, no money, and all the while, will still have to be myself. A repugnance."* You write of wanting "out of it all: no pain, no waste, no memory." After, you rail against your self-pity, not because you can admit to its uselessness, but because you don't "deserve" grief: you are so insignificant. But self-hatred, you say, is just another conveyance for narcissism, a darker vessel for the me, me, me, me. Who were you to others in this time? Hardly a thought for anyone else's suffering. You witness nothing of the outside. You're enslaved by what Plath calls the "shut-box" of personal experience.†

"I'm falling into the pit," you write, "I must stop looking inward, I must learn to write what is worth someone's time."‡

* Friday, August 23, 2013
† Interview with Peter Orr for *The Poet Speaks,* 1962
‡ Sunday, August 25, 2013

The night before leaving you dream again of the Diplomat.[*] Your mother and sister are there, and though they don't observe the event—for this is what you name your rape by him, "the event"—afterward, they edge backward, watching you with damp pity. You are embarrassed and hysterical, and your sister helps you build a wall around the stoop where "the event" occurred. Together you close yourselves in. Beside you your sister stands looking "worldly and solemn." You wake weeping.

You will never get over it, you write, not ever. The trouble, you say, is that it didn't begin with the Diplomat. It hadn't ended with the Man in the Gray Room either. This curse was on you from the jump; this violence is the knot at the center of your life. If only you could make out what it is inside you that draws these men your way—you believe you could really change, you could remake yourself in a safer image. Never seeing, as I wish you'd see, that there was nothing you did, nothing in you that earned it, that the knot was not yours for the unraveling because its origin exceeded you, it was in the rope being looped around your throat.

* Saturday, August 31, 2013

At last you set out. You'd booked a van, but at the lot a man hands you keys to a seventeen-foot truck. You're edgy on the ride, but calm yourself singing to *Hejira* and *Scarlet's Walk,* to *Have One on Me* and *Little Girl Blue.* Past the windshield a universe uncoils itself. What sort of a woman will you become? The future stoops on your chest, a stone slab. In the evening you get lost in the Bronx but finally you make it. You arrive. You have five roommates, only one a man, all drunks. On the second day you walk to the nearest market, one you're later told is for the neighborhood's robust Hasidic community. You've never seen Orthodox Jews before so you just think they're Amish. You're in daisy dukes and a crop top, which you hadn't realized would be inappropriate. The children stare like they've seen a flying saucer.*

"So much is happening already," you write, "it's good & exciting & unnerving & big."†

On the sixth day you go out with a man from OkCupid. You are stupid—he's dull and a poet; he says he stays up drinking and writing "like Bukowski" all night. He says he must "suffer effectively" for his art, but even this admission is offered without affect. He escorts you to the premiere of a friend's film and abandons you with strangers for thirty minutes while he does

---

* Monday, September 2, 2013
† You'd begun reading Woolf's diaries. You admire her abuse of the ampersand, trying it on for yourself.

coke in the bathroom.* You ask yourself why you're still there and realize you can just leave. So you do. The decision is minor but feels momentous, you write of being proud of yourself—how astonishing to find you can still say no, and doesn't it prove you aren't ruined, you aren't nothing, and you don't have to endure men's bad behavior to be loved, a love they aren't extending in any case.

You write how you weren't supposed to be going on dates anyhow. You are meant to be "inhabiting solitude." You're still rereading Sarton on the difference between it and loneliness.† Solitude, she says, is a way of making room "for that intense, hungry face at the window, starved cat, starved person. It is making space to *be there*." But you see you don't know how to abide self-presence; you are sucked too easily into blankness, an astronaut unloosed in the soundless void of space. Sarton nearly killed herself in Nelson that year, twice, and ideation, she remarks, resembles another feeling she'd had: one of being "close to a mystical experience of unity with the universe." You take her advice, though, and busy yourself, as "boredom and panic are the two devils the solitary must combat," she says. You start looking for a goddamn job.

---

* The film is a John Waters rip-off. Your date doesn't even offer you a bump.
† Her journals were about all you could stomach in the wake of the Diplomat.

On the eighth night you go out with another man, not the Bukowski boy (who texts to follow up but who you refuse to see), though this one, too, is rich and a name-dropper, he works in fashion, he also bores you.* You get too drunk and too nervous to head home from Manhattan at three a.m., so you crash with him in the East Village, where he lives in a two-bedroom alone. You blow him because you feel you owe him and in the morning he faintly fucks you. He pays for brunch after, which helps, because you're hungry all the fucking time. You're down to your last twenty dollars.

You write of having trouble being alone at night. "I want to assume nothing bad will happen. I don't want to live in fear." You tell yourself you've survived the worst already, and either way you'll be fine. Your life, you say, is only just beginning.

* Sunday, September 8, 2013

By the eleventh of the month you've located a half-dozen bars where you can get two beers for six dollars, and three that offer a free slice with every drink purchase. The pizza is more like flatbread with a dusting of plastic-tasting cheese, but countless times over the next year, this will be all you eat in a given day.*

Even though your committee's refused to approve you for further funding, you continue work on your dissertation. You tell yourself you might salvage things, prove them wrong, but a more substantial part of you is resigned already to failure, and you're wary of further effort—you know you don't want to do it anymore. Dutifully, though, you go to a café each afternoon. You refill the hot water in your mug until the tea bag runs clear. You tinker at your chapter on the *Ariel* poems: "Focus on the Holocaust, the McCarthy era, SP's ties to Modernism. Be more political. SP-as-War-Poet, a poet of conspiracy. Draw the committee back in—they might stoop low enough to care."

Everything you write toward the project is trite, cobbled from academic studies you haven't read in years. You scrawl lyrics in the margins of your diary: a line here, an image there. These too are bad but at least they excite you.

Felix visits. Everywhere you go people crawl over themselves

---

* Wednesday, September 11, 2013, a day you note is the two-year anniversary of the Waltham murders

to sleep with him. You no longer envy this, writing how obvious it is it's your self-hatred that makes men recoil. You are the engineer of your anguish. Why can't you pull yourself up from the muck? But there's something "untenable" in you, something "monstrous. They all see it. How I'm just a fuck hole."*

You wonder if this is what you want: total evacuation. Or is it the spectacle of abjection, the way (you feel certain) others apprehend you, their supposed knowledge of your shame, your debasement?

* Tuesday, September 24, 2013

Cautiously you reconnect with Serena. You convince yourself she never knew what happened that night. You were both so fucked up, and maybe she couldn't hear your screams, your banging, maybe the man she was with told her not to answer, maybe he, too, had been dangerous. The two of you see each other most days. Now it is cooler, you walk the length of Manhattan, or down from Murray Hill anyhow. You take the train to Herald Square, Museum Row, Washington Heights. You wander Central Park in little outfits and too much makeup, while everyone acts like they've never seen sluts before. You're walking provocations. The exhibition delights you.* No matter where during the day you travel, you both end up shit-faced each night at the local dive. The staff lets you stay after close: they adore Serena, she's beautiful and can drink, she laughs easily. The bar regulars are all artists or musicians or poets or filmmakers. Pratt kids. Ex-Pratt kids. People say they're really *into* your dissertation but later you realize they were just coked up. (Don't condemn them. Soon you will be too.) You write of waking at two p.m., feeling you've missed out on all the city has to offer. Still you're at the bar by five. Now you're looser, men take an interest in you, all sorts of men—straight men, queer men, married and partnered men, older, younger, drunk and sober, rich men and otherwise, as your ego balloons.

* Monday, September 30, 2013

You instruct yourself to curb this. Remember what you are, you say: a fetish object; men like you because you're forbidden.* You sense it in the tempo of their touch. They're starved, the panic in their grip unmoors you. The volatility in some of these encounters echoes violence, but isn't quite. You count your flings like a rosary. They're useful, you tell yourself, they prove you are able, still, to be desired. To costume yourself in a shroud of sex. You don't write of your own desire, or how sex feels for you. Is this pleasure? But you've decided on it, you're an agent in your life, you are finally free of what was done to you. You *are* free, you write. You are. You are. You are.†

* Monday, October 7, 2013
† Tuesday, October 8, 2013

Through October, the bad days pile up. You don't find work. More boring lovers. The house increasingly unstable: two of the roommates enter "recovery," which seems to mean they abstain for two weeks and—having proven their facility in temperance—proceed to go on ten-day benders. One of them fucks the only man in the house. She falls in love and tells everyone in the building about it but him. He recoils. He gets that caged feeling, the feeling of men. She, meanwhile, is all pink, a smiling pink mouse. Another man moves in, replacing one of the women, and he and the first man spend their days guzzling Natty Ice in the basement. The cans begin crunching by noon. The first man sleeps with another woman in the house. The pink mouse loses her mind.

Now her sadness is infectious; now you shun her. You are cruel. "She is too near what I was," you write, "my dark double . . . she's what I ran from."[*] You're embarrassed for her. For your new friends at the bar you twist her into a sad joke. You find her slouched with dealers in the living room at all hours, her face slack, her pinkness ebbing. After being confronted in a house meeting, she sits with her dealers on the stoop instead.

You pity her and know you *are* her. She's no ghost of days past. She's you in a strawberry-blond wig.[†]

---

[*] Wednesday, October 9, 2013
[†] But first she is herself. How can you not see this?

You command yourself to limit time spent at the bar but don't. You're up until seven each morning railing lines with Serena and the other leftovers who stay after the gates roll down. "You're a coke whore," you confess, "or becoming one. Put a stop to this."* But by the evening, I read, you're sending texts—wondering who will be out. You know you're unraveling but there's always another key being held up to your nose, always a baggie or a vial in some pocket, always another "guy" to "call." Once you start you can't stop. The high sharpens you to a single, imperturbable point. Cocaine allows you to dazzle. You effloresce. It's the only thing that lifts you from ego. In the radiance of a coke flare you become entirely exterior, all attentiveness to others and your surroundings; you become a rushing rapid of words. You never pay for the drugs, which is crucial, first because you have no money, and second because buying it would mean you have a problem.

You begin sleeping with a bartender friend down the block. He lives alone and his drugs never run out. He's cute. He has a nice laugh and is gentle, but you both know you're using each other. Sex with him is different than with the others, more textured somehow, and playful.

"I've started getting my body and my health under control," you lie after three sober nights.†

* Friday, October 11, 2013
† Tuesday, October 15, 2013

You go on a third date with a man you sort of like. He's older, thirty-six, and on his nightstand he keeps a framed list: How to Be a Good Man.* He says it's from his mother and makes him feel close to her, which, in turn, makes you want to feel close to him. You fool around. He's tender and intense but you say you'd like to wait to go further. You tell yourself this is what other women do, the sort of women men respect, but of course you have no idea what normal women do or what a usual sexual chronology might be. Certainly you've no clue how to command a man's respect. You've never waited to have sex before, you write. When a man wants to, you do it. You're calculating your position within purity culture, toeing a border. What if you manufactured a new erotic model of yourself? He doesn't need to know what came before. It's not dishonesty. It's tactical omission. You think he'll view your decision as a sign of your sexual assurance, your integrity, your continuing interest in getting to know him as a person, finding out what makes him a good man.†

He suggests you see sex as a "miraculous mile-marker in a conventional sequence of events." He says you have hang-ups,

---

* Saturday, October 19, 2013—although I'm furious with you for not recording the list!

† That you equate integrity with the withholding of sex isn't surprising, but I can't cosign it.

he calls you frigid. He says you should leave and you don't hear from him again. Can you blame him?*

By the end of the month you wonder why you hadn't ended things in Boston. "Weak," you write, "too fucking weak. Disgusting. A worm."† Though I'm glad you didn't. How embarrassing to have died in Boston!

You try sleeping pills—not in the suicidal way, just to keep yourself from drinking. You figure if you take one early enough in the evening you'll pass out rather than go to the bar. For a week it works, but the chaos in the apartment escalates. Now you spend each night out to escape the house.

"I can't enjoy casual sex," you write, though you've been having a lot of it. "If sex wasn't such an ordeal, if being vulnerable with men wasn't death, I might be OK." Sex terrifies you still, yet you force yourself to endure it, and constantly. By now you're well acquainted with the word "dissociation," but aren't using it to describe the place you go while getting fucked by bar strangers. You're drunk, and high, and what you are is a good-time girl. You want to provide men with a good time. The flagellation comes after: "I owe sex to whatever man will settle for me," you tell yourself. "I can't force someone to care for what they don't care for."

You see your need of love as a "constitutional weakness." You long to feel less. Everything is oversaturated. It's all in brash Technicolor. It's a "lack of sophistication," you say, wondering if "maybe I'm borderline." You watch *Girl, Interrupted,* you reread *The Bell Jar,* you read everything by Jean Rhys, while the stories distend in your chest. You grow light-headed, you get the volatile feeling. Like a star collapsing.‡

* You blame him.
† Tuesday, October 22, 2013
‡ Thursday, October 31, 2013. What you gather from the stories, though, is not self-diagnosis but a clearer sense of the systems and institutions that failed and destroyed

In November you use the word "rape" unequivocally to describe what happened in Boston. You won't share this with anyone else for some time yet.

A recurring horror in these months is the specter of "unstructured time." You tell yourself you're spiraling because of the vastness of dead hours. You say you must read, you must read, and wonder how it's possible you need encouraging. You are— or were—the sort of woman who'd devour four books in a week. In the three months you've lived in Brooklyn, you've finished only three.

You're photographed by Ryan McGinley, you're photographed by some talent scouts, you walk in a couple go-sees, but don't land the jobs. Nonetheless you feel the city opening. You see Neko Case in concert, you see Anna Calvi in concert, Zadie Smith is your first customer at the volunteer gig you start at the end of October. You don't let on you know who she is. You think how if you were British, life would have been simpler, more comprehensible in some way, you feel convinced it might have sounded like a wondrous, if Gothic, novel.

You're partying a lot. You go for an STI panel when you realize it's nine months since the Man in the Gray Room. You

these women: medical, ideological, familial, romantic. You're reminded that Plath's novel opens on the execution of the Rosenbergs, that Kaysen's boyfriend at the time she was committed was fleeing the Vietnam War. But you still can't see your sufferance in a broader social fabric. You are cast out; utterly singular. The failures are all your own.

were tested twice after but remind yourself there can be delays between infection and appearance. The not knowing is its own paralysis, you write, as it denies closure.[*] You've carried with you the possibility that part of him might remain in you forever. The results are negative.

<hr />

[*] Thursday, November 28, 2013

You start seeing a Columbia graduate student in literature. He's dweebish, and not all that handsome, but seems sweet, and he wants (or says he wants) to commission you for a panel on Plath.* One night he gets so drunk he accuses you of flirting with other men at the bar where you're having dinner. His face goes red and his whole body tenses. You'd be happier, he yells (really, he yells this), if I were pimping you out to every guy here. You fucking slut. You fucking slut. The people seated around you look over before staring determinedly into their plates. The bartender glances at you and busies himself with the dishwasher. You refuse to cry. You throw your last twenty on the bar and walk out.

The man's insult freezes you in time. You write that you're a matter of convenience to people in your life, and what of it? You admit: you're too guarded. No one feels they really know you. And anyway, the man was right. You *are* sleeping around. You'd thought it meant you were in control. You fucking slut.

Doris Lessing dies. You try rereading *The Golden Notebook,* but the words crowd and blur on the page, they overwhelm you. You stop.

Instead you see a movie where Jared Leto plays a trans woman dying of AIDS.† Watching it you feel only pity for some alter-

---

* You think this could put you in your committee's good graces. You don't consider any conflict of interest in this mixing of your sex and professional lives.
† Tuesday, December 3, 2013

nate version of yourself, one who'd gotten less fortunate news in the little room at the clinic. You hate this inward turn: the machine-gun fire of the I, I, I, I. You have a sense of everything cracking up.

You spend your days alone now. Is this the solitude you dreamed of?*

You loathe the happy people you meet. You feel occluded by their pleasure. You feel awfully blotted out.

---

* Sarton here feels useful again. She invokes Louis Lavelle, who divides solitude in two: the "painful solitude" of self-alienation and ignorance, and the solitude of communion, where we reckon with our "inner responsibility" while also accepting the "impossibility of being self-sufficient." We have a need to be with and *for* others.

You visit your mother outside Philly for the holiday. She accuses you of talking down to her and you admit (to yourself, in your diary) there's some truth there.* You're never open with her. You write of the panicky feeling, your sense that for your mother you were always her last defense against the world's disorder. To have poured your troubles in her cup would have shattered it, and you had to be solid—for your sister, too, who you helped raise. To be mothered now, you say, would be a humiliation, impossible; a shameful belatedness.

When you return to Brooklyn, you end up again in the bartender's bed. With him you do molly, you do coke, you smoke a joint, and drink whiskey—neat—from a crystal tumbler until the sun comes up. Against all odds he gets hard but doesn't penetrate you, a fact you recount with relief. You don't narrate your rapes for him but allude to an obscure grief, and he holds you as if you are a rare gift. You are shocked by the flood of feeling you have in this moment.

A week later he sleeps with your best friend.† You abandon yourself in an affair with a married man. He threatens to leave his wife, a woman you've met before. She's pretty, a lawyer, she has studiously white teeth. She's done nothing to you and yet

* And for this I want to shake you, to make you see you two could be comrades, could commiserate over your common history. Instead you both conceal it. You clam up with each other.

† Which, I see now, was within his rights, as you had no claim on him. Still, it hurt.

you're vengeful, you say sure, why not? Then he too sleeps with your friend. The same one. On the promise of leaving his wife he reneges.[*]

You rarely eat but run and bike and do yoga almost every day. You're undergoing a process of debridement. You direct yourself to lose ten pounds before another shoot for McGinley, which will again be nude. You pinch the skin of your stomach. Theatrically, you bloat out your belly and show it to people. You're six feet tall and grant yourself eight hundred calories each day.[†]

By now you're bartending two or three nights at an upscale Mexican restaurant in Williamsburg. Occasionally you buy your own coke and hoard it. You stop sleeping with men for a month, writing that you're too disgusting to be touched, you don't deserve tenderness. You long to decontaminate yourself through chastity. You write of numbness and loss of appetite, the black suck of depression after a bender.[‡]

You think to get a dog but dismiss the urge. What's the use, you wonder, of becoming accountable to another being while still rolling the "matte pearl of suicide" on your tongue.[§] You write twenty pages of your dissertation, all of it bad. You read *The Years*. You start *Villette*. You read *Cruel Optimism*. With the few hundred dollars you've set aside from the new job, you visit Boston, then you go home.

---

[*] On December 20 you write: "I am a specimen, a curiosity. A fuck-and-run."

[†] Sometimes fewer. In January you record your diet as such: a half grapefruit during breakfast with black coffee; an apple, a granola bar, and tea at lunch; one scoop of brown rice with greens for dinner.

[‡] On the twenty-ninth: "I seem to be expanding with a kind of nervous energy, a permanent mania."

[§] Tuesday, December 17, 2013

Winter is long and the snow is always yellow. The sidewalks are "aluminum sheets of ice."[*] You acknowledge that your partying has drained your resources, that you're falling from a "zone of poverty" into something less anticipatable. Your job exhausts you and you've little to show for it. The money is plainly bad. You try reading the paper each morning, thinking it will ground you in the present, but go on drifting—you remain prone to the "stabbing wormhole of the I."[†] You copy a passage from *The Years* as a warning against this: "But how did they compose what people called a life? . . . Perhaps there's 'I' at the middle of it, she thought; a knot; a centre," but in hindsight, I can't see how this would have disturbed your egocentricity in the least.

You write of a mind going gossamer, your thoughts are thin somehow, and flitting. The gaps between entries in your diary expand. "I am lazy," you confess halfway through January, "and nothing new ever happens. I'm always whining about the same shit. So what if I want to die, who doesn't, and so what if no one loves me. I know what I am. That's more than a lot of people can say."[‡]

You surrender again to the married man, who says he's stayed single since he last saw you, but once you've let him fuck you,

[*] Sunday, January 5, 2014
[†] Wednesday, January 8, 2014
[‡] Saturday, January 18, 2014

Serena tells everyone and everyone, in turn, reports that the married man has lied about his separation.

You run into his wife in the city and the two of you make small talk, but you see the hatred swimming behind her eyes, wet and hot. She longs to watch you suffer. You think of telling her you *are* suffering, you are, and it's all you've ever done, but this time you've earned it. You deserve her hatred, and really, perhaps you ached for it, maybe you'd calibrated your whole being toward it. You picture her slapping you hard across the face, you think of guilt blooming in the shape of a red hand on your skin. You know you've fucked everything up.*

* And drunkenness, you write, is no "explanatory framework . . . being blitzed is no excuse."

Your committee doesn't demand a leave of absence but intimates they'll no longer support your project. Instead you quit the program altogether, a simple and purifying act, like stepping out of a rain-soaked dress. In a manic fit you apply to a dozen publishing jobs, you apply to internships you can't afford to accept, you apply for second bar gigs.

One afternoon you chance on the married man in a café uptown, on the East Side—a neighborhood you're never in—where he tells you he's telling his wife that it's over.[*] The uncanniness of the coincidence unnerves you; you wonder if you've been snared in some *Truman Show*–style madness.[†] He sees your panic and says his wife works around the corner—it's a bizarre accident. You're getting up to leave when you notice her walking in, and you turn your back to her, praying she doesn't recognize you.[‡] In a matter of minutes, she storms out in tears. "She looked so defenseless," you note. The man leaves without looking back, as you knew he would. It doesn't mean anything. His "freedom" changes nothing, for he doesn't love you and never did.

You go to bed and remain there nine days. By the fifth you can't conceal your stricken state any longer. On the phone your mother worries, and you feel bad but don't have the energy to

---

[*] Tuesday, January 28, 2014
[†] Less seriously, you wonder if perhaps he followed you here.
[‡] "I am her dark shadow," you write. You are the vile replicant.

pretend anymore. Words again are unintelligible. You can't read, and can't write, or not really. The loose scrawl in your diary stretches and loops across the white expanse of its pages like a mist, the letters bleed together. You stop reading *Villette*. You seem to remember Esther Greenwood suffering this symptom just before her breakdown, but though you've just reread the novel, you can't summon this detail.

Briefly you consider checking yourself into a ward but don't, as you feel sure you'll never get back out. You think of withdrawing all the money from your bank account—there's hardly any there—and mailing it to your mother. You write how you'd like for it all to be done, to be nothing, and yet.

I 'd like to pause here and intervene.

It occurs to me I expected a deeper attention to the rapes in these diaries, but they puncture your record only occasionally: shadows peering out from the backdrop of a dismal dailiness. Mostly you're avoidant, but I should've expected this: you were quite literally on the run.

At moments I wonder if my writing this book—digging through your history in this way—is unethical or dishonest, if I'm exposing you. I wonder if the rapes were less disruptive than I'd imagined. Do I thrust on your experience a traumatic significance that wasn't there? Is it my job, or perhaps my crime, to assemble plot, to force on your behavior an ineluctable causality? It's entirely possible I gather your confessions from the wreckage of your accounting to pathologize you, to frame your actions like the motion of a rubber band snapping back.

For example. Was it rape and rape alone that pushed you into the arms of the married man? It had something to do, of course, with your perceived betrayal by the bartender, but do I draw too neat a continuity between your sexual abjection and the affair? Do I smooth your edges? Do I make you the victim, do I tidy you? Worse: Do I absolve your wickedness.

Or perhaps my urge is diagnostic, litigative; maybe I feel a need to put you on trial. Slut.

You of course were only yourself. Nonrepresentative. You weren't a novel, a story. You couldn't know you'd be the subject of this book. Perhaps what I do to you is another violence. I am your architect. I erect my edifice of horror.

B y the middle of February, miraculously, you're reading again. It's not clear to me how you dug yourself out of the hole. You are nonverbal on the matter of those dark weeks. You read Sarton's *Plant Dreaming Deep*. You inhale three collections by Alice Munro. You reread *Sula*. You finish A. S. Byatt's Frederica Quartet. You encourage yourself to produce a routine through the week, not just the bar work, but an hour of reading and journaling in the morning, and regular, coordinated exercise. "Six months of inertia," you write, "I allowed things to happen near me, I refused to see myself as an agent. I don't own my body but want to change, I have to. Or death."* Still you eat hardly anything, but the schedule helps.

Your dreams this month are consumed by rape, though not the rapes you lived through, they're new ones, with further men, and in them, the men mutilate you, they gut you like a fish, beat your face to a pulp, shove enormous instruments up you until there's blood and pus and shit all over. You wake in cold sweats. You feel you're not sleeping at all. "I am more and more permeable," you write, "my boundaries are diminished. There is no self." One day your hands stop working, and on the

* Thursday, February 27, 2014

next you write that the "way I move through space has become incomprehensible."*

On the twenty-eighth you go home with a Yalie. In a way this is the real rock bottom.

* Tuesday, February 11, 2014

You read Frank Bidart. You read Adrienne Rich.* You buy a new diary back in Boston, where you are visiting Jean, Edie, and Felix. The Professor hears you're in town and texts repeatedly.† You ignore him. "Sex is so uninteresting to me at present," you remark, offhanded.‡ Back in Brooklyn, the married man fucks his way through your friend group. Him you block too. You stop seeing the bartender, because you "can't be bothered with men—[they're] exercises in masochism. I am knowingly entering situations that will hurt me."

You write of a sense that you're looking over a great ledge; you write of feeling like an enormous phantom limb; you write of "corporeality without nerves: I am a shadow, the shape of a body but without pain or sense—an imitation of life." You tell yourself you're in mourning but feel separate from all of it. These revelations arrive in the doorway of your intelligence carrying no weight.

You watch *True Detective,* you reread *The Line of Beauty.* You admire Hollinghurst's obsession with James and think of rereading James's *Portrait* but don't. You plan to exfiltrate yourself from your friendship with Serena. You're toxic to each other,

---

* You don't know yet how involved Rich was in the genesis of Janice Raymond's screed of anti-trans propaganda, *The Transsexual Empire,* a note I include here because no one talks about it, and more of us should.
† Though you've blocked him, you suspect he's stalking your social media from a burner.
‡ Saturday, March 8, 2014

enablers. Besides, you're too sexually competitive; you use men as pawns to claw at each other. Not, of course, that you're wanting sex. You say you long for nunnishness. You loathe desire's surfacing—that forgotten hum. "These debasing sparks," you write, "they are small and flinty—I want but cannot kill them off."*

Mostly you're alone now. You wake each day "with a running catechism of my idiocies, my mistakes, all my awful humiliations."* You imagine falling like a petal onto the tracks at Bedford Avenue but shove the vision back—Felix is coming to visit; where would he stay if not with you? More cocaine now. Your apartment is unlivable; you're a "prisoner" there. Degrading yourself with the Yalie wasn't enough. Now you go out with a Harvard man, you sleep a few times with a bar regular, you have a one-week stand with a graffiti artist. You return to the married man, who has become, in a more official capacity, the separated man.

On March 17 you wonder if psych meds could even things, but are nervous of being "flattened, sanded down somehow."† You read a book on string theory and write of dreaming up "a me somewhere, in some alternative universe . . . happy and healthy: a me who smiles and laughs—I mean really laughs—a Jamie who is loved."

On the twenty-fifth you pillory this naïveté, your stubborn faith that things might change. "Look at my mother," you write, "who at 51 has never escaped poverty, who, despite her work and her hope and her force of will, will still be slogging and poor at the end of her life. Like my sister will. Like I will." Is *this* optimism cruel? you ask. Does *this* belief keep you from peace?

* Monday, March 10, 2014
† But what is it, I wonder, you worried you would lose? How numb you were then, and exhausted; how senseless and miserable. What else would be flattened?

Three weeks pass unrecorded.* In April you write of wishing you could quit partying, but this would mean staying home, and the apartment is a "trap house" with all the comings and goings, the strangers and chaos, the yelling, hysterical laughter, and roommates perpetually moving in and out.† "No solitude, no quiet, no peace." Why check into a madhouse? You are already living in one. The bar of course is a bar, but it's also your refuge. A friend there asks you to play keys in his funk band. You learn the songs, you rehearse, you do a few gigs. Your birthday passes. It doesn't feel like a celebration.

* Though you scribble dispatches from the outside world, as Anna Wulf does in *The Golden Notebook*: an Ebola outbreak in Guinea; Russia's annexation of Crimea; the trial of Oscar Pistorius; Courtney Love's claim that she's found Malaysia Airlines flight 370.
† Sunday, April 6, 2014

Y ou sleep with a man who ties you up and shaves your
cunt. He instructs you to call him "sir" and "daddy."*
At first you think he's joking and begin to laugh, but
an unnerving (a familiar) expression possesses his face. You
play it off as flirtation. When he fucks you it's too rough; you
tear; you bleed. You consent to everything—anyhow, you don't
revoke it—but feel shame even as it's happening. Worse later. "I
think," you write the next morning, "I've been treated too badly
to enjoy that . . . I wasn't afraid but didn't like the way it felt . . .
what he thought he saw in me, what he thought was appropriate
for my type." But it's easier, isn't it, to go along with what men
want from you. It seems to me you've no notion what you yourself desire. No pleasure in these pages. I search but find no signal
that you experienced sex beyond what was demanded. I don't
judge you, but I wish you'd interrogated your participation in
these scenes. What was it you wanted? What turned you on?

You read Monica Lewinsky's essay in *Vanity Fair* and copy
this from it: "Perhaps by sharing my story . . . I might be able to
help others in their darkest moments of humiliation."†

You read the diaries of Anaïs Nin. By the time the Germans
invade Paris, she's living here on Bleecker Street, befriending
Dalí, fucking Henry Miller. You read Muriel Spark. You reread

* Saturday, May 3, 2014
† Thursday, May 15, 2014

Isherwood: *A Single Man, Goodbye to Berlin, Christopher and His Kind*. You read the first volume of Sontag's journals, envying her chilly remove.

Of your own diaries you're embarrassed: maudlin exhibitions, marred by extremism, with no art or style to speak of. No recognition in them of causality, which is to say, you go on making the same mistakes. The plot doesn't build. You wonder what makes a great diarist and worry that academic training has stamped out your language, it's got your tongue, and you're only now returning to yourself, coming back to writing.

You wonder if everyone you know is an artist or if they're just drunks.

The same could be said of you, but you defer the thought and join a book club, where you read Hemingway and Homer, Holleran and *Myra Breckinridge*.

"My body is more excitable," you write at the end of the month, "I feel a stir of desire. I'm not frigid, I'm *not*—a relief. I want to write again, I do: poetry, stories, a memory maybe. And of course a novel."

In June you instruct yourself to "avoid the interior. Surround self with others. No need to be with the self. The 'I' is a hole. Happier lately. Though not happy."

You write nothing else until September.

In September you read *Crash*, you reread *Cat's Eye*, you read a sort of trashy novel you see everyone on the subway holding, because you've decided, now you've Left the Academy, that a book need not be labor to be worth your time. You aren't writing because you seem, lately, not to have much in the way of a self. "I'm at work or with friends," you say. "It's wonderful how I've pulled it off . . . sidestepped my ego." You move out of the frat house and into a shithole, but the shithole, for a time at least, is mostly quiet. You make new friends. For one of these you stage an intervention after he starts smoking meth.[*] You of course don't have a problem; you just have fun. You work at the dive bar now, the Pratt bar, and the people there ply you with free drugs for free drinks. You never black out because there's always a bump of something to set you to rights, to even you out after all the shots you're expected to take.

It doesn't occur to you most people aren't blitzed or high on the clock, but (you tell yourself) New York bartending operates by a different playbook. Sobriety would be a signal you aren't *enjoying* the work, that it doesn't please you to serve people. Really, these jobs persuade you, it's the perks—like the free-flowing liquor—that expiate the long hours, the shit money, the fact that each day your whole body aches. As for coke, everyone

---

[*] Which is funny, I think, since you went on doing coke with him several nights a week.

you know in the industry shoves it up their nose, and constantly, it's no secret. Really, it's an asset. Half the time the owners of these places are kneeling over immaculate white lines right there beside you, and gathered in your hunched mass, you are manic sinners at the hands of a tight-jawed god. It's easy now to slip beneath the dark waters of your own life. There's no outside to the bar anymore: you work four or five nights a week. The others you end up there anyhow. Your friends go nowhere else, you drink free, time stops.

Occasionally you swim out to other parties: On Top, Holy Mountain, Bathsalts, anything late at the Spectrum. You nearly knock Amanda Lepore over in a crowd one night, but she's dainty and gracious, the whole room calibrates around her glow. Some other time you're ordering shots at a dingy spot between sets and find Björk leaning against the bar right next to you. You ask if you can buy her a shot, and she says, Nǒ thænk yoǔ ☺ I am vęrý drǔnk ãlrēædŷ. Across the room, Matthew Barney is standing on top of a Skee-Ball machine. This would have been just after they separated. You bartend for pop stars and A-list actors with relative frequency now. They know they can drink at your dive without bother. But famous people don't interest you, or rather, you feel bad for them, because celebrity seems alarming and soporific at once. How awful to be always looked at, you write, inspected—to feel enslaved to an endless performance of amenability.

You're never dressed for these occasions: you have neither the money nor the talent to put together the kind of looks everyone else does. Instead you slap on pasties and booty shorts with pleasers. You look cheap but decide that's the joke. Your hair is silver, now fuchsia, now lavender, rose, cerulean. What's unchanging is that it's fucking fried. You master the art of the Brooklyn barter. Your friends not in service do hair or fashion, they tattoo, or deal coke. The dealer friend is how you get into these parties in the first place, and you know it, because your friend sells to half the people inside them. When you feel anything through the haze what you feel is an ambient glamor. Proximity to pleasure has become quite enough.

The university notifies you you're no longer enrolled there, and you wonder why they emailed at all. That girl is gone. She died back there. No men in these months: "I'm done with all that now, sexless. There's a truth in my body that sees this is best."[*]

[*] Thursday, September 18, 2014

The diaries end there, but don't worry, darling, I can play the biographer. I'm telling your story. Trust me.

First, your new housing falls apart. There are rats, to start, that chew through the walls of your roommate Dee's closet. She wakes to them writhing in her bed, crawling over her bare body. They loot everything in the pantry; the whole place reeks of rat piss. When you come home from work at four in the morning they dart around the kitchen, squirming flashes of horror. They aren't afraid, of you or anything. Some nights you snatch stray cats from the block and bring them inside. It's October, getting cold, so mostly they don't mind. You submit applications to dog rescues, prioritizing ratters. You start fucking men again to sleep somewhere clean.* Briefly you date one, a sweet guy, but you're not ready and don't want to be having sex, though you have it. Another endurance test, you tell yourself. No matter. It's just a body.

Of the five renters in the apartment, just you and Dee try to broker something with the landlords. They don't budge—in fact, that you've protested at all inflames them. They're frenzied, accusing you of lying to avoid paying what you owe. You document everything. You put rent in escrow. You hound 311 until they send an inspector, who confirms the infestation. After this, the landlords break in and threaten you. They post goons outside

---

* This is relative.

the building who slash your bike tires and wait by the door to intimidate you. This in particular is immobilizing—considering the rapes and that you're getting home from work in the middle of the night. You go to afters, stay at the bar until sunrise, sleep at friends' houses or in friends' beds the nights you can't stomach a man. The other roommates pretend nothing's happening, they pretend not to smell ammonia or see the shit. They treat you and Dee like hysterics. You call 311 again but it's your last move. The landlords return; they kick Dee's door in. You rush to see what's happening, and find Dee naked and screaming.

Out, the landlords tell you, out within an hour. Whatever's left we'll burn.

Serena rushes to you from a hookup's place. She's violently hungover or maybe hasn't slept. You both look like hell. She helps you shove your clothes, your bedding, and most of your books into a stolen Home Depot cart. Together you truck your little life to another friend's place. Most of your shit's in storage, so it's simple to sleep on couches awhile. You move around a lot. There's a month-long sublet on Flushing, where you rent a tiny room from an influencer. The place is three blocks from the dive and the influencer is amiable enough, but you're grime in their home, all shame and drunkenness and obvious poverty. The influencer, meanwhile, is manicured and gleaming, and hosts other manicured, gleaming influencers for brunch every weekend. It's unclear what any of these people do for money, but it's not your business. And you should be grateful. You crouch in the place like a troll, certain your clothes still smell of piss. When you creep out of your temporary bedroom you wear enormous sunglasses, protecting the smiling beautiful ones from your awful, stony glare.

One good thing happens in this despairing year. Five days before Christmas, Olive bounds into your life. The influencer lies to the agency; they claim you're on a permanent lease and say they'll assist with the dog's care. For this you're ever in their debt. But it's the first Christmas you've been apart from your mother. Neither of you has the money this year to get you home. You cry into Olive's fur for hours, for the rest of week you get drunk enough to stay drunk. On the first of the year, you wake up—still drunk—and move, with Olive, out of the space.

It's 2015. You are in the wormhole. Light disperses. Light falls apart from you. Maybe you're Madonna in the "Ray of Light" video, racing, you're speeding—toward what? The irrevocable. Shall I spoil it for us? Expose the plot. Perhaps I could guard against what's coming. Or someone else will. No. I should step back. It's the ethical thing, really, as I'm just your observer: an archivist. Anyhow the nightmare of your life threatens to suck me back in.

For a while you rent a room in a three-bed with two bar regulars and a frat boy. Everyone treats it as a crash pad, and you're a mess these months, drunk all the time. The only thing you're good for now is loving Olive, which you do with all of yourself, you're broken up by your love of her, transformed through it, see you must go on living because of it. Care gives form to the dead hours; time like an old body settles into the procedural repetition of her need. No matter how hungover, you take her to the dog park each day, glorying in her emotional clarity, her curiosity, all her panting, doggish aliveness. Her world she loves, loving everything in it and all its little creatures. That you cannot no longer bothers you. It suffices just to be near her. She's six months and rail thin, a boundless force: a smiling pandemonium of squirrel-scampering, terrier-humping, mud-rolling pleasure. Her paws are white mittened. She likes you to hold them as she naps. Nights, she curls against you as a baby, so you sleep in the fetal position, giving yourself over. She *is* your baby. The only one you'll ever have. Your breath syncs; for the first time you sleep peacefully. Before rescue she'd been starved, beaten, left in the rain and cold. Still she knows joy. Still she wants more life. Her dexterity with trust astounds you, her crystalline resilience. She is everything. You're alive because of her. Know this.

Then March arrives. You're fired from the bar you've let supplant your life. You deserve termination,* but not for the reasons given to you,† and surely not for the reason disseminated by the bar's Svengali to its most callous and gossipy regulars.‡ For a month you hold it together—you make rent, you're approved for unemployment and food stamps—but soon the scaffold collapses. The net is tugged back. There's no money left. A week, then two, you manage with forty dollars. Instead of eating you buy a bag of dog food. You can't afford train fare anymore, so you jump stiles or walk everywhere, pounding pavement for hours each day, dropping résumés across the city, no matter how impossible the commute. You are frightfully thin; most nights you shake with hunger. No one can find you a job, but most people will buy you a beer. You age rapidly: you look like a woman in a history book, some Dust Bowl tragedienne.

The month dissolves. Rent, again, is due. You have to leave the apartment but have no place to go. A friend asks why you don't just go home, but there's no money to flee and nowhere to get to. Some dumb night you wander back to the dive. Your former coworkers pity you; they get you drunk and high for free. Then there's an afters, which you go to with Anna—a friend's

---

* You're too drunk (like everyone else) but not holding it together any longer, you're absenting yourself, it's indecorous, really, and the amount of coke and booze you're stuffing your body with should have killed you, but hasn't.

† Invocations of your indisposition to authority: the (correct) charge that you hadn't read a shitty self-help book you were asked to.

‡ There are shadowy insinuations about money, but no one seems able to keep the story straight. After the owner asks you to rejoin her staff two years later, it's apparent this was a fabrication—what sort of entrepreneur would invite a thief back to the garden?—but you agree to return, if just to clear your name.

girlfriend—in Sunset Park or maybe Bushwick (the cab she pays for is a blur), and everyone dances until dawn. Anna says she doesn't know you from Eve but can't let your dog live on the streets. She says you'll both move in with her, that there's a couch with your ass on it as long as you need. She's got four dogs: two large, two small. Olive will have to get along with them. Your money's no good to her, she says, so don't bother offering. Not that you have any. You agree. Together you sob—a strange start to the friendship, but it's the start you've got.

After three months you land another gig, just a night or two at a venue each week, but the owners are kind and have a vision for the space. They're more settled than your other bosses, it's no party job—just a job job. Through summer you attempt to right the lurching ship of your life. Mornings you read the paper over coffee, then bike or take the A train to the Rockaways. You roast in the sun a few hours before returning for work. You need, though, to save enough money for a new apartment. Anna's a saint, but cleaning the dishes and walking her dogs won't change the fact that you're a burden in her life—a ghost in her home, a wedge in her relationship. Anyhow the couch is lumpy and too short. Two shifts a week won't cut it. The sugar daddy website yields nothing good. Just time wasters, bored rich men window-shopping for pen pals or live-ins, but you don't want to be someone's girlfriend. What you need is cash, and stacks of it. What you want is freedom. Some of the girls you know are dancers or do cam work, so you ask around for advice, but none do full service. You see now it's the only way you'll marshal two months and a deposit. You can wing it. Danger finds you, sure, but you've cultivated an instinct and haven't been killed, or not yet. Let's celebrate that. You calculate an hourly, ask a friend to take your photos. In them, you blur your face, shop out your tattoos. With a few friends you construct a check-in system. Someone besides the men should know where you are.

The first time, yes, you're petrified. On some plush velvet couch in a Midtown hotel lobby you try to sit like a stone while your body trembles. You pretend to read a book. I don't remember which. The priggish men behind the front desk eye you warily, but there's not much they can do to stop you. You're a guest of a guest, just waiting for your uncle to come down with the room key. It's normal for a woman to be dressed like this at three p.m., or could be. Maybe you're going to a very slutty funeral. The client, as it happens, is obliging, even handsome, on business from Auckland, well-dressed and well-groomed. A nice cologne: woody, notes of bergamot. Let's call him S. In the elevator, S is chatty, surprisingly easy to talk to. In the room he pops a bottle of champagne—the real shit—and pours a glass for you, from which you take hummingbird sips while he tells you of his trip, his work, his narrative of family life. S's daughter (of course) is "around your age." You remember you've shaved some years off your history, and so ask what she's doing now she's just finished college. "Uni," he corrects, but he's proud of her, and this pride radiates from his expression in bands of shimmering light. What's next for her, you press, because honestly, you're curious. It animates the writer in you, the dream of other lives, but S pivots, asking what brought you into this "line of work," what you're studying, how long you've been doing "this." You're at Columbia, you say, and summarize your extinct dissertation for him. You've got a stipend, you explain, but New York is just *so* expensive. You don't tell him he's your first. You like him fine, but no man should own that knowledge. Of course you both see what's hovering at the edges of this chatter: his fear that his daughter might end up like you. Delicately, you assure him he has nothing to worry about. The wealthy daughters of rich johns would do this only if they really wanted it. S has a nice cock. Actually, he sort of turns you on. When he fucks you, it's resolute but physically considerate. He repositions you often: "I want you every which way," he grunts. You try not to drift else-where but do. It's nothing to do with him; you hope he doesn't notice. You're talkative and affirming and it goes on a while and then it's over. He pulls out of you and tears the condom off to cum all over your tits, then relishes in the sight of you below him, graffitied and glistening. With your ringlets fanned across the pillow, he says, you could be a Botticelli.

After this the work comes easy. You advertise on Craigslist and Backpage. Other sites, too, but these are where your clients come from. FOSTA-SESTA is three years in the future, but the crackdowns have begun already. You play it as safe as you're able. Most of it's common sense: in writing, leave little trace. Don't put a price on The Act, because what's paid for, you remind the men, is your time, which has immense value, and when you think of it like this, you're a CEO, a stock trader, a goddamn fucking billionaire. You think of all the years you've wasted. How luxu-rious now to imagine your body gathering cash like debris along its shores as the hours and minutes slip past. At last your time has matter. Time in your body *means*. Occasionally you answer a work call and hear the telltale echo on the other line, tinny and forensic. "How much for a blow job," some thick, stuffy voice asks. "Extra for kissing? What about raw?" You hang up on these men quickly, because the last thing you need is a record. Your approach, though, is hardly professional. You're too broke to be high-end, but you're thin and young and white and techni-cally, you've cornered a "fetish" market ("hashtag TS"), so you command a decent rate. With the money you earn from S, you buy a secondhand LBD and sensible heels. A pair of stockings without runs—a godsend. The rest of the cash you stuff in a sock and hide in your suitcase. At the Duane Reade on Nos-trand you swipe a fresh tube of red lipstick and a box of cheap dye. It's time you return to your natural color.

You book sparingly, partly because even a two-hour date will suck up the whole day, and partly because you're lazy. But the clients you take on, you genuinely enjoy being with. Escorting unhooks something wondrous in you. The transparency of the encounter—its front-loading with clear communication and a smooth transactional index—relieves you, it makes sex an experience with a set of rules to be abided by, guardrails past which a man travels at his peril, past which you not only can, but must be compelled to, say *no*. Almost by accident you've authorized yourself to make demands in these scenes, and besides, the performance of pleasure is all you've ever done with men. It's familiar, so now you perfect the skill, studying slipperiness, prancing and playing in your own erotic field. Scrupulously you knead the dough of your personae. You know, at base, what you're doing is "survival" sex work—that you can't live without the money you make off these men—but it's more than this, too. Really, you feel powerful, you're a rare jewel, you are even present in your body at times during sex. You can't remember that happening before. Readying yourself before Anna's full-length you find you are beautiful. You'd never known this.

The summer drags. In August the city clears—clients grow scarce. So does the bar money. It's a hard month for gig workers, as usual. You have enough to move out but you and Anna have a rhythm now; you've grown close. You're running again, and swimming. Drinking less. Anna's at her boyfriend's half the week, so most nights you've got the place to yourself, and stay home with the dogs, watch movies, or text the person you're sort of seeing. She's funny, brilliant really—a filmmaker and musician—but your life is a wreck. You know this. What could you possibly offer anyone, what use would you be in a serious relationship, while crashing on a couch, bartending a couple nights a week, hooking anytime you're bored enough to shave your legs? Things must be set right and you're trying. Really, you are.

You know what happens next, though.

I don't want to say it. I won't.

There is a detonation. All your life and the next four years blown apart. You are a chaos of atoms. You are utterly gone.

Part IV

WE

The Present

We meet over Zoom.

Though I'd requested in-person sessions, my insurance is precarious and I've been stalled on the waitlist nearly a year. The administrator says office visits will likely open soon, but we both know she's bluffing, and pressing this now doesn't seem worth the trouble.

Before our first session, Helen emails, brisk and professional: Hello Jamie, she writes, I'm looking forward to meeting you! Together we settle on Friday mornings.

When she appears on my screen I'm startled by Helen's youth. I'd avoided googling her, wanting, I suppose, this encounter to be unpolluted by our respective histories. Though I don't ask her age, I suspect I'm older, which doesn't bother me, or not really, except through the automatic anxiety: Have we been moving through the city in overlapping circles? Do her friends know me? Have I—a dreadful thought—bartended for her before? I feel certain she will have some reason, any reason, to despise me, and I long to feel anonymous in our work, at least at the outset, to be free to account for myself in such a way where I am that self's sole author.

During our first three sessions I mainly discuss the genocide of the Palestinians by the Israeli government and my mother, and the latter of these topics feels more unanticipated, like I didn't think there was much to parse in my relationship with her. On Gaza I tread cautiously, unsure where Helen's politics lie, not wanting her, I guess, to decide we can no longer meet. My instinct is cowardly, and I am shocked, too, by how quickly I've come to see these hours as indispensable. I realize, suddenly, I'm in crisis, and they seem necessary because they've become my lone buoy.

There are days, yes, I feel undone by this book. Stewing in the most debased moments of my life has made me unutterably soluble. I am often alone now, and feel I have no footing. What's worse, most days I seem to have no identity at all.

Partly I see how this is my fault, the slippage toward solitude. Early in the process I thought I'd include Charlotte and Harron more extensively in the writing of the book, but after sharing an early version of the second chapter, grew shy of them, disinclined to shove all my tedious trauma off. I don't want them to turn from me; I know the impossibility of bearing another person's wreckage. In those years I was a chaos of atoms, the bondswoman of my trauma, never seeming to take human shape. The discontinuous feeling returns. I picture my self radiating out over the sea; I imagine light landing on me and refracting, I am bejeweled by a million iridescent scales.

Before our fourth session I write: How do I establish better boundaries around my empathy without cutting people off? And then walk through my sense that writing is the space—perhaps the only space—where I am able, properly, to be with others. A cold fish, otherwise. I don't think I'm a particularly likable person, which used not to rattle me, and now does, all the time.

In the hour of the appointment, however, I settle again on talking of my mother. Is this deflection? Table setting? Maybe, I tell Helen, I'm seeking a genealogy of trauma here, trying to find what I've inherited from the women who wear my face. It's sort of obvious, isn't it, this line of continuity—the thread of male violence stitching us together. Maybe what I'm doing now is holding a convex mirror up to the parts of my history that exceed me; situating "my" "trauma" in a larger story, one that defamiliarizes my singularity, one that makes me, in a generative sense, non-exceptional.

(Crucially, I have yet to recount my rapes in detail.)

It's not, I say, like I don't see rape's vastness. Rebecca Solnit calls it a *"pandemic* of violence by men against women." She names it "the longest war." A tension of the book for me is learning how to articulate individual experience within systemic ruptures. God, sometimes I think how fucking stupid it is I'm fixated on this darkness, particularly as rape happens to so many—I mean, to truly uncountable numbers, especially minding that those numbers are self-reported. Rape's not at all irregular as an experience. Solnit argues that lurid stories rise above the ambient static of sexual brutality, but that, as a culture, we refuse to establish or acknowledge any sort of pattern. We go on talking of rape as a private, intimate shame, rather than viewing it as a crisis, a human rights issue, an entire matrix of sexual subordination. This, I tell Helen, was one of #MeToo's central failures: it consolidated the fiction of rape as anomalous, and positioned the narratives that resonated—Weinstein, for example, or Epstein's island—as horror movie stories coordinated by conspiracist cabals.

But then, I continue, the very fact of writing about my rapes means I see my suffering as singular, doesn't it?

Helen regards me expectantly.

Like, why would anyone care, besides me and the people who love me? To tell "my" story demands exceptionalism, it's premised on the notion that my particular life has, or should have, a range of possible audiences—different people with whom the narrative can connect. Art, in my view, should transport those who encounter it, should be larger than itself. The act of turning my rapes into an art object, making of them a kind of *thing,* presupposes that this thing does more than record or relay a sequence of events. The *thingness* of my survival mandates import.

I pause. My breath is shallow. Helen goes on looking.

You know. I really haven't thought this through.

Helen nods.

For the fifth week, I make a list of topics to discuss with Helen, and when I feel sure we'll have enough to talk about for the hour—as each Friday I live in terror of dead air—Olive and I walk to the park. Though it's nearly Thanksgiving, the day is warm and overcast, thick (as for so much of this year) with the threat of rain. I've squashed my frizzing curls beneath one of K's baseball caps.

Where the trees crowd, a dozen squirrels are nutting, while a horde of dogs run and tumble between them, with one another, off leash in the park's center. Their owners revolve in a misshapen circle on a small dirt hill there, a smug clique that, in recent months, has gathered its power. The Real Yuppies of Ridgewood. Where I used to let the friendlier dogs greet Olive, now the very fact of her being leashed—while they are not—marks Olive off to the clique as a Bad Dog, erratic, disobedient, in any case untrustworthy, surely not around their Gigis and Rubys and Sadies and Shadows. When we pass now the owners shout in a chorus: TO ME! COME! HERE!

We are cast out. We are not of their little band. In some dubious fashion I've failed in my position; I am, as it happens, a Bad Mother. Olive tugs at my arm, looking back at my face, unable to countenance my heartless denial of her freedom. I remind her of the night, nine years ago now, when her harness broke and she made a run for the park, but was hit, on our block, by a car, which didn't stop before speeding off. And how I'd thought

204 | JAMIE HOOD

she was dead. And how she lay on her side, unspeakably still, and how no one on the street helped in the slightest. And how, in the seconds it took me to run from where I stood to her limp body, she leapt up and began, again, to run. And how I chased after her. And how I ran and ran—but she was too fast. And how, when I was out of breath and out of hope, I found her, at last, waiting at the entrance to the dog park, shivering before the locked gate, her right paw aloft, bleeding, yes, obscurely injured.

To Olive now I say, don't you remember when I carried you— all sixty stubborn, helpless pounds of you—the mile back to our awful apartment?

But perhaps you've put your trauma to rest, I say, and this seems right.

She lifts her dark brows, blinking inquisitively. Good girl.

L ater, in session, Helen and I discuss nothing from my list. Instead we talk about my worry that I perform for her, a kind of actress, out of that automatic and sort of female desire to be liked. I write nothing in my journal after, and the hour slips, vaporous, almost immediately from mind.

In week six we return to my mother. I note the tiredness of this, the hammy Freudian phantom hanging over my belaboring of the topic.

What intrigues me, though, is how this talk hews to spatial frames—questions of distance and proximity, the asphyxiating feeling of too closeness, even though, for fifteen years, we've lived in different states. I had a need for separation, I say, to get out from under the funereal pall of my youth, the swampy melancholy of Virginia. Too much grief there, with us or in us, and each violence another heap of dirt over us, slowly shoving all the air out. I felt effaced by our family tragedy, I say. There was no room for my pain. I'd never own my life there, become my own woman.

I feel ashamed of my flight from them: my mother and sister. The shame of exile, of splitting their pain from mine, like any of it's unconnected. Guilt, too, over leaving my sister to be the good daughter, the (borrowing my friend Ruth's phrase) "daughter-caretaker," the one who carried things after I left. But shame lived at home too. Class shame, for one. We were white trash, or a hair's breadth from it, separate by virtue of our passing better. How meticulous, the excavation of the South from our voices, and I, the most dexterous, identifiable only by the punctuating trace of *y'all* on my tongue. How we grasped stickily at my education, the dream that I'd better myself, get tenure, become a "public intellectual," a famous writer, the dream that I'd lift us from this mess.

Solemnly, Helen *hmm*s.

But I couldn't write. I couldn't write when I was near them, and in grad school it all rang false, it was cheap theater, my desperate play at bourgeois ascension. Later, when the words at last came, it was dredging seawater from my throat. Silt there. This was many years after, I say, and didn't happen, I see now, until I began processing my rapes.

I ask if Helen knows Plath's poem "Medusa," I say Plath fled America as a way of extricating herself from her mother's grip. And how Aurelia Plath was drawn, in Sylvia's poems—and as Mrs. Greenwood in *The Bell Jar*—like Woolf's angel in the house, that feminine specter that must be killed so the sovereign female artist might be born. I say I think of "Medusa" sometimes, with its image of a telephone cable slithering across the Atlantic, inescapable . . . the medusa jellyfish's little roaming suckers . . . the violent umbilicus chaining the daughter to her gelatinous mother. The cord that must be cut. Must be overcome.

I say I feel I'm digressing here. Anyway my mother isn't Mrs. Plath, not even close.

Helen asks about my fight with K the other night. I say I felt condemned, like I'd been named Bad Daughter, because I don't call my mom as often as he does, and because he thought I wasn't disturbed enough by the news of her possible vision loss. The cold fish thing, I remind Helen, I go icy when faced with an irresolvable problem. It's my need for control, or rather, my emotion becomes the one thing I *can* discipline in a crisis that exceeds my authority. When we argued I asked K what he'd prefer me to perform—what would make him believe I felt something. I saw how I was jabbing back but I didn't care. I can't, I told him, let worry consume me; it's inert or else obstructive—nontransformative. And then I began to cry, overwhelmed because I never seem to offer people what they want from me. I never seem to be the right sort of woman.

And then of course he apologized, I say, because he hates when I cry, but *I* hate that I *have* to cry for him to see me as feeling. I hate that crying is the only tool I have to elicit sympathy from people. Why is it so impossible to imagine a woman might go inward with grief? It's irrelevant, besides, because half the time when I cry, that's read, too, as fake. Because I'm customarily so imperturbable. Because my surface is so often smooth. I'm fucked either way.

It feels typical, says Helen, that I began policing my emotions in the wake of trauma. Shock often robs people of "normal" affect.

Well I've never felt like a believable victim, I tell her. (I pause. I say I'm using "victim" provisionally.) Because of my unlikability, because I rub so many people the wrong way. It's like they think bitches don't get raped. Or because the way I fell apart was into chaos and sex, I couldn't possibly have suffered, for if I suffered—*really* suffered—I'd have worn it like a badge, and everyone would've known, they would have witnessed me wandering around, all mopey and silent and celibate, a dumb doll.

We're coming to time, Helen interrupts, and says she needs to be mindful about ending by 11:55. But she was "interested" in our discussion, which is why we ran over. I'm strangely smug over this. How I dread the possibility of boring her. Though perhaps it's a tactic to convince me I'm not unlikable—or in any case, not unlikable *to her*.

I write to myself after: Don't fall prey to your desire to fascinate. You're here to process and manage trauma, NOT be your therapist's favorite storyteller.

In the seventh week I write nothing down, I remember nothing. The session is a void.

I'm angry with myself over this.

Before our eighth session I try assembling a makeshift Chronology of My Life and Trauma. What if I pretended that the plot was linear, and of a piece? What if I allowed myself the pacifier of conventional story, what if I said my experiences of violence bled into one another in explicable and narratively meaningful ways? Do I do myself a disservice—do I disavow the possibility of "healing"—by letting it all float here, fickle, a havoc I can't or won't impose order on?

I write a list.

In the beginning I am born.

I remember nothing of my first years.

When I am four, or maybe five, the man who will become my ███████ erupts, he is magma. The particulars elide me. When we flee him I am six. My baby sister has just been born.

I ride beside my mom in the U-Haul. The trailer is empty. My ███████ called to say he'd be back early from the work trip, so we left everything behind in boxes, three lives gone—a clipped victory. We wind down the treacherous mountain highways of West Virginia toward the coast. I seem to remember there being no guardrails, and for years I believe this is an illusion in my memory but my mother confirms it later, saying many roads then just hung in the sky, utterly boundless.

The drive is an adventure and lasts one hundred years.

I will come to miss the fury of the Appalachian snow. Just before we disappeared I lost my Barbie in a drift outside our house. No. *His* house. I dream of her shivering beneath the avalanche. I dream of her rescue. I blot out the rest. I obliterate that place where I learned what men's hands do.

In Virginia we wait in my aunt's house on a quiet street, I know not for what. There are old people everywhere and my sister wails all the time. Colic. By contrast, I'm what adults call a "quiet child," which means I get in no one's way. I am six and my only friend is twelve. He has a dog I love, but it jumps the fence one day and is struck, crossing the road, by an enormous truck. I witness this. When the tire rolls over the dog's torso, his nose floods with blood, a deep, thick brick red. A ripe strawberry pinned to the end of his darling face. I cry for hours. I'm convinced it's my fault.

One day my friend leads me behind his shed—"where no one can see us." He pushes me to my knees and undoes his pants and shoves himself in my mouth. Grown-ups do this, he says. I can't move my head. The times this happens I go limp, I'm an absence, a rift in space-time. I learn to step to the side of myself and travel. Sometimes I stay, watching my small body where it kneels. It looks like a Precious Moments angel. It doesn't fight. It's an urn. I hardly think about what my friend does because I'm not there. The Precious Moments angel has nothing to do with me, although I suspect this, too, must be my fault.

In his house one afternoon I feel his desire close in. I know "we" will play grown-ups, but before he's able, I run and hide beneath his bed as far back as I can scoot. I know he's too large to fit there. I look at the dust where it's gathered on a single sock and pray God will kill me. We're not a religious family, so this prayer is the only one I know, and I whisper it often, then for thirty years after. It hums in my head even now, sat beside that dusty sock, the shed, the bruised knees, all that followed.

In the house of my ███████ something awful happens. I convince myself it's a bad dream. I still don't know for sure.

Time passes.

Now I'm thirteen. I spend my afternoons at the Barnes & Noble on Virginia Beach Boulevard. I walk there along the railroad tracks. The train passes twice a day, very slowly, so you never worry you'll be hit, unless you want it, which is something I know people want now and then. I'm scared to look down where the tracks cross a small bay of water, because that's where the men go, we're told, men and addicts, which are mostly the same thing. Never play under the bridge. Bad things happen there, especially if you're a girl.

At the store I browse the magazines, because I borrow books from the library and no one gets angry if you read magazines without buying them. I pore over *Seventeen* and *Bop* and *Teen,* thinking one day I'll meet Ryan Phillippe or Josh Hartnett or Milo Ventimiglia—maybe even at *this very bookstore!*—and they'll see me and know I'm destined to be their girl, and they'll pull me from the trash heap of my life. They'll hate fame by then and have so much money of their own that they won't care I'm poor and a nobody, and they won't need to know what happened to me before, because all that matters is our future, which we'll plunge into with open hearts, together, for forever.

One day while I dream there of the sea change I feel certain is coming, a man corners me among the shelves. He's old and bald and has a visible erection tenting his khakis. He starts rubbing himself on me. I go still. I'm under the bed again. He's smiling and whispering something to my body about where his car is parked in the lot, and couldn't I just follow him there? My body doesn't reply. It doesn't scream. When a store employee turns in to the aisle he flees. The woman's face is red, red as the dog's strawberry nose, and she storms toward my body, snatching a *CosmoGirl* from its clenched hands. BOY TROUBLE. GET YOUR CRUSH TO WORSHIP YOU. THE BEST JEANS FOR YOUR BUTT. She says I should be ashamed of myself, she says how disgusting I am—there are *children* here, she seethes.

I am thirteen.

When I'm fourteen I decide to find a boyfriend to prove that I exist. I spend hours in AOL chatrooms, writing to whoever will see it my age, my sex, my location. Then the deluge of private messages, all from older men: men in their thirties, forties, and fifties, who say they *just know* I'm beautiful—they can tell from my screen name. They say how mature I am for my age, and I believe it, because I am. I have been very old since I was six, I say to myself, I'm immeasurably ancient, a tree that's withstood a thousand suns. Some among these men say they love me and I believe this too: Why would anyone lie about love?

I "go out" with a few of them, which means I let them pick me up in their sedans from the Barnes & Noble parking lot. The store provides a cover. I can tell my mother where I'm going without it being too much of a lie. I think how funny it is, how I'm proving the red-faced woman wrong. Look how desired I am, and how adored! Look how I am filled with light.

By now I'm so tall and thin I feel I'm floating off. When I get into the men's cars they look shifty, they wear dark glasses and baseball caps, like we're being tailed. Perhaps we are. I, who have never known men, suppose this rather normal. It's not unusual, I convince myself, that a forty-seven-year-old divorced real estate agent would want to "date" a girl going into the ninth grade. One man commands me to pretend I'm being picked up by my father. I say I never had a father, and he laughs, he says, well that's all right, honey—you told me you're in the theater club. How about you just act?

The men's houses are sparely decorated and sort of haunted seeming. I let them touch and manipulate my body however they like. None of them fuck me because I say I'm too scared to go that far just yet. In my way, I remain a virgin, but they do everything else. Before I meet them I feel powerful. While I'm with them I mostly feel nothing. I ask if they really love me and just before they cum they say yes, of course, I'm precious, their little angel, and when they're spent and quiet, I ask again, because I need more than anything to know I might be loved. After, though, their affections ring hollow, and I find myself missing our previous communications: the black, clanging weight of the written word.

One time a man I'd met calls the landline while my mom is home. She summons me to the phone. I hiss at him, I say never call here again, and when I hang up, my mom stares at me, bewildered and fuming. Where the hell did I get off? Hadn't she taught me better? Don't I know there are men who'd love nothing more than to hurt me? What I didn't know was there was any other kind.

Now I am sixteen. My mom's boyfriend has been sliding a hand mirror beneath the doors of my and my sister's bedrooms. We don't acknowledge it but his desire clots the air in the house. His need infests us, it sticks in our throats—we choke. We choke. One night I get into a screaming match with him. I hate you, I say, I fucking hate you. You're sick and you *know* what I'm talking about. I have to be the one to say it. My mother and sister are so small they can barely see him where he stands. Faggot, he shouts, you goddamn faggot. He throws a chair at my head but I duck and it breaks apart against the wall behind me. I grab a purse and my phone and dash toward my car. The keys, I realize, are still inside the house, so I start running and don't stop until I'm out of breath, until I'm panting and dizzy. When I still myself at last I see I'm at the old bridge. I stumble underneath it and hide for hours. I dream of being murdered. I dream of transformation. The next morning the boyfriend is gone.

More time dissolves.

Now I'm eighteen, a college girl, and like a lot of college girls I discover if I get drunk and high enough, the hazards of womanhood start to look cinematic, almost sexy. The drugs let me be fun. I dance on tables and fly across campus to the same bland frat parties wearing next to nothing. We writhe to Britney, Rihanna, Gaga, Beyoncé. My best friend nearly dies falling off a swivel chair while performing a striptease to "Buttons" by the Pussycat Dolls. His back is a havoc of blood. We laugh and laugh and laugh.

Still no one loves me. My friends find boyfriends and girlfriends and reform their habits, they cultivate new self-images. Meantime, I revolve, a black hole, in the narrowing universe of our small circle. Where before I was the life of the party, now I dissolve in tears before the end of each night. I embarrass myself and my friends in public: I'm a fury, filled with directionless despair. I've become *that* girl, the mess no one wants to be saddled with. People pull away.

Instead I start a secret life. I throw up most of what I eat, I drink alone in my dorm, I invite strange men over two and three nights a week. What I remember of these liaisons is thanks only to Adderall. The woman from the Barnes & Noble was right: I'm disgusting. A pestilence.

In the mirror I sneer at my doubled image, I tell the mirror woman how revolting she is, and how unlovable. I no longer care who the men are. I don't ask them to love me. I want only that they use me up. I long to be exhaustible. I want to be disintegrated in their disregard.

The years slide apart from me without notice. I know I'm waiting to die. Will it come soon, God, please, I whisper, please let it.

I stop writing. I can't go on.

I don't tell Helen about My Chronological Life. I haven't decided if I'm able to share it with her. Too much feels too raw, too humiliating; I'm one enormous, exposed nerve. In truth, I don't think about my childhood. Teenage years. That time like a current drags at the edges of me, sucking and pulling, my pulse goes all slow. Already I felt spoiled: bad meat, a stinking affront. Instead I talk to Helen about a termination that happened just before the pandemic. I'd told my bosses at the dive where I was working that I didn't want to serve rapists, and I said they seemed to be letting an awful lot of those in lately. Some of the worst guys who'd moved through there started coming around again, men who'd been banned for years, but who felt emboldened to return because the place was under new management. Three incel types had taken over, I guess because they thought it would get them girls.

One night while I was working, the dealer who coordinated my gang rape showed up, with a pretty woman and his slimy smile, and before I could react, began ordering drinks from me—not recognizing me, I guess, or pretending not to know who I was. I panicked, I tell Helen, in an instant my skin went clammy. I couldn't breathe—my heart *literally* skipped a beat, I say, I felt it drop in my chest and thud back into motion after a lost, interminable second. It was the strangest sensation, like falling from a great height. I was hyperventilating so badly I couldn't speak. Eventually I asked my barback to serve him. Only later did it occur to me I might have kicked him out. But in the moment I was frozen—where would I have found the force?

Helen nods. She asks how my body feels as I describe this experience. I realize I'm in it again. My breath shallow; my forehead damp. I want, though, to finish the story.

Shortly after, I continue, I brought the incident up with the bosses. They'd ambushed me after a shift with some bogus meeting. I see now they were already plotting how to oust me. They didn't like how I talked back, which has always been a problem between me and authority figures, but I knew that bar and the job miles better than they did. They were underwater, and I wasn't going down without a fight. I see now it was a labor issue, which I wish I'd been more competent in talking through at the time, but even though this was post-#MeToo, plenty of industries remained pretty unshakable. It's simpler—though of course still daunting, still urgent—to renegotiate the conditions of your work if you have, say, a union to back you up, or some other legal scaffolding that erects protections around your employment. If you're in service, or undocumented, or freelance, or a sex worker, it's another matter entirely. There's always a line of bartenders waiting outside to replace you. I had a thousand dollars to my name and a mountain of student debt. What was I going to do? Hire a lawyer? So I told them what happened in that encounter and I said I thought the lifting of certain bans was making it unsafe for women to be there—staff and patrons both—and I was told, in turn, that because the rape hadn't happened on the premises, it wasn't the business of the bar to deny the man who raped me entry.

He used the bar as a hunting ground, I protested, and he'd done this to other women we all knew. Which, incidentally, wasn't why he was banned by the previous owner. She'd done it because he was robbing people—stealing wallets and so on. But I was told, again, that because these assaults weren't *in the bar*, it wasn't in their purview. What would I have them do, they asked, interrogate every man who walked through their doors about his sexual history? They weren't the police, and anyhow, because of the nonproximity of the event, and because the evidence was nothing but hearsay, the police would tell me the same.

A month later, the bar was shut down for "renovations," and when it reopened a few weeks after that, I was the only one on staff no longer on the schedule. This was the sort of place that survived on its regulars, and the meeting I'd had with the owners happened in the bar backyard while several were present. In point of fact, a couple dozen people overheard the whole thing, but it was nothing to them. Then one of the owners began telling people I was crazy, saying I threatened him in the meeting, and was a liar: a hysteric, in short. But as there were witnesses, no one really believed his line. Still, I was stained with suspicion. And because the dispute had to do with a rape, my credibility not only as an employee but as a victim was now in doubt. Friends I'd known for many years, and who'd known about this assault awhile, began to see the story differently. Even though the experience itself had an autonomous life outside the conflict, even though this man *had* done this to other women known to that particular bar's milieu. I was interrupting everyone's fun, and there's no greater crime in the industry than stopping the party. Anyway, when word of all this got back to me, I texted the boss and told him to keep my fucking name out of his mouth. It occurred to me if people already believed I was guilty of menacing him, there'd be no harm in saying that much.

On the other side of the screen, Helen regards me a moment, quietly. I wonder, she prods, if there's residual anger there.

Where before my heartbeat was slow, now I find it's racing, I find my cheeks hot, my breath quick—like I'm squaring up.

I don't think about it much. There's something in that period of my life that's just gone. Like a movie you haven't seen since you were small. Or time as a sketch: a cloud of intensities. The funny thing is, I *wasn't* there. Or rather, my body was, in the material sense, as in there was a creature with fleshly form moving through my days, but I wasn't present. It all seems to have happened to someone else; it's alien; I don't remember the tactile feeling, the texture of that era at all.

I think now how the oddest part is it wasn't like there was a Dissociated Me and a Conscious Me, but that there seemed, in fact, to be *two* doppelgängers—a chaos agent who orchestrated my self-destruction, and the hollow doll that bore it, the vessel. Meanwhile I was floating over them both, a distant onlooker. It's sort of science fictional, like *Invasion of the Body Snatchers,* or like I'd become a Stepford Wife. Totally lobotomized. Even as I imagine this, I can't find myself in that past at all. It's a closed door, and for four years I was behind it, or outside it, while the two replicants battled things out. But perhaps this is the rationalization of an addict. I know it's easier to say I wasn't in charge of those obliterated years, the boozing, the drugging, the slutting. Yet it felt like a possession. And when I woke, that time had the hazy, shimmery quality of dreams.

Suddenly I feel nauseous. Bile rises in my throat. I try to breathe, deeply, a belly breath.

Sometimes I think how if I'm responsible for my self-destruction in the aftermath, then maybe I'd been responsible for the rapes, too, you know, like I'm implicated in all of it. I know this isn't helpful; I know it's irrational to think it, but I do.

I pause. Helen glances rightward. I don't mean to interrupt, she says, but we're at the end of the hour. Are you all right?

I tell her I am and exit the meeting, but find I have no idea. Am I?

In the ninth week Helen apologizes for how we left off in our last session. She bemoans the limitations of time.

I say I understand our hours are necessarily interrupted, and interruptible. Like life. It falls apart from us. Just skin.

After the last session I felt fragile, but I always feel fragile after, or perhaps permeable is the better word. I tell Helen I've been writing everything I can remember about each session in my journal once we close. I want to be better, I say, for the process to accumulate. I don't want our work to go up like smoke. When I'd finished writing the week before, I longed for light. There's been so little this winter. Gray days; gloomy days, where for years I remembered the high, clear blue of January in the city, azure piercing its remote cold. Olive and I trekked to the park when I'd set my journal aside, and circled the loop there once, twice, three times. So quiet in the early afternoon: the birds few, the others few. Mainly the old Polish women humming to themselves along the benches, their eyes seeing everything.

I say to Helen she's become a part of the book now. I ask if that's all right.

It is, she says.

I want to braid our work with the writing, I tell her, and I've been doing yoga every day, and daily walks . . . I ride my bike now year-round. I want to hold all this together in a somatic process, thinking (as I often do) of CAConrad's work, their poetic rituals: "I had been treating my poetry like a factory, an assembly line," they've written, and what they sought out in place of this were "structures where being anything but present was next to impossible." So much of my paralysis with trauma has had to do with temporality, an inability to inhabit self-presence. I leave my body when the memories surface, so how could I expect (I say, turning again to Helen) to heal that body from a distance?

Writing, I think, is another technique of bodily evacuation. A necessary one for me, but absenteeism nonetheless. Rachel Cusk writes that the artist, particularly if she's a woman, "must leave the moment in order to access a moment of a very different nature, and each time she does it a cost is exacted, the cost of experience." It's a separation from dailiness, all the sediment of the ordinary world.

I find myself recounting the reading I'd done in Flatbush the other night. When Helen asks if I was frightened, I say that, actually, performance enlivens me, it brings writing back *into* the body in some vital way. I feel myself repositioned in language, it reminds me all story emerges first *from* the body, and in these writings my individual body lived through these stories. That I was there for them, and they happened, and I survived.

Because the reading concerned him, I tell Helen about the Professor, our affair, the way I ended things. I tell her how I was sharp and cruel when he tried to reenter my life. It was the first time I understood repudiation as an action over which I held power, and that I'd never before felt capable of saying to a man, *fuck this, fuck you, you're disgusting. I* was the monstrous thing. *I* had always been the one fucked. And usually I'd brook whatever a man offered and just loathe myself after.

Hmm, hmms Helen.

At times I want more from her reactions than she seems willing to give, and feel guilt over this, as if my desire is the desire of a dictator, like I fashion myself the sole arbiter of our dynamic. In other moments I suspect her method is the best one, because my grief has never been given space, I've never felt attended to or truly *heard* by others. Space and time Helen offers. Her non-interventionist approach keeps me from spiraling into shame over talking about myself in our shared time.

I return to the moment.

Then something funny happened, I say. While I was writing this sequence, I decided to google him—not to reach out, just to get a sense of where he ended up. I thought I'd discover where he was lately teaching, and instead, I found he'd been #MeToo-ed. I wasn't even surprised.

I feel laughter bubbling in my throat, but why? I pause, I sip water, as the giggly feeling bucks around inside me. I'm trying hard not to float away.

Helen looks on.

So I couldn't stop thinking about that temporal overlap, how, *at the same time* we were seeing each other, he was groping students, and sending them dick pics—attempting to coerce them into sex. And this feeling wasn't shock!

I begin, nervously, to laugh and apologize for laughing. I don't find it funny, I say, I just feel deeply disoriented—disturbed, I guess—while walking myself through this.

In the right-hand corner of my screen I watch a tiny Jamie speak there, my digital ghost—another splitting, me and not at once. Now I sit, entirely still, trying to unknot the mess of my thoughts. Helen doesn't rush me.

Suddenly I'm inside a memory: we're careening down the interstate in his car, it's late, I'm drunk, and the Professor pulls his cock out of his jeans. Of course he wasn't the Professor then; mostly he was S to me. The car (I'd noticed just before this) is going eighty. He's hard already, though that's typical. He grabs me by the hair and pulls my face down on him. He's been drinking, too, he reeks. Then the salt smell: it's summer, his balls are sweaty, heavy. I take him down my throat, as there's nowhere else for his cock to go. I'm drowning. Later I will think of that poor girl Ted Kennedy left to die in the water, aching toward an air bubble in the sinking Oldsmobile. You chose this, I tell myself. And I had.

Helen coughs, discreet. I'm in my body again. I sigh.

In rooting out this story, I say at last, I saw I had to remap the whole relationship. While the reports didn't transpose perfectly over my experience of us, the parallels were all there, and I began thinking how *of course* there was a nearly seamless line of continuity between his behavior with me and what he did to those other women. Men too. His predation was nondiscriminatory. What frightens me, I suppose, is that the affair not only occurred in the same timespan he was violating other people, but *also* while I was dealing with two of my own rapes. Events I didn't grant proper names for a while, sure, but that I fully understood as nonconsensual. Meanwhile, with the Professor, I believed I had this magic power, that I was the boss of us. I ended things by humiliating him, an ending oddly empowering to me, because I learned in that encounter a method of refusal that seemed actually to work. It wasn't that I thought I acted nicely—I didn't come out of our affair thinking I was a *nice* person—but there was a thrill in the experience. A thrill of expansion. I grew larger. But as I read the testimonies of these other students and saw myself ineradicably in them, I thought, did I have any power over him at all? Which isn't to say I had no agency, but the idea that I was in control there, that I wasn't compromised by the disparities in our positions, seems shakier now. I think how maybe I didn't recognize the Professor's actions for what they were because I'd been getting raped my whole life.

With him I was an adult, but something about this odd-knotted circumstance forced me to look at how I'd never been young, to see that my youth was stolen from me, and that I never had the chance to learn appropriate boundaries. I slept with much older men as a teenager, too, I say. Daddy issues. What a fucking joke. None of this explains the Professor, but I can't extract it from my way of seeing, my erotic worldview.

In my diary I quickly scribble: FIRST MEMORY OF DESIRE?

Helen asks if we can continue the conversation next week. She says she'd like me to describe the feeling of looking backward in a word or two. What is it, do I think, that ties the teenage years to this affair?

We're at time.

After she vanishes I bundle up and set out on foot, walking deep into Queens, turning down streets at random, deciding to settle wherever feels right. I pass the yuppie café ("rancid vibes," I overheard a zoomer say of it once), and then the pleasant one, then the used bookstore, the new bookstore, the awful bagel shop, and the one that's just OK. I go on walking. House finches hopping everywhere in my path. What was my youth? For years I thought myself a kind of Lolita, in the pop cultural sense: Liv Tyler and Alicia Silverstone in that Aerosmith video, heart-shaped glasses and pink lip gloss, impromptu lollipop-oriented oral performances. It was years before I encountered Nabokov's narrative, years before I felt mirrored by Dolores and horrified by Humbert Humbert's seduction of his reader. Now I mostly see my past through the frame of sexual violence, but it's a splintered frame: I crouch within it a moment and then leap back, pricked and bleeding. Finding the container dubious. I hadn't wanted to identify as a victim. I thought it meant I'd be forced to cede ground, that I would be, somehow, less fundamentally sovereign. With my later rapes the terms were clearer: I was drugged or overpowered. I was brutalized: banged about, choked, torn, robbed.

What I want to say to Helen is that there are gray areas in my sexual history—the way I slept around, my sluttishness, the abundant sex in my life that I sought out, that I *chose*, whether or not it brought pleasure—and there's something in me that wants to preserve that ambivalence, the slipperiness of my eroticism. My character, as it were, is thorny. I find there's a danger in infantilizing survivors of sexual violence, like we have no capacity for decision-making. Not in our lives before rape, not during the experience of it, and not after. Which isn't to turn responsibility back on us, but to say I'm uneasy with being made reducible to the choices other people make for and about our bodies. Perhaps I resisted calling myself a "victim" or a "survivor" (even now, see, I set these words off in scare quotes) because I felt such naming required me to be a nonparticipant in my life. If I wanted to be believed, it was imperative I understand myself as a helpless receptacle, a sort of perpetually rapeable mannequin, drifting far out to sea. When I first began speaking about my assaults, I needed to believe in this vacancy, a provisional identification that allowed me to forgive myself for what happened, which of course wasn't my fault at all. To have been an absence meant, at least, that I didn't ask for or earn my rapes, that these were only things that happened. For a hole can't warrant how it's filled.

But as time passes, abjection feels less useful to me, I think because I want to be a subject in my life, an active player, particularly in a sexual sense. I want to learn my pleasure, to own my desire. I want to fuck, and not from some broken place. This image of myself as emptied—it only reinforces the notion that I was ruined, that I'm beyond repair, and I don't believe that. I can't.

Was there a word that came up for you since we last spoke, something to describe the backward looking, Helen asks in our next session.

Curiosity, I say. I want to make sense of my disorder, while also granting credence to all that's ambivalent and irresolvable about life. I tell her about my walk after our conversation, I say I've been thinking how precarious the political moment is for survivors, one that obliges us to speak while also disciplining the boundaries and representational possibilities of that speech. I'm meant, for example, to narrate my experience in unequivocal story beats, as in: I was innocent when I was found, virginal, really, and morally unimpeachable, then those drooling beasts stumbled on me and held me at gunpoint or knifepoint or I was tied up, and it was wartime, and when they were finished, my sexual life was done for, but I devoted myself to God, I gave my body over to the nuns. And thus I make myself believable.

I live in deep fear, I tell Helen, of not having been the "perfect victim," which is funny, because so much of the impetus behind the book I'm writing has to do with upending convention, disaggregating the usual narratives of sex trauma. One of the great disappointments in #MeToo was its reconsolidation of the status quo, the way it calibrated around monsters and angels. It was like, Harvey Weinstein?—a monster. When we put him away, great, we've solved rape. We got him. And the women the movement was kindest to were those most proximate to power, the A-list actresses whose careers were torpedoed, the CEOs of Fortune 500 companies whose careers were torpedoed, and so on. Not to delegitimize their experience, just to acknowledge that the media didn't give a shit about domestic workers being assaulted by their wealthy employers, it wasn't particularly interested in the testimonies of nonwhite women, and it said fuck trans women. Even today we see a racialized specter of rape being deployed in service of genocidal war propaganda, just as it was two decades ago during the "War on Terror."

In the story of trauma, it's risky, I say, to represent oneself in a way that undermines or deviates from a politics of innocence. Spectators feel unable to track the plot; the narrative becomes less intelligible. But that's *because* of rape culture and misogyny; it's *because* of this kaleidoscopic matrix of anti-feminist rhetoric. If you produce this impossible ontology (the Perfect Victim) so no one's able to embody it, you create the conditions for systemic incredulity, the fiction that sexual violence doesn't happen, or isn't serious, that it isn't endemic to life under patriarchy. The fact that I slept with a lot of men in the wake of my rapes becomes a crack in the porcelain: now people can claim the assaults were only reverberations of my usual bodily habits, or say I misunderstood some foggy nondistinction between them and the sex I agreed to. I think, too, of my time escorting, and the decision to write about it now—how this will render me even less credible for many people. Because our culture is so wildly suspicious of women who treat sex as capital. Because women's bodies aren't "meant" for *our* power or pleasure. They're meant reproductively. As usable resources. But all sex is transactional. For the time being, there's no outside to capitalism, though I dream it. We don't fuck beyond the borders of the market. People refuse to face this brute fact, they perfume it, and fashion fables to conceal it—which is the more insidious maneuver, to my thinking. To measure sex in hourly rates exposes the lie of sociopolitically uncontaminated romance. That's why it drives everyone so fucking mad.

In my video feed I watch Olive, behind me, stretch her long dog body up onto the couch. She turns her head to stare at my back. I sense her impatience. I laugh.

I'm mindful, says Helen, of our time. We part.

On the train to the surgeon's office I think of something Helen asked me earlier: whether I feel able to be "human" in our sessions. If I can shirk my anxiety about perfectibility, believability. Certainly I feel able to make mistakes, and contradict myself. I can grasp and marvel at my hot anger—a dangerous thing for a woman to grasp, but I grasp it. I guess in other circumstances, even with people I know well and trust, the story must be hemmed and tailored. I have to make its shape recognizable for a variety of possible audiences and interlocutors. Even with K, I think now, I'd been cautious while describing the horizon of my sex trauma. Three years in, and I hadn't really told him about it, or not in any detail. Even with him I tidied things. When he began to cry I switched to the abridged edition. I was so scared he'd leave. Other boyfriends had.

Men hear "assault" and get cagey; they see you, suddenly, as breakable, and seek distance from the wreckage. Or rather, men *want* you to be breakable, but they like to control the terms of that fragility. When I was single, men loved telling me how sad I looked. I saw how this turned them on. It unsettled me. I couldn't make sense of it, except to suspect they were imagining hurting me themselves. The fact is, I *was* sad and didn't want to be, and surely didn't want it to contrive the nature of my desirability. I think often of a scene in *Mad Men*, when her charming equestrian crush says something to Betty Draper about her "profound" sadness. "No," she tells him, "it's just my people are Nordic." Which has always struck me as funny, because Betty's totally dissociated for *years*. Still, I admired her flintiness. I learned to guard my sadness. I tumbled myself like a stone.

I remember the note I scrawled in my diary, the question of when I first felt desire, and can't pinpoint the moment. I can't even narrow it to a fucking year. I remember the first time I willingly gave a guy a blow job, I was thirteen, he was one of my best friends, but I don't remember if I really wanted to. I knew he wanted it, though, and I wanted so badly to please him, I wanted so badly for him to think I was beautiful. Maybe he did. I wonder now if I've ever felt it, desire I mean, as in properly felt it, a desire of my own, and nothing to do with what I thought men demanded, what I believed I should perform, beyond sensations unfurling inadvertently *in response to* a stimulus. Where is the origin of my longing, what is it I want? Have I ever known?

In the blindingly white Midtown office two doctors ask me to disrobe. I seem always to be in doctor's offices now, on the phone with doctors, on the phone with my insurance company, having my blood drawn by bored nurses, being examined, poked, prodded, and photographed. My body is not my body. It's an assemblage. Behind their masks in their white coats the doctors breezily discuss my vagina. I am there and not. I want to go home.

The next time I see Helen, I say I need to return to the Professor. To return to what he did to those students. Their stories are theirs, and this discovery seems, also, to be a fracture in the brittle bone of my own story. If I want to say I was an agent in our relationship, that I decided on the fucking, and years later I find he'd been preying on other people simultaneously, is my account of my relationship to him reconcilable with his broader behavior? That is, does his predation revise my understanding of things, does my knowledge of it render unstable the "mutuality" of our connection? I understand why I need to feel I was in control of the affair. It represented for me one of the few occasions in my life where I seemed to be authoritative, where I wielded the power of refusal and was understood as having that power to wield. Anyway, when I ended things. But was I sovereign before that moment? Did I own myself when he first approached, when I first relented, when sex with him became habitual? Was I present when he fucked me? Did I feel pleasure? Or just wanted. There's something insufficient in our definition of agency: that it's something one has or else doesn't. What if agency is more dynamic than this, a structure of feeling rather than an object to be held or discarded or seized? What if it passes between people and reformulates itself, texturing an infinite arrangement of possible parties? What if the disparity between him and me compromised my position without this lack fully negating my choice in the matter?

Olive sleeps beside me on the rug, her wide furry flank rising and falling with her breath. Her leg twitches, desperate: a dream, or a nightmare? I nudge her haunch with my foot. Helen waits for me to continue. Sun breaks through the clouds, illuminating the kitchen.

I guess what bothers me, really, is this specter of guilt.

How do you mean, asks Helen.

It occurs to me my relationship with him might have spurred or emboldened him to do what he did to those other students.

Helen's brows knit toward each other. Without lifting her head, Olive yawns.

In my heart I know it's illogical, but still I can't help but ask myself if I made his abuses possible. I guess that's what trauma does. It plants its little seed of shame, that tiny, needful thing, and inscribed on the seed is a message: that I'm to blame for the violations, for all of it, and then this message festers and grows inside me, watered there by my grief, sopping it up, until finally the seed splits, and the awful message blooms and expands its murky radius, gathering every burden to me, each action, as if all events in my life and everything that's occurred around me are compelled to attest to my disgrace. And these guilts become the dense thicket I'm caught in, the thorny tangle I can't see any way around, or through. And one of these guilts is that I'm accountable for what he did—not to me, but to the others—as though my saying yes was what made it impossible for him to hear when they said no. Like I was a mirror, and in me, he saw only permittance and absolution.

The clouds again amass outside. The kitchen surrenders to shadow.

After we spoke last week, I saw I felt this way, too, about the older men I slept with in high school. It didn't matter I was fourteen, that I was too young to consent. It didn't matter that I'd been molested as a child, that maybe I was acting out as a manner of processing or punishing myself for the earlier damage. By meeting them and "allowing" them to use me I came, later, to suppose I'd enabled their proclivities. I don't know what those men went on to do, of course, but with the Professor I know now. I know what he was doing while he was also fucking me. I know, too, that he faced a reckoning, and that's perhaps a small blessing.

On the screen I see my eyes are red, and tears are welling in them. I want to go on and the idea of continuance is a torment. Finally I tell Helen about My Chronological Life, and that I'd been unable to send it to her. How in it, I at last unearthed all the things from my childhood I'd shoved in a box. I tell her about the woman in the Barnes & Noble, the one who called me disgusting when she found that old man rubbing himself on me. I never thought before how the woman might have stepped in at that moment, offered to help, to protect me. Instead, she decided the sin was mine to carry. As if my being assaulted was the very thing that *proved* I was not a child, and rather that I, at thirteen, was exposing "real" children to the polluting force of sexuality by being, myself, abused. I'd never felt like a child, so this sense of myself as a contaminant was simple enough to assimilate to my ego, which was fractured already, I already understood myself as a sort of rot. That I was disgusting seemed perfectly sensible, considering I knew something putrid had transpired in me, within the borders of my body, and I believed that foulness had colonized everything about and of me, had seized me and was slowly seeping out. I thought everyone could see it. I felt like that dirty poor kid in the *Peanuts* comics, the one surrounded by a toxic cloud. I saw I wasn't a child then, or even a person really, but a place—the place where rape went, and where rape belonged. That anywhere I was, rape would find me.

I stop to catch my breath, and Helen says, but you *were* a child.

Not really, I tell her. The years were few in me. Which is a different thing altogether.

I am staring at the fire escape. A pigeon's perched there, rustling its feathers. The light shifts. The pigeon shits into my pot of wildflowers and shuffles side to side, cooing companionably.

I'm trying, I say after a silent minute, not to imagine myself as the steward of others' ethics. I can't keep people from committing harm. But the uncertainty nags: What if I could? I had every reason not to report my rapes, and I have to believe that was the right call. Still I'm haunted by the possibility that my failure to speak spawned further harm, and I hate it, I hate this awful ghost, but it's sitting there, watching me, and I cannot fix or banish it.

Helen frowns.

I look at the clock.

I'm sorry, she says, but I'm mindful of our time.

When we hang up I spend twenty minutes crying at the kitchen table, ugly, heaving, red-faced sobs, the kind of crying you see in movies where the actress is gunning for an Oscar. I remember the neighbors across the courtyard, and feel suddenly shy, hoping no one has seen me. Would they feel pity or disgust? The *stradone,* I call the courtyard, like I'm living in a Ferrante novel, like the lives of everyone on these blocks are intertwined, gossiped about, like I, too, have become a necessary character in the story of our neighborhood. The ego!

Emily arrives at noon. With Olive we walk to the park, circling the track while I tell them about Helen. We haven't seen each other lately, Emily and I, as they've been working twelve-hour days at the theater again—opening a new show. They ask what my process has been like. It's good, I think, to have this third space for the grief. I'm tired of holding it all myself, I say, or withdrawingly inviting loved ones into it. I tell them Olive's been keeping close to me, as if sensing my tumult. I correct myself: not "as if" sensing, because she just is, she's sensing it, like she always has. We talk awhile about animals and the porousness between our emotional lives and theirs, their bottomless receptivity.

Charlotte shares videos of children in Gaza saving their cats. I read Adania Shibli's *Minor Detail*. I read Vivien Sansour, who writes that "I have never been prouder to be of people who love birds and bread and whose humble existence has shaken the core of those who are scared of life and who continue to destroy all of it—human and non-human. Call me human animal—it honors me to be from humble people who value all life." How to carry this grief? I wonder. How to stop it?

At the beginning of a bar shift, one of my regulars comes in to tell me he "doesn't feel safe" patronizing the bar anymore. While he's talking I realize he means because the owners canceled an event in solidarity with the Eurovision boycott. I want to ask him whether he thinks fifteen thousand children "felt safe" while being murdered, but he's already gone, and I stew in my fury for the next ten hours of labor.

The twelfth week is pandemonium. We host friends for a potluck, then I find the holidays have arrived, and K's parents seem to be in town, so I put my writing to the side. Always I want them to like me, and, always, have no clue if they do.

In session I tell Helen about their visit and recent tempests at home. I say K and I are like a pendulum, swinging between contradictory extremes. One day, we're communicating better than we ever have, while in the next three I feel I'm standing on a cliff edge of dissolution; I grow certain we're careening into breakup. The book seems to be a pressure point, I say. It's cast a pall over us. I'm convinced he resents me for writing it. I know he resents the time and energy it's seized from me, which is to say from us, but I'm unsure if he's even recognized that resentment.

The book's removed me, too, from my sexuality. I'm dissociating again, even if it's not a total separation. I don't feel near to my desire. It doesn't originate with me. I'm merely responsive to his want—this, my forever tendency—his randy feeling, and even then, I'm often too fragile. Is it normal to not feel like fucking when every day I'm knee-deep in sex trauma? I don't like being conquered by the book, or the sense that I'm failing as a girlfriend. Because it *is* a failure, I say, I know I'm not meeting his needs. And if I can't do that, what am I good for?

I don't feel ready to talk about this. I ask Helen if we can change subjects.

She asks me, instead, to return to where we were before: to guilt and shame, to the sense of responsibility for the violence suffered by others. Or maybe, she offers, I could talk in a broader sense about how it's been for me, reliving these things.

It feels like shit, I tell her, and I see I have to claw my way out of the muck. The book's the hard part, really, because it's where I'm entirely alone in all this. In my head, my language. I say I began writing in 2015, or rather, I began documenting my self-hatred in a private, locked Twitter account only I had access to. This was just after the gang rape. I was at my lowest. I didn't see how I'd come back from it. Those words weren't particularly deliberate, certainly not aesthetic. I'd get drunk and post all the vilest, most annihilative things I could think to say of myself, like how I deserved to get raped even more times, and I'd talk about what a rancid nothing I was, call myself a fucking slut and say how I should pray to be murdered the next time men deigned to defile me. I was merciless, stabbing at myself again and again, rolling like a pig in my muddy sickness. But after a while, the delight I took in it—that manic, absented feeling of total self-obliteration—lost its charge. Little spider veins exploded across the surface of my abjection, and I became opened in a different way. I exorcised something, I guess, and came, unexpectedly, on a longing to rebuild my life, or at least to fashion a sort of self again. I didn't understand, at the time, that what I was doing was writing toward a feeling that would eventually become this book. I had no clue then why I would write such a thing. And I'd kept everything secret for thirty years; I'd told hardly anyone, so how could I imagine making all this public?

Of course the spark of writing, like desire, is often opaque to us, it has its own beingness, or (lacking a better term) its own soul, and if you're a real writer (can I use that term?), you understand the writing must carry you elsewhere, outside your-self, your ego, well beyond the boundaries of your control. This is how you identify *true* writing, or art—the good shit: whatever you want to call it. There's a mystery there, an enigmatical quality, and the person recording that soul is indispensable to its transposition but also, necessarily, exceeded by it.

Part of the mystery for me was about entitlement: as in, who gave me the right to tell this? And what about my history had earned this telling? I'd wanted shame not to be the project's prevailing tone, the dominant animal, but what I'm realizing as I move through it is that's what the work demands. Shame is its psychic detritus. But then there's also something about authorizing myself to witness myself, and I hadn't considered this before now, that I'm trying to prove to myself, by writing this book, that all of it happened to me and shouldn't have. That I didn't deserve it. And the book is for a public, yes, it's a cultural reckoning, sure—but maybe *that's* where the tension lies, in this self-recognition that's always evaded me, which is my story's importance *to me,* I'm seeking in it some affirmation that what happened to me mattered.

Is it, Helen asks, a search for legitimation?

I don't know.

The doorbell rings. Olive's ridge rises; she's barking; I apologize to Helen. I say I'll be back in a minute. In the stairwell I think how it's been impossible to imagine any part of my life mattering. Good or bad, in truth, despite my obvious fixation with my self, my relentless, compulsive need to document my existence. But it's deflating to navigate a world that cares nothing for you, that, in the best of circumstances, grants you the relief of inattention. At worst, that world will want you dead. Maybe the compulsion is to leave some trace before it gets me: my fortress against death. I faced violence nearly every day, I think, not always sexual, but there was never a time when my future nonexistence stepped beyond my line of sight. Even as a child I saw how deeply and determinedly I was despised. This

242 | JAMIE HOOD

contempt wore many faces. Our poverty, first, marked us as interlopers. Our classlessness. And I was never suitably situated in gender. I was a faggot, a sissy, a girl. And then when I was a girl, that too was wrong, and I was taunted and threatened and named, then violated: physically, psychically, sexually. My body was never mine, not in any context, not at any time. There was no outside to violence. Even when it wasn't happening, I writhed in anticipation of it.

The front door closes behind our mailman. I seem to have lost time. Olive's stopped her barking. I return to the computer.

I've lost where we were, I say, but I was thinking about how loath I am to connect all this to my positioning as a woman. How politically insufficient that coupling is. If I admit to the gendered quality of my experiences with sexual violence—if I acknowledge the rapes had something to do with the way I and this body have been sexed in a social world—the legitimacy of my womanhood gets called into question, like the whole reason I'm a woman is *because* I'm traumatized, a premise I find moronic and insulting on its face. But these experiences are inextricable, too, and even though not only women are raped, rape disproportionately happens to women because of woman hating, because of the misogynistic stratification of life under patriarchy. And this sense of having mattered, of having been someone for whom life has matter, is bound up there too, in no small part (in my case) because this world doesn't believe trans people have a right to exist at all. A few weeks ago I told you about my ousting from that awful bar, and how simple it must have been for the owners to paint me as crazy and a liar, to weaponize discursive panics about hysterical "victims" and degenerate trans freaks. So then I found, later, that some of my closest friends kept hanging out there afterward, kept chumming around with those men. Which was a stark reminder of my *place*—that these people I'd spent nearly a decade with were so willing to discard and discredit me, and for what? Some dingy, broke-down, rapey little dive. My friendship was totally inconsequential when weighed against a buy-one-get-one IPA at happy hour. I was worth less than a free beer! I had never felt so small, and it was stunning—as in it laid me out; I was stupefied—and it was entirely, ridiculously predictable. That revelation confirmed something for me: that it was wise, even in moments when my whole world was razed, to minimize my pain and compartmentalize, to make a mockery of myself. After all, I was a joke. What else was there? Rote continuance. I could have killed myself, but when the worst arrived, I looked at it and said, well, I guess I have to keep fucking living. And then that life, too, felt of nothing. I'd wake each day and think, what the fuck am I doing here? But I went on getting up.

My history of the period is foggy, and I've realized lately it's because I just wasn't there. I was gone. I remember thinking then, well, does the philosophical meaninglessness of being an amoeba paralyze the amoeba? Does it wail and thrash and ask God why it's stuck on this rapidly less-green earth amoeba-ing, or whatever it is amoebas do with their days? No. It's a biological phenomenon. It functions. It persists. And when I stopped my screaming and my crying and I shed my bewilderment, that was me. I was an accretion of time, passing. And now this devastates me. I look back and think, how awful: all that time wasted. The whole of my twenties. Half of my thirties. This second half has been much better, I can say as much. The last four years are the best of my life. I'm more present in the world, more open to people, and I'm excited, at last, to be alive. Not all the time. Things are shit sometimes, too. But I want to be here. I hate looking at the past and seeing how absent I was. I think how I could get hit by a bus today. I ride my bike all over the place, it's really quite possible. So I try to inhabit pleasure, I try to be here, and be generous with others—I try to feel that my existence is urgent, and filled with wonder. And I consider, now, not only the way my life might have matter to others, but also how it matters *to me*. And that life is a thing I want to have. And I want to live it.

Helen is smiling.

I'm mindful of our time.

At the end of the session, I am blown open. Immediately I send a voice memo to Charlotte and Harron, recounting my "I want to live" moment. I tell them it was like in a movie, just before the narrative climax, when you begin to really cheer your heroine on. I make myself sound like some doe-eyed ingenue. But there was an electric feeling there, undeniable. A lightning bolt of transformation, as if sent from the heavens. In my diary I write how part of my joy was to be found in the purity of the utterance. It was a simple, absolutely observational statement that felt, nonetheless, like arriving at the highest summit. Because it wasn't true for so long, this wanting to live, or maybe I never knew what being alive felt like. I wasn't living. And now I am broken, but in the good way. Now the beauty might peer in. Olive climbs beside me and nudges my hand with her snout. I cry.

The next week Helen asks me to dig around in my sense of wasted time. Is it grief there, she wonders.

In the days since our last meeting I've been abandoned to the dense smog of depression. An emotional descent meant (I cannot help but think) to give the lie to my newfound desire for *more life*. It's the winter, I convince myself, which is long and silent and sunless. It's the book, which hangs over each day, merciless and sneering. It's the drama of my fights with K, which recur as on a loop without resolution, shit-slinging back-and-forths that are always the tedious same. On Thursday I try fucking myself with a toy, conjuring some silly fantasy, but nothing doing. Thoughtless, my body clamps against it. I miss fucking, but abstractly. Desirelessly. How awful.

It's grief, yes, I at last tell Helen. A decade gone up in smoke! And what came before those years was hardly better, it's just time that's farther from me. It threatens less. I say to her I want, also, not to devalue those years or the people I knew in them. There were decent people, too, not everyone was a rapist or an apologist. And I don't want to mischaracterize anyone's life, even if those encounters seem shallow now. The shallowness, at times, was my fault. I couldn't be honest about my pain; I couldn't trust anyone, or not really, I couldn't extend generosity. How can you love anyone well while trapped in the tunnel of self-hatred? I couldn't recognize the complexities of other lives;

my imagination was shrunk down to a tiny, threaded knot. My heart was small. I was totally cold.

Now we're in this cynical moment where you're not supposed to admit to being wrong. But I lacked empathy. I held people to such rigid standards, which often meant cutting everyone out, shirking them. I hope this isn't only a novel way of punishing myself for my damage, but knowing I approached care from lack seems a useful thing to document and work through.

Beside Helen, a money plant stretches toward the sun.

I was thinking yesterday, I tell her, of that cliché about surviving trauma. That it makes you stronger, or makes you the person you are, teaching you profound lessons about the sort of life you should want to lead. Instinctively I retch—it's grotesque and patronizing, like you're some fairy tale dolt who can't see the moral of a fable until you've been savaged and left for dead in some sad forest. I could easily have been a strong, resilient, astonishing person without having endured decades of violence. Countless people lead perfectly interesting, valuable lives without such suffering. But there's the rhetorical imperative, bobbing its stupid head above water, and it forces you to say you feel you've learned something, that there's an edifying capacity to your pain. You know what my rapes taught me? To think of myself as worthless, as nothing, just meat. To hope for death each day and never trust or love other people. There was no fucking lesson in them. Rape is the opposite of meaning.

Then I wonder: Is it commodity culture? Is it the nagging demand that all experience be objectifiable, *optimized*? The trouble is, I can't say rape *didn't* shape the person I've become either, because I believe our history is accumulative, that we gather all our mess up into the narrative of a life, and that, as time passes, this story becomes denser and denser. It crystallizes. There's no part of me that believes in a "true" self—a self that exists as if before the world, in a kind of metaphysical vacuum. We are the products of our world, and in turn, remake that world by living in it, by being with others as, simultaneously, we all move through it.

I begin to laugh. Helen looks confused.

Sorry, I say, it's just that that Kamala Harris clip came to mind. With the coconut tree?

Helen shakes her head.

It's classic Kamala, I tell her, utter nonsense projected through what I imagine must be a haze of Quaaludes. She's talking in a press conference about god knows what, and out of nowhere says, "You think you fell out of a coconut tree? Well, no!" And then does that unhinged laugh, like someone's squeezing the air out of her. "You are," I say to Helen, doing my best Kamala (not good), "the product of all that you are, all that came before you, and all that will ever be." Something like that. It's very Buddhist, in a way, and it's the funniest thing I've ever seen, so obviously I watch it all the time. Kamala brings so much joy into my life, even if, like all politicians, she's fundamentally evil.

Anyway. So we're accumulative, right, and importantly, we haven't fallen out of any coconut trees, which is to say I can't undermine the events that have led me to this point. And I also don't want to harden into a way of being; every day I want to be *more open,* expansive, full of possibility. My death has always seemed quite real to me, deeply, horribly tangible, I suppose because of all the violence, the abjection. My rot seemed determinative. But sometimes I think rape might be the more radical repudiation of life, because you're carved out of your self but have to remain in the world nonetheless. You're evacuated, but the outline remains, the formal gesture of your personhood. Rape is death entering life and dancing there. Death looks into your face and smiles. Death blows you a little kiss.

Maybe for religious people, that's the space hell occupies in their minds: the nightmare of eternal suffering, death-in-life, et cetera. If I believed there was something past death, I'd be more frightened of death, but we don't know where we go, we can't, and never will. I'm frightened, yes, by the thought of pain, but the afterlife is materially unspeakable in the way we think of trauma being. But trauma has a language; we just convince ourselves otherwise so we aren't forced to face it. Or perhaps we're convinced it's unspeakable by those who wish us not to speak it, who know silence protects them. So someone says being gang-raped is "beyond" representation, a statement that's demonstrably untrue. Solnit speaks of this in her piece on "the longest war." Even counting *only* gang rapes that have occurred on buses, she writes, we have an entire cornucopia of narratives. I think, too, of Bhanu Kapil's *Ban en Banlieue*. I've written one hundred thousand words on my trauma. Is *that* unintelligibility? Rape effaced me and yet I speak it. It stole my face and my name, and I'm still fucking here. It remains in me. We live in rape's presence, and its presence infests us. This pretense of wordlessness is a tool of the tormentor. It doesn't serve.

I realize I've been ranting for some minutes now and apologize to Helen, who raises her eyebrows.

This is the space, she says.

I hear birdsong just outside the window. It isn't spring, but spring is coming, uninterruptible. In the dream I had last night I was in the backyard of a restaurant. There were picnic tables, and seated all around them were friends, though none I knew from real life. On the gravel there was a starling curled into itself, unmoving, and when I took it between my hands, its body began to twitch. It was alive; it tried to fly off and couldn't, and I held it there, calming it, carrying it to a dish of water. I woke.

Grief, Helen interrupts, grief is where we were.

I see my face in the Zoom square: a far expression. Though not sad, or not exactly.

The grief comes when I imagine other lives I might've led. Would I be writing this book—a book that feels to me so vital and strange, my pesky little rape baby—if I hadn't endured violence? Of course not. But I could have written other books this entire time, I could have dreamed another sort of art. I might have been finishing my seventh now, rather than spending a decade here, in trauma, trying to disarticulate its feeling, its form. Maybe I'd have been some brilliant novelist, a Rachel Cusk, a Virginia Woolf, or what if I were a painter? What if I hadn't had such an implacable need of words? Perhaps the visual would've sufficed. But then I think it might have been far duller. Maybe I'd have been someone who posts GIFs from *The Office* on Twitter. Maybe I'd have worked as a tech girlie, coding twelve hours a day, perched on my barrels of Bitcoin inside some grim loft in Downtown Brooklyn.

Does art live in me—not *because* of trauma, but because I sought beauty where there was none? It's sadists who suppose all art must be borne of suffering, and I'm not one, but I could be persuaded that the soul of art demands friction. That it often thrives in the absence of wonder. It arrives to supplant lack. But perhaps it's another of life's irresolvable queries. Who would I have been if I wasn't who I am? This question isn't revelatory. You get one life, and it vanishes so frightfully fast. Boo fucking hoo. When I was a child, adults always told me time passed quicker for them, a claim I was dubious of but that I now see is true. The years are gone in seconds. I'm learning to make peace with a notion of doors closing. The horizon contracts, yes; the map of possible paths turns to dust. It needn't be an awful thing, but there are only so many careers to try on, a finite number of love affairs to become entangled in. I know this. And yet imagining the lives I might have led if I wasn't imprisoned in suffering, so bound to the mechanics of survival—what Agamben calls "bare life," life's shorn, biological function—is difficult. It wounds me.

I'm nearly forty and I've only just started living. I grieve this. I do. I'll never get those years back. I want to be OK with this. But it's hard not to dream of other lives, and maybe that dream is the current that carries me to writing. Perhaps it was my imaginative escapism that animated the desire for creation.

We're coming to time, says Helen.

And I see we are.

K and I fill the fourteenth week with our fighting. We both seem to be going a bit batty. I reread *The Golden Notebook* for the first time since moving to New York. Before, I'd read it once a year at least, but the novel now doesn't help matters at home. I'd forgotten the sequence near the end of the story when Anna Wulf and Saul Green (the neurotic, radical American) dissolve in the madness of their violent but seemingly (at any rate, in Anna's sense of things) fated romance.

What I feel in this week is anger, and I want to scream but can't. The anger sits in the center of my diaphragm like a peach pit. I don't want to worry Olive, I can't, and the agitated heat between K and me just flattens her. She'll spend a whole day lying quietly, soaking up our bad affect. She'll be ten in two months: my precious girl; my universe; my toasted croissant. Her muzzle's gone gray this year. Even her little eyebrows are turning white. I want every hour of her time on this earth to be filled with love and pleasure.

For years anger was the only emotion I let myself have, a kind of insufferable, nose-thumbing righteousness. I hate that I felt obligated to be impenetrable, to be hard—let's face it, to be a real bitch. It's not a pleasant way to be, that living in fear, but I thought any revelation of my vulnerability would lead to pain, to further violation. I hadn't known anything else. I felt inexorably, terrifyingly unprotected. I was the only one who could keep me safe, and why would I think anything else, but then, my iciness hadn't rendered me inviolable either. I knew if I let myself inhabit other states—grief, sadness, desire, rapture—I'd disintegrate, and there'd be no getting back.

I sidestepped a nervous breakdown by the skin of my teeth. I see this now. And part of how I did it was by becoming a fortress in myself, while for others I was a sage, a mother, the solemn, distant advice giver—which is hilarious, like I knew anything about leading a good life. And I've always drawn in men who need my strength, who often sap it, who like to steal it for themselves. I begged K not to ask this of me now, because the book has been so destabilizing, and for good or ill, I must sit in that instability, I have to stay in the bad place, and relive it all, so I might be honest in my writing. I'm unable to be the rock of our relationship for the next while. But here we are, with him shuffling me into my usual role. I don't believe it's deliberate; he's just so used to my caretaking. And that caretaking is so invisible. He doesn't think about it at all. But I can't fall apart right now, even if I'm a woman on the verge. It would be bedlam.

When I tell Helen this in session, she asks what it feels like, in a somatic register.

I wake in a panic every day, I tell her. My mind racing, my heart racing, a kind of cold dread in my belly. I'm nauseous often, and my appetite yo-yos: it's nonexistent or I'm ravenous, I'm entirely empty or I have a need to eat all fucking day. I have no sex drive to speak of, I haven't even been masturbating. Sorry, I say, I hope that's not too much information. I'm trying to institute regularity, to keep time by movement, to sustain sanity in motion. I do yoga every morning, Olive and I take a turn around the park each afternoon. You can't forget the body keeping the score, or whatever.

Olive hovers at my feet, circling; she settles, she closes her eyes and immediately begins snoring.

In writing, I continue, the craft questions seem fine, sometimes even good, because I can look at them and say, well, here's a formal trouble to turn my intellect against: a riddle to decode. But as I come to the end of things, I have to hold it all in one place and take stock, to see who I am and the person I've been. I have to stay present in it. And it's tough going. I feel like shit all the time, and I feel stupid complaining because *I'm the one* who sold the goddamn book. So then I wonder: Is the project another innovation of my self-destructive impulse? Is its writing an advanced procedure of harm? I'm in this period of deep solitude, because writing, of course, is solitary, but also because a lot of what I'm wrestling with concerns histories I don't feel able to talk about with others, or maybe it's just I don't think I can talk about it with K. I trust that I'm loved, but it's less clear to me lately if I'm held, if I'm heard and properly understood. Though maybe it's only stress talking, maybe the pressure of finishing is sharpening me to an incredibly thin point. Anyway it fucking sucks.

Helen says when I talk about my relationship, I often raise a question of my "role," and my dexterity or incompetence in performing that role.

Always the actress, I think, but do not say.

When I speak I tell Helen I fear I'm mostly positioned maternally, that I end up being the manager of my relationships, or (worse) the disciplinarian. Which is funny, because for so long I was the Lolita, pliant and helpless. Now it's the men with mommy issues who sidle up to me. I'm not, I admit, always good at being tender, but I wish my vulnerability was encouraged, my delicacy. With K, I'm always training him to be attentive, and when I mother him toward my care, it defeats the purpose of that care in process, in some perhaps indescribable way. I hate it but I feel like his mom sometimes, and while I enjoy nurturing, I don't want to be anyone's fucking *mom*. Except Olive's.

Below me, her beautiful ears twitch.

I know I'm being awful, I say, I can hear the shrillness in my voice. It's just been hard between us. For one thing, I've been utterly alienated, sexually speaking. What a shock, I guess, that sitting in my rapes eight hours a day has shut my body down, but it's like a switch was flipped, and I haven't been (I hope, I say to Helen, you hear the sarcasm dripping) *inhabiting my eroticism*. It's so cliché, so "get thee to a nunnery" vibes, or whatever. But I take responsibility for it, and I know it's been really tough on him, and obviously I think sex is a necessary and wondrous thing for a relationship, but my god, it isn't easy for me, either. I feel incredibly disempowered. I feel numb, and finally, it's *my* body that's malfunctioning. I want more than anything to be this sexual, sensual, fuckable woman, and *of course* I want to fucking cum. If I could cum twenty times a day I'd do it. I think there's an idea he has that I don't want it, or that I hate sex, but I don't! Even if so much of it's been bad, even though it's often been a site of violence. But it's not where my head is at right now, and I hate that. Lately I'm in a terror. I think: Am I frigid? Am I experiencing frigidity? Is frigidity a condition analysts still diagnose women with?

Helen is silent.

It's awful even saying all this, like I can't distinguish bad sex from rape, which I am entirely, perfectly, unequivocally able to do. This discursive slippage is something you have to fight against when the apologists and reactionaries come out of the woodwork with their shitty little "Has #MeToo Gone #TooFar?" essays. The last thing I need is some "post-feminist" in *The Atlantic* telling me I can't parse the difference between fucking some guy I regretted waking up next to and being roofied and passed around by five men in a trap house. There's this idea that rape victims, or survivors—whatever—are so idiotic and traumatized that we lose facility with differential thinking. Anyway, this is a tangent. K and I still have a physically affectionate relationship, and we do other things, but I just can't be penetrated right now. I freeze up. Even alone, even with toys. It's like my whole body shrinks into itself. So even if I'm sucking his cock every day, having his cum blasted all over my tits, getting eaten out—the fact that he's not finishing inside me feels like a really calcified lack, an enormous monolith between us. And that monolith stands in the center of our apartment, casting a phallic shadow over us both. I feel terrible about it.

As in guilty? asks Helen.

My stomach drops. My mouth has gone dry.

Yes. Guilty.

Helen pauses. I can see she's waiting for me to elaborate.

I fail to fulfill my proper function. And there, the shame blossoms.

Proper function?

With men, sex is my one reliable asset. It's what I've had to offer, and what men always sought in me. Not to be like, *hmph! all men want is sex!*, because I'm not some sitcom housewife and I don't believe it to be true. But most of the men I've dated saw me as a fetish object. For almost all of them, I was the only trans woman they'd encountered in real life, or so they told me. So it was trans women in the porn they jerked off to, and then me. Which doesn't mean porn is evil or men can't witness or engage with sex work in complex ways, but if you can't fathom that the woman you're with has a coherent, autonomous consciousness and reality in the material world, that psychic gap is harder to bridge, I think. And many men don't care to try. Like, they *could* approach me as something other than a fantasy on which to work out their transmisogyny, but why bother? I wasn't a credible partner. No one was posting me on the grid, there weren't Thanksgiving dinners with their families in Westport. I was an experiment, a symbol of their rebellion against certain sexual prohibitions.

You know, I dated two men sort of seriously just before K, and in both cases, it was obvious they stayed because I was their sex doll, and they thought themselves quite radical making me their cum-covered little trophy. Then they could go tell their greasy faux-communist buddies they were "doing the work" by fucking trans women—and what's more, being seen with us in public, though always, of course, at night, always, of course, in bars. I wasn't the girl you took photos of on the steps of the Met, I wasn't the girl you were lathering with sunscreen on Beach 90. How shameful to verbalize this; how pathetic. And maybe it was only me. Maybe *I* was the problem. I haven't known many trans women who primarily date cis men. Everyone's a lesbian now, and good for them. But a desperation lived in me. I was so utterly alone. I would have done anything, because I needed a man, in that time, to prove I was on this earth for pleasure, as well as for the pain I'd lived through. I needed to feel protected, and of course, never did. I suppose I thought: if I let them use my body eventually they'll love me, but the trouble with that is you don't *love* the objects you own. You just own them. So now that I'm not as sexually available in my relationship, I'm back in my paranoid era, I feel I'm not giving K what he's owed. Which is to say I know I'm failing as a girlfriend and a woman, and I fear that soon he'll leave me for it. Never thinking about what I want. Never thinking if I want to leave. Rationally, I know he's not with me for sex, that I'm more than my use value as a hole for his cock, but the terror persists, it's sitting just over there, a dingy little ghost in the corner of the room.

I see this image snag Helen's curiosity. She leans forward.

I'm trying to visualize these things, she tells me, the ghost in the corner, the monolith at the center of your apartment. These descriptions of your fear and grief—do they feel dense? To me it's fascinating that they have mass, they have shape.

There's a sort of weight on my chest, I think, even in the

moment I consider her question. And the air is thick. I can't seem to draw it smoothly into my lungs.

I don't know, I say.

Then you mention a split: the traumatic body versus the rational mind. It's all very spatial, isn't it?

I don't know. Or I need to think about it. Certainly there was a spatial dimension in my response to the rapes. One of the truly shocking things for me was how a person could look into my face, and see me, and decide I was *nothing*, decide I was just slop. And this feeling made whatever they did to me morally imaginable, even justifiable. Because I was meat. I was laid on the butcher's block and they didn't care at all. How does a person move forward with this knowledge? I suppose I assimilated it, and for a long time, I despised my body, I starved myself, I puked up meals. I ran forty miles a week for five years to pummel my disgusting body into oblivion. But it made me agile, too, and I learned a different sort of physical endurance, so that the self-defensiveness and the self-obliteration were both in there, all mixed up. Then when I was sleeping around, there's no doubt in my mind that the riskiness of the behavior was a way to confirm what my rapes had me believe: that I was dirty, an abomination, and it was my duty to invite men to soil me. That was the purpose of my life.

But I've been thinking, lately, how we're supposed to say rape isn't about sex, it's about power, but this doesn't sit right. Yes, rape as a political event is inseparable from systems of subordination, but the brutality is also inarguably, elementally sexual. The proposition that rape might not, in the first instance, be *about the body* is bullshit. Rape installs a horror of the body's sexual porousness. It exploits our fundamental beholdenness to the other. Rape infests our eroticism. The rhetorical elision of sex to center a generalized inequity, I think, effaces the material impact of rape, which has many faces but is, ineluctably, a meticulous and gruesome technique of rendering intimacy abject. Pretending it's about power, and power only, allows people to ignore the fact that it's a weapon predominantly used against women, and to ignore this ignores the way rape consolidates women's bodily disenfranchisement in the patriarchal order.

A manic, electrical feeling circulates through me.

So sex and rape don't collapse into each other, but become alternating transparencies, or each is suffused with the other in the psyche. I can enjoy sex, and my erotics are also bent by this history of evacuation. The specter of defilement darts in and out, and I think this feeling became exacerbated in the way I was treated by men I dated over the years, who weren't raping me, but who were nonetheless using sex with me to make my insignificance known. I remember I was casually seeing this man at the end of 2019, and he was so sexy, he looked like a seven-foot-tall Jesus, and we went out a few times, he came to a couple of my poetry readings, where I read early material from the book, back when it was a collection of poems. Which is a convoluted way of saying he knew about my rapes. I remember one night he planned to pick me up from a happy hour shift I was working so we could go to dinner after, and he showed up with some other woman, much younger than me, dressed somehow sluttier than even I was, and she was all over him, right in front of me at *my* place of work just before he and I were going on what I'd thought was meant as a proper date. Meanwhile, this woman *also* believed she was on a date with him, as, I suppose, she sort of was, and he'd thought it was appropriate to bring her to my bar before taking me to a second one. We weren't serious, but this seemed a totally insane method of humiliation. Like, who fucking does that? He was forty years old and divorced! Now I guess I knew why his wife left him. After that night, I was over him and not, and then stupidly texted him a month later because he had cried and apologized and we were maybe going to try again, and then he replied to say he didn't think he wanted to date me after all, because really, the only thing I was good for was a blow job, and—

Oh my god, Helen interrupts.

—yeah. It was totally sick. And in a more usual circumstance, maybe I'd have thought, fuck that man, he's just some piece of divorced shit, but as these experiences of dehumanization accumulated alongside the trajectory of my traumatic history, it felt like a moment of utter clarity, and what was clarified for me was a truth about my life: that this really *was* all I was good for. I was a hole, a cum slut, a rape girl, a nothing. God. I'm sorry—I can feel the hour coming to a close.

Helen nods.

That's our time, she says.

And it is.

Once we part, I wonder why I resurrected this memory of Jesus. I had liked him but there was nothing meaningful between us. What was it about that experience that so disturbed me? I feel shaky sitting in front of my shut laptop, and sort of breathless. By the time I met him I thought I was "cured." My last rape was in 2015, so I guess I believed the grief was gone, that I'd processed things, and then found all it took was one horrible text message to take me right back. I was under the bed. I was in that bookstore, being told how disgusting I was. There was spit dripping down my back while I waited for the sound of footsteps to recede. And there was nothing violent in what Jesus had done to me, but it somehow verified my innate worthlessness, which seemed to me a rather widespread belief held by men—a pattern, really, among my boyfriends. Right after Jesus there was G, who started choking me during sex even though I'd told him I didn't like it, that it frightened me. There was L, too, who'd threatened to get physical after he came on my face. No one could know about this, he said. So there was no outside to fear, and I don't conflate these events with my "real" rapes, because to do so feels unrigorous—it doesn't serve me— but to pretend there's no line of continuity between the unpleasant and abject is laughable.

I've been reading this book by Katherine Angel on desire and consent, and in it, she discusses the way a legal framework can cloud the distinction between bad sex and rape—how it's more difficult to grapple with the political gravity undergirding women's miserable sex without writing it off as misadventure or hardening it in the language of violation. I had never thought before to take bad sex seriously as a social failure. I hadn't realized these problems were also politically addressable ones.

Then the fifteenth week is a blur. My baby sister is ill, and I'm underwater with freelance work. The same arguments at home. These fractures tug me from the book until I feel I can't write, and that *this* is my first thought—a view of my *real* life as an inconvenience to my writing one—nauseates me. But the deadline approaches. My labor cannot stop.

Helen is out of office on Friday and asks to reschedule. That this absence overwhelms me seems pitiful. I think how I'm becoming dependent; I think how I'm allowing myself to be made, well, weak. I'm more indebted to the people around me than I've ever been, and this disorients me; I'm unaccustomed to such reliance. But I'm so much alone now. With everyone wildly busy: Harron finishing her book and moving house; Emily in the thick of a new job; Charlotte hours away in D.C. Separations that are no one's fault and yet I wish we were together oftener.

K and I seem to be dissolving. Days I think we're salvageable. We walked through the bitter cold on Thursday to our local bar, an always-empty dive, and talked about our projects while that kinetic writerly feeling darted between us. Tipsy, just enough, and back at home, while I made dinner, we played records, we danced to CAN and Boy Harsher. Later, more quietly, Patsy Cline, the Magnetic Fields, Fleetwood Mac. We kissed, and my body warmed and opened. I thought I'd die if I didn't taste him. I lay a pillow on the floor and knelt there, needful, looking up to watch his face as I took him in my mouth. In the reflection of his pleasure, I felt beautiful, teasing his orgasm out, wanting to bathe in the light a little longer, having escaped—for a moment—the fragile feeling that's dominated my days, my sense that I'm frighteningly changeable. We went to bed together, unusual. He's been staying up late lately, leaving me to lie alone in the room, reading.

As I fell asleep I grew certain we were still *right,* still affixed to each other. Then more storms, the moods, the bafflement. Talking makes it worse. Not talking makes it worse. I feel leaden and foggy. I am panicky in our home. It isn't sustainable. It just isn't.

I begin the sixteenth week by telling Helen something strange happened the night before.

Oh?

I'm out of it still. I went to a reading series last night, one I've read at before. I was by myself, and went to dinner ahead of it, where I had two drinks. At the bar where the reading was, I had a glass of wine during the performances, and another glass and a shot with the bartenders when it was over, because I worked with them many years ago and it was nice to catch up. Then I was talking with a man I know from the internet, and he left, and I spoke with someone else a minute, and suddenly I'm waking in bed at five in the morning. The last I'd remembered it was nine p.m. I'm fully clothed, my contacts are in, K and Olive are beside me, and I feel loopy, just totally discombobulated. K thinks someone put something in my drink, which is possible of course, but why?

Helen asks about the drinking, if the number seemed usual to me.

I'm a tank, I tell her, and I don't say this proudly, but I am, because I've bartended so many years. I can drink almost anyone under the table. The thing is, I've been roofied before—multiple times—and though I feel hollow today, I remember the hangover feeling like death. The fact that I'm up and keeping food down and speaking in complete sentences seems atypical. What's more—everything's accounted for. I'm OK, and noth-

ing scary happened, or I don't think. K said I got home about
9:45, and the bar is a thirty-minute walk from my apartment.
I checked my bank account. I didn't take a car, I didn't spend
money anywhere else, and on my phone you can see in the activity log that I walked for about thirty minutes just after nine,
so in reality, there's maybe fifteen or twenty minutes that are
opaque to me. I'm worried I was a mess at the bar, but my friend
who was working said I seemed fine—

I'm glad you're safe, says Helen.

—yeah, me too.

What does this bring up? You used the word "hollow." You
wondered why someone might do this.

My breath is short, and my chest muscles are clenched. A
mourning dove lands on the fire escape, the first I've seen this
season.

It's scary, of course, and I thought I was past all this. I'm
old now, and classy—not obliterating myself at bars six nights
a week. Not that that would mean I deserved it, or . . . well,
maybe that's residual shame speaking. Have I mentioned two
of the rapes happened after I'd been drugged? When I woke
this morning and could tell I hadn't been penetrated, there
was a kind of relief there. I'd made it to where I needed to be,
unbesmirched, and Olive was safe beside me. K, too. He said
I seemed all right when I blew in; chaotic, yes, and he thought
very drunk, but not upset, not hurt. There's so much to get done
today, but on the other hand, I think, well, I wasn't raped again,
so who cares?

Helen waits.

I've been writing about it this week. One of the two rapes
where I was dosed.

Helen waits.

I tell her about the Man in the Gray Room. I ask if she thinks
it strange I took a ride from him.

She says it sounds like I did what I needed to do to get home. I scan her face for contempt, and don't find it.

The other one—where roofies were involved, I mean—was blurrier even than that. It feels impossible to dredge up.

I try breathing deeply, uncertain why my mind circles that night. I feel as if I'm talking in a manic fashion, jittery and searching. The words catch in my throat, little silver hooks.

What details remain salient, asks Helen, if it feels useful to particularize the experience in that way. If you want to continue down this path, I mean. You don't have to. I hope you know this.

I am absolutely still. Not breathing. I consider turning back. I could shut my ears against the call, refuse the memory, stuff it under a thousand layers of silt, and don't. To Helen I say, no . . . that's helpful. I say there were four men, a couch—sad and old and beige, I feel sure of the color. I seem to remember them all smoking cigars, but it might have been just one, or maybe two. At least one, though, I tell Helen, because the air was thick with smoke, and it's different with cigars than weed or cigarettes, it hangs heavier, like you're in a room where a fog machine's been running. Besides, the odor was familiar: my ████████ smoked them constantly. His walls were caked in tar, and I'd get nauseous whenever we visited his house. He was a bad man, too—probably still is, but that's for another session.

I knew one of the men. The one who carried me to the apartment. I've probably mentioned him. He was a regular at the dive where I'd been recently fired. A coke dealer, and his shit was bad, the drip always tasted like gasoline, but everyone bought it when the guy with the good shit wasn't working. He used different names with different people, I realized later. To me he was Pierre, which was funny, because there wasn't an atom of Frenchness about him. He was really proud of being from Brooklyn. He hated the transplants taking over Bed-Stuy, and I, of course, was one of these, so it didn't matter that I was poor, and living on couches, or that I was hooking—I wasn't from here, so I was one of *them,* no different from the trust fund kids at Pratt, no different from the snobby nepo babies who looked down on him while they bought their baggies. Despite myself, I represented the elite. Occasionally, I guess, the facts matter less than the feeling of a thing. Pierre was handsome; I can admit that much. He had a striking face: cut jaw, strong chin, low forehead, but with delicate eyes and pillowy lips. I'll know that face forever. Of all my rapists, he's the one I'm branded by, his image entirely eternal. In the apartment where they were taking turns on me I remember their laughter, I remember thinking to myself, what's so fucking funny, like I'd caught the second half of a joke one of them told, a joke from which I'd been ejected. Later I'd think, my god, you stupid bitch—*you* were the joke! Because of course I was! What a laugh.

It wasn't easy situating myself in the moment. There was the smoke, and the roofies, and the room, of course, was a mess of limbs. I just kept being filled, you know, like every time I thought it was over, my face was shoved in another lap, another pair of hands grabbed my hips, repositioned me, tugged me backward. Again, I tore. It was a bitch to shit for weeks. Odd, how my body seemed sort of gluey, like there was no flesh or bone or blood in it anymore. I seemed to be without sensation, nerveless kind of, and because of that, I wasn't as scared as the other times. I was dead already. There were even moments I felt bored, which probably sounds crazy, but by this time (you have to remember) I'd been getting raped with some regularity for twenty years. Any pain can be banal. I asked myself how long it would take, as in: How many hours can four men spend on one woman? And as I thought this, I saw it might go on a long while. I was sort of in and out, but I longed for sleep. I just wanted to see my dog. I remember wondering if they felt gay, because these were all really macho guys, right, and I was thinking how they all had their cocks out in front of one another, so it occurred to me this might undermine their masculinity somehow. But I guess it wasn't about them, or they'd rationalized the event in some other way. Maybe forcing me affirmed something more profound for them about their manhood. Maybe raping me helped them feel impervious, invulnerable, utterly unkillable.

There was a moment when my head wasn't being held down and I was able, for just that instant, to glance around me, and I saw another room. Its door was ajar, and in it, I saw the shadow of a bed, and the outline of another man sitting on it, I guess a fifth man, the nonparticipant. Or anyway I don't remember him joining the group, but like I said, I was between states. And in the middle of the body's outline was a small red light blinking back at me through the darkness, like the light of a camcorder as it's recording, so that I saw then what was happening was bigger than I understood, or more serious, because the nonparticipant was making a document of what was being done to me, and this fact made it suddenly impossible that I separate from the scene entirely, as I'd been doing, because the scene existed now in a more material way, it was in the process of being immortalized. And all the dissociation in the world wouldn't erase that.

I lost consciousness again, and when I woke, I was outside; they must have thrown me in the street when they were finished. I came to in a pile of garbage on the curb. Revolting. I wasn't thinking of the rape in that moment, no, because I was paralyzed with fear of the rats I was sure were rummaging all around me. I was dressed, I saw with relief, but it took a while to stagger up from the trash. After this I crawled. I wasn't able to walk. My body was wobbly and gelatinous, and I was crying, loudly, when I passed some man on the sidewalk. I remember looking at him and asking for help, but of course I must have looked a fright—like one of the neighborhood crackheads—and I pictured myself from his view, dirtied, a wild animal. He kept walking. Fuck you, I screamed, but he was already gone, and I didn't mean it, or not really. I wouldn't have stopped either. It just wasn't done, certainly not at four in the morning. Halfway to the apartment I managed, at last, to climb to my feet and hobble forward. If I woke the friend I was crashing with, I didn't know it. Most nights she slept at her boyfriend's, so it's possible she wasn't home at all. The dogs all woke. Olive, then her four: Penny, Patron, Buckley, Gaza. They crowded and wrapped me in their love. I blacked out again until morning.

My first thought on waking was practical: What if the video gets out? Of course I thought the rape was my fault. It didn't matter I'd been drugged, it didn't matter there were five men, and they were all huge, and I was being held down. These truths were tertiary to the plot, which was that I was a slut and I'd been doing Pierre's coke with him in the bar bathroom on and off for months, that I'd left my drink unattended on the bar like an idiot, and that—this was essential—these men had put me back in my place. Rape Girl. Everything I'd done in the thirty months since my last assault was diversionary, I'd merely costumed myself in someone else's life. And done it badly, besides. So I worried, mainly, about the video, as I was sure if it circulated it would be interpreted as porn, that everyone I knew would think I'd gotten myself caught in some Girls Gone Wild scheme.

It seemed impossible I see the recording for what it was—evidence. Anyway it never did surface, but I couldn't fathom even one person believing me. And that doubt remains—it's in me now. It's hard to think anyone has ever believed me. I mean, I never reported, so there's no documentation but my own account, and people love nothing more than poking holes in women's stories. There will never not be people who say, well, I think she's lying, I think she's doing it for attention or money or she's seeking revenge—trying to ruin some poor man's life. Like this attention ever goes well for a woman. Imagine hearing about Christine Blasey Ford going into hiding after the hearings and thinking, I bet she sure loved all that attention! Imagine seeing what happened to Amber Heard and thinking, here's that attention you ordered, mama. I'm not even naming anyone. There's one man in the entire book who people could, with great diligence, identify, and he's already been found out! But I have to remember I'm not writing this to be believed. I'm writing to open space in myself for other books, to offer solace—I hope—to others who've lived through this. I can't write for my worst readers, and there's no amount of evidence that would satiate people, there's nothing to do or say that could make a person "good enough" as a victim. It's why people like us best when we're dead. As if death is the only proof possible, like: oh dear, see what happened to that poor girl, and now she's gone. Better we can't speak. Better our corpses be the books left behind us, interpretable to everyone but ourselves.

I'm mindful of our time, Helen says now, but I want to ask: Are you OK in this moment?

Yes, I tell her, in fact I feel sort of indignant. I feel fired up.

Email me if anything, she says. Until next week.

In the park, I dash a few pages off in my diary. Beside me, Olive is silent and regal: my gray-faced sphinx. She's watching an old man throw rice for the pigeons. Only her brows move; her whiskers. Above us the sky is clouded and grim. Months of gloom.

I realize I haven't shown Helen the Chronology, and see now I won't. It's too much an imposition. I wonder, suddenly, if this project is art at all, and then I think, well, who gets to decide what counts as a woman's art in the first place? I fought with K over Ana Mendieta last week . . . god knows why. He said she was nothing special, and this shocked me, in the way the art world's continuing support for Carl Andre shocks me. Now, of course, that fucker's dead. Rest in piss. Less and less do I feel inclined to justify or legitimize confessional art. For years I wrote defensively about the diary as a literary mode, on autobiographical poetry as an insurrectionary act of self-making. And I believe these things, I do, but do I care anymore that others don't? For me, Kathy Acker's cut-ups are art. Anne Sexton's therapy poems aren't her best work by any stretch, but they're art, too, and I look at Cindy Sherman's freaky Instagram filter posts and think, well, OK, that too seems to me to be art.

Why is it when I arrive at my own work I falter? I end up asking: Have I adorned my trauma effectively enough that the labor will be recognized, or will I seem to be merely exorcismic, purgative? I think of that line in one of Plath's last poems—

"the blood-jet is poetry"—and how it's been used as a proof she never worked at the lyric, that she only bled on the page. Ridiculous, if you look at the juvenilia, its laboriousness, the way she suffered constructing imitations for years before coming to the *Ariel* voice. I've battled these condescensions forever, and now here I am, launching the same tired, woman-hating claims against the work I've done. Another tactic of self-harm, maybe.

But why should I make my rape book artful? Why be cowed by this obligation. Shouldn't trauma be a mess? What if I let it be a performance, a public flaying—is it not better to provoke than appease? I won't prettify it. And I can't trust any impulse to aestheticize my violation. It's an unsettling imperative. It pivots on the belief I might make my rapes beautiful, and then who would I be? I must remember I'm Leda, not Yeats. I'm Philomela, not Ovid. Or maybe I'm all of them; maybe I need, in this book, to demonstrate the fact that I can do it all, that I might be the sufferer and the engineer of that suffering's narrative. In writing the story, I enlarge myself—not, perhaps, in a sense of overcoming, but by eliding the trap. No longer feeling I'm nothing but this story. Because I am more, and by so much. A fact I see with greater clearness each day.

The next time I see Helen I turn the tables to ask how *she* feels when I tell these stories.

It's sort of funny, she says, because she'd been thinking of asking if she could share her feelings with me. If I would be comfortable with it, of course.

Please tell me, I say. For months my curiosity about her sense of things has swum around in the back of my mind. I feel electric.

Helen says she finds herself sort of speechless, because she seems to be *with me* while I relive and resurrect these experiences. She, too, is transported. Her feelings, also: horror, sadness, disgust—disgust, she clarifies, at what was done to me.

She pauses.

It *was* disgusting, I say, taking note of her phrase here: "done to me." A solace. I am not blamed. Which is also to say, I'm believed. We talk for a minute about this. I say I feel incredibly cared for and attended to in this space, and then grow shy.

I ask if Helen's familiar with the work of Virginie Despentes. She shakes her head. I've been rereading her novel *Baise-Moi,* I tell her, and a book of essays, *King Kong Theory.* She has a #MeToo book coming out in the fall that I think I'd like to write about. *Baise-Moi* is a rape revenge novel, in its way, sort of like a more fucked-up *Thelma & Louise,* while the essays deal with porn and sex work, rape and ugliness, the French working class, and so on. She has this long meditation on hooking where she talks about the way there's an abundance of stories by women

274 | JAMIE HOOD

who sell sex, but hardly any from johns on the subject of buying it. No accounts of men saying, yeah, I pay for sex, and here's how it makes sense in my world, here's where the money comes from, and so on. And let's face it: the client canon would be a fucking nightmare. When I line all the men I and my friends have fucked for money in a row, the bad politics and awful prose become a tidal wave. Every novel would be titled *Heyyyyy Kitten:)*. But I was thinking about how this is true, too, of rape. The entire onus of narrativization falls squarely on the survivors of it. Only we speak it into the world. You never hear men saying, well, yes, I raped someone and I'm taking accountability for it. I want to understand what justice could look like—I want to work toward reparation. The burden of the telling lies always on us, which is perhaps why people are so prone to skepticism. The scales seem so wildly uneven.

The doorbell rings and I ignore it. No bark, I tell Olive, but she squares up by the door, stubbornly growling. Now I think how stupid what I've just said is—why should I offer a more powerful platform to the rapists of the world? My dumb optimism rearing its head again: the willful faith I have that some men might thrive in the opportunity to be better, that they might accept responsibility for their behavior and seek rehabilitation. But I also wonder: How can we imagine ending rape if the only strategy is forcing victims to talk about it and throwing the people we convict of perpetrating it in prison, forever? We make martyrs or spectacles of survivors, while rapists remain in the cover of shadows, or else get locked up, where they rot, unseen and unheard, utterly beyond the scope of transformation.

Finally I tell Helen I haven't thought this through yet. Maybe the bigger problem is that most of these men don't believe what they're doing is rape. They commit these atrocities and rationalize or compartmentalize them. I wonder at times about the men who raped me: Do *they* think of themselves as rapists? Probably not. Probably they just thought I was some fucking slut. Which is mostly what men tell themselves, I think. That we got what was coming.

I'm mindful of our time, Helen says.

I see I've been going on.

Perhaps I write to be honest about the sort of woman I am. The women I've been. I worry, yes, that confessing my messiness will discredit me, which is, I guess, a funny way of looking at it—like the book's publication will be the rape trial I never had. But I needed not to tidy too much, I needed it to be more than the place where I went to say, here's what happened to me and, gee, I sure hope you believe it. The writing had to slip the limits of my control.

Another doctor's visit. I find myself trapped on the N train between stations and start thinking of the desire that lives in writing, what is opaque or unintelligible to the author, or should be. Desire, I consider, is snuffed out by knowledge and experience. Desire, to survive, must remain *just over there*—animated by distance. Distance and deferral. I felt I had to make something more slippery than I was, a book that shattered my capacity to narrate a dozen bad events. I had to lose the grip of it. But I find myself swatting at a competing thought: that the experimentalism is itself a method of detachment. What if, I think—noticing the construction worker across from me nod off to sleep—I play in this collage of forms to isolate myself from the trauma? Am I hiding? In turning, say, my rape by the Diplomat into a grad school *Dalloway* about dissociation, am I, in fact, refusing to look at what he did to me? I've recorded the brutality, yes, but do I couch it in the rest to persuade myself it's an addendum to something larger? That the violence was just a cog in the greater machine of meaning, that I had some other purpose there? Does my transformation of the event allow me to pretend I was never on those cobblestones, torn and bleeding, with his spit dripping down my back?

The train chugs into motion. An empty Red Bull rolls into the aisle from under the seats.

In our last session, I'd told Helen that my deliberate *artfulness*—that is to say, the *art labor,* which is not the same as its aesthetics—opens an escape path, one I might travel to outsmart myself, to divest the process from violence's materiality. I make it into *work*—

A voice over the intercom: CANAL STREET. I exit.

—but rape has always seemed to me a trouble of form; that is, an interruption in or explosion of narrative. It demands something different of storytelling—

Above ground the sun is bright. I put on my sunglasses, threading through groups of men selling knockoff purses. They call to me and I smile, walking quickly. I'm late.

—which is the revelation, I think, at the heart of Ovid's *Metamorphoses,* or with the story of Philomela, anyhow. There's no undoing her rape. It's over. She's defiled, as I was. Experience passes into the rearview. What is left in the aftermath—and this, I think, is what haunts and galvanizes so many of us—is the call to language, to testimony, and eventually, to writing. In antiquity, weaving and poetry were linked. Philomela, then, becomes a poet. She can't reverse time, but she can tell the rocks and the trees of her grief, she can demand witness. When she's silenced, once her tongue is cut, she learns to shift modes, you see. She masters the visual. Raped women in Ovid are always turning into heifers or sheep or laurels or stars, but what's singular about Philomela's rape and mutilation is its metamorphosis of the narratological field. It makes of her a writer. Rape muted me for many years, but when I began to write into the chaos,

I couldn't stop. I needed to puzzle through it in every way, in tweets and poems and essays and criticism. Public and private. Because every form was stained. All art was.

I check in at the front desk, and am told to seat myself in the waiting room. So I wait.

In the nineteenth week Helen asks if I worry I'll be read hysterically.

I tell her I appreciate the ambiguity of her phrasing, its smirking double knot: that as the artist, *I* might be understood as a hysteric peering out from the frame, but it's just as likely my reader or critic is the hysterical one, or we both are, hysterically, inescapably together. I say I don't believe it's possible for women to make art from life without facing a paranoid reading, the one that exiles confessional writing from the Eden of Real Art. To Helen I say I wrote about this in my first book, and that I'd been thinking, lately, how funny it is Knausgaard gets worshipped as this perfectly objective interrogator of twenty-first-century subjectivity because he wipes his ass and tells us about it. Which is fine, I say, but is it representative? All the suicidal literary men are geniuses failed by the disintegrations of history, while the women are made into jokes, just raving dolls, yellow-wallpaper women. Did Sylvia Plath burn her head off? No, you fucking dolts, haven't you ever used a gas oven?

Helen laughs. I think how wonderful it is to make Helen laugh and remind myself I'm not here to entertain. And yet . . .

I yammer on awhile about the cultural backlash against #MeToo, and before I know it, we're at time.

Through the twenty-second week I dream of the end of the world. These dreams, of course, are not unusual—I've always been apocalyptically minded. Some mornings, before I've woken fully, I let myself imagine the visions vanishing after I've completed the book. My god. I have this embarrassing fantasy—how silly!—where I submit the manuscript to my publisher and bam! That's it! I'm cured. And I never have to think about rape again, while my little exorcism, when published, succeeds fabulously and secures for me the stability I've long longed for and never had.

Over breakfast I chastise myself. How awfully bourgeois I sound!

But I can't bartend another ten years; I can't live paycheck to paycheck again. I'm just too tired. And I know none of this will happen, or in any case, not how I picture it. Anyhow, grief doesn't evaporate, and processing trauma won't reverse time. It won't undo my history. Still, for one glorious instant, I let myself pretend that by finishing the project and letting go of it at last, I could quite literally close the book on my rapes.

When I tell Helen about this, she asks where I believe my fantasy originates.

Isn't it obvious, I say—it's the fantasy of control. Writing is inextricable from domination. No wonder so many of us are animated in art against injustice, the sites of our subordination. I couldn't keep men from hurting me, but I held on to my sovereignty in my ability to tell the story of those wounds. Not all women are so lucky. I feel deep gratitude for the fact that I'm alive, and I've been able to do this work, to communicate something of these horrors, even if I know the language remains inadequate. So much is left unsaid. The question of authority, though, loosens in process, because when the writing's really good, you experience a loss of control. The writing flits past you. There's something, nonetheless, in the call of that song that yearns to master experience. How could it not? You become the god of a story. So part of me suspects I'm writing to discipline my violations, and punish myself for my reckless submission to abjection afterward. And maybe there's something in the process that's protectionist too, like, if I can face what happened, I'll prevent its repetition. Maybe I make the book a sort of talisman, as if I could lock the nightmare of my life up in it. The trouble is, I could be raped again, easy. When I was roofied at that reading, my fear came flooding back. There's nothing in the world to protect me. Sometimes I wonder if publishing the book will sharpen the target I always thought was on my back. Like I'll manifest more rape, rather than purge it.

Always I was baffled by the recursivity of this violence. I became convinced it was something to do with a metaphysical fact in me: that I was *immanently* rapeable. With distance I'm better able to see the system at work—rape culture in the long view, I guess. I'm lately thinking how invisible trans women have been made in the conversation, despite our being at an escalated risk for sexual and other forms of intimate violence. But no one fucking cares, and this is partly because transmisogyny makes us, in a discursive sense, unrapeable. The status quo's sexual prohibition against trans women means we're not even understood as fuckable, let alone lovable, and if we can't be fucked, how could we possibly have been raped? This is the "logic" undergirding the Trumpist disavowal: "She's not my type."

This banishment of trans women from the horizon of accept-
able desire *also* entails that any sexual experience we *do* have we
must have been desperate for, experiences we not only begged
to have, but were granted as an act of fathomless generosity.
Men I used to sleep with would talk about me being "lucky"
to have gotten it from them, which is a rationale at the heart of
all rape culture: that women must be grateful for whatever cock
we get. Like cock is so fucking great. Sometimes, sure, but the
bedrock of transmisogyny is the claim that we aren't reliable
narrators of our own existence, that we're sexually confused at
best, and insidious fabricators at worst. Ontological deceivers.
Phobic presumptions about the inauthenticity of our identity
become mapped onto everything we say and do in the world—
this notion that we aren't who we say we are renders all aspects
of our self-accounting dishonest. Add to this the current sex
panic, which paints anyone who's not cis and straight as a moral
pollutant, a trickster, a violator. Trans women are receptacles
for so much of our culture's erotic terror. We're fundamentally
monstrous: body horror made manifest; cobbled-together doll
parts. It's total dehumanization. And when you dehumanize the
other, you can justify any violence you enact against them.

Helen's mindful of our time.

With Charlotte and Harron later, I recount the conversation, and think through continuing news out of Gaza. Not to
equate my experience with the genocide the Palestinian people
are suffering—a genocide authorized and paid for, of course,
by the American war machine—but to articulate something
about the global network of sexual violence and its mytholo-
gies. Earlier in the week, *The Intercept* published a debunking
of the *Times* article "Screams Without Words," which alleged
mass, coordinated sexual violence by Hamas fighters on October 7. The reporting there incited a classification of Palestinians
in the mainstream political imagination as "human animals"

against whom any annihilative violence is permissible. Meanwhile, Israeli soldiers are stripping and abusing Palestinian men in the streets, they're stealing the undergarments of displaced and murdered women to pose for photos in them. The Israel Defense Forces is using rape as a tactic of war and no one will talk about it. Nearly every major news outlet disseminates the same Islamophobic propaganda—painting the Palestinian people as barbaric—that fanned the flames of the War on Terror. It makes me fucking sick. And it's hard to think of anything else.

W eeks pass and I no longer count them.
Instead I mark time by the coming of spring. Daffodils start to surface—they look just like green onions, green little reeds peering out from sad dirt patches all over Queens. Trash surrounds them: empty Coronas, piss-filled bottles of Polar Spring, avocado shells, cigarette butts. Then the glory of the flowering. Loud, early, unmistakable. The mourning dove I named Morrie last year returns to the nest beneath our AC unit. At first light, he's at it with the cooing—frustrating K and stirring Olive, but when they leave the room I return to him, and coo back. Mostly he flies off. Mourning doves are so nervy, a far cry from the stubborn, curious pigeons that ramble, fearless, over every sidewalk in the city. Probably it's not the same bird; probably he isn't Morrie at all. But it's nice to think he could be.

Most sessions I tell Helen about the writing: process, deadlines, my terror of letting this grief go. All week I've had the panicky feeling, I say, but I know the stress is normal. No need to pathologize myself for it. Anyhow, it's where I thrive: in the eleventh hour. If something worries me as I approach the end, it's my inexorable porousness, how perilous for me to sit in this shit. Have you noticed, I ask her, that I often use the language of contamination to describe myself? Not just the rapes, but with my emotional receptivity, too. I'm really spongy, you know? I feel unsettled. And imprintable. We're not supposed to talk about empathy anymore, there's no more of this "I'm an empathetic person." The concept is anathema, it's this bizarre conceptual boogeyman on social media, and everyone in literary criticism is suddenly *against* empathy, god knows why. Inventing a problem, in my view, to seem more radical than the common folk. What use, I wonder, in pretending we aren't social beings, interconnected, and that we remain beholden to the experiences and feelings other people have. Or we should! Identification with others doesn't mandate a blotting out of their singularity. We're so paranoid, now, about connection. Paranoid about everything, really. We live in an age of conspiracy. But I don't say I'm "permeable" to claim moral goodness, either. It's a hazardous state, and as I look back, I can't separate my present from my past, and I start to feel sort of feral, which reminds me of the dissociated years, my black hole of self-annihilation. So I'm unmoored, and yet I can't burn out those feelings, or I won't be able to write honestly. Being in the writing is frightening lately, I say. A kind of collapse: all my selves appear before me. And they're waging war with one another.

I ask Helen if I sound totally crazy.

Not at all, she says, do you feel you're being peculiar?

Well I've been so isolated lately, I tell her, so in the tunnel of writing, and in that solitude, you start to lose perspective. Most days I don't talk to anyone until K comes home from work, or I'll go out to get a coffee, just to feel like a person.

What's the tunnel like?

Helen jots something in her notebook, just below the camera's frame.

It's the dark matter, I say, the chaff excluded from visible life. There's so much I don't tell people, but with the book I'm bringing my nightmare into full view. The writing is where I go undersea. It's how I establish and then habituate myself to others. Writing allows me to *be with* others in ways I've otherwise failed to manage. I was thinking the other day about how imperviousness never protected me. Shutting myself off for so long didn't keep me from being hurt, it just kept love out. Which I know sounds cliché, but sometimes that's where the truth lies. For years after my last assault, I said if I was raped again, that would be it. That was my limit. It's why I couldn't let people get close: I didn't expect to be here long. When I started seeing Pierre around the neighborhood again, I felt my life was finally over. At last I was ready to be done with it all, and this knowledge flooded me like relief. But then I was terrified of him, which is sort of funny now, because what else could he do that he hadn't done? Except kill me, I guess, but maybe *that* was the fear, that he could steal death from me too, as he'd seized my life and my name, like he and his friends had, like all those men in all the other years did. And in those months I was nothing; I saw nothing; I remember that time hardly at all. Little remains. I didn't read. I didn't write.

Now I look back on myself with such guilt. I have a wish to shake that Jamie and tell her how stupid she was being. I can see, though, how I was in survival mode; see, yes, that always it seemed impossible I should make it through even one day. Each hour was an enormous mountain to be summited. Or I was an animal in a cage. Future slop. There's still part of me that condescends to that animal. I feel smug—I think, you fucking idiot, if you'd only turned this or that corner, none of it would have happened. None of it was fated, because that's not how life works. I was no nymph. I wasn't stuck in some Greek myth. I look at it all laid out here, and find I've seen the movie before. I know the ending. I regard my previous selves and I'm screaming, you stupid bitches, the killer's in the closet! You're blathering on the phone instead of running! I needed to gather my precious force, but I wasn't putting things together then. Everything in me was dispersed.

As a child, as a teenager—those violations bewildered me, I think. I had no language. Maybe they were more formative. It's possible they're the real cracks in the foundation, but they don't feel as disruptive as what came later. They're fuzzier somehow: blown-out photographs. And when violence, again, interrupted my life in New York to requisition this new woman I was meant to be, I thought, how could this have happened? I'm not supposed to be that girl anymore! I'm free of that! But I *was* her, and I wasn't free at all. God. That rape was such a blow. The paranoia returned; I felt I was on the run, and I'd been found out. Creating this narrative of the last decade has been tough, I tell Helen, because story asks us to imagine life as causal—a logical sequence of events—and when I look at the aftershocks of my trauma, it's quite easy to establish continuity between my behavior and what was done to me. I mishandled my own body, right, so what was it to me if others mishandled it too? I feel such shame. With the married men, you know, I cared and I didn't. No one was leaving anyone for me, so I wrote it off. I thought because I was a nothing, I had no impact on others, and now I look and see I did, and there are actions of mine I have to be accountable for. So when I think about that, it seems rather usual to blame myself for the rapes too. In some ways I became a monster—a careless little cunt—because I wanted to be despised. I wanted to position myself as a woman who deserved it. I know it's not possible to deserve it, I swear I know this, and also I know there's part of me that wanted to be the kind of woman people looked at and said, well, she really *got hers*. I know at times I still have those feelings, which I guess must mean I'm Not Cured. So funny. To go through all this and still have days I'm back at the start.

Helen asks what I hold in that insight. Anger?

I don't think it's anger, I tell her . . . maybe disgust, which is bound up with shame, except shame is more of a negativity.

Disgust is active, you see. Shame is just a fog. You're in the fuck-ing muck of it. I felt disgusted by myself, yes, which was simple, because men kept treating me like I was disgusting. Anytime I'd get on my high horse, I'd remember a hand around my throat, a jellyfish body heaving itself into me. I'd remember waking in garbage, crawling down Nostrand Avenue. A bloated rat. And I'm so stubborn, right, I really thought I was *showing them* by upping the ante of my own abjection. So there's ambivalence there, too, and I won't cover up those lapses, I have no wish to pretend I'm above the fray. I haven't miraculously healed myself. It'd be so easy to write that memoir—one where I'm beyond it all. Easier still to write the story where I go, oh dear, I was so helpless, and so perfect, and don't you feel bad for me? But I don't write to elicit sympathy. I've got no interest in mak-ing myself an angel or martyr. I never saw myself as a victim, because to see yourself as a victim, you have to start by seeing yourself as a person. I surely wasn't that. I was an absence in my own life. I knew violence from the time I was six, which is to say there was no *before* violation in my life; I have no origin that precedes trauma, because the formulation of my ego was bound up in it, so I felt, yes, *of course* this is the matter of my life. To understand yourself as a victim means you've got to believe you deserve better. My whole life, I didn't believe that, and now I do. Anyway, a lot of the time. I have a broader language to hand, a support network. I've changed plenty in these last years, and am not in active violence, which helps.

The weeks go on passing, I say, and spring comes in fits and starts. Two warm days and seven cold. The other morning I saw two crows on my walk to the M train: slashes of pure indigo against a cobalt sky. Enormous! I forget how enormous crows are, and I felt in my marrow they were telling me how much is yet to come. Animals are never bad omens. Really, they're only ever themselves, but to be near them in this world is a balm.

Olive (it's funny) is underfoot all the time now. She knows I'm nearing the end. At the park I point out starlings, finches, a single hawk. At dawn the wrens sing, and though I can't spot them among the trees, I know they're near. The mourning dove is on the sill again. Marilyn Mourning Dove, I think to call her.

To Helen I admit I see myself as a person now—not a perfect one of course; only human. I don't think I deserved what happened to me anymore, even if I fucked up and did thoughtless things with my body, even if I slept around or enjoyed the tiresome pleasures of married men—I didn't deserve my rapes. And the rapes don't explain my life, either, they aren't determinative, or in any case I refuse, now, to let them be. I think I needed to get through the book to recognize this, to see that my life was bigger than the cruelties of a dozen men. Then there's so much I've kept out of the book, which pains me. The joy isn't there, I'm sad to say, and there's been plenty of it. How strange: I protect my love and pleasure from view, but how right, too. Those things are *mine*. I must keep them close. The rapes were only what was done to me; I don't own them; they aren't my cage. I can let go now. And I know that's what this is. A separation. Different, I think, to the dissociative impulse, because I no longer turn from my life. I look into it, and my life is no still image. And having faced things, it's funny how bored I've grown with "my" trauma. Maybe because it doesn't seem to be mine any longer. I'm handing it off, as every act of writing is an offering: you must give your words to whoever comes. And maybe they're heard. Or else they rot. It's immaterial. I'm already gone. And no one has to hold this for me, either, but I hope others feel less on their own.

The revelation after coming to New York—thinking I'd be somebody else—was that I'd always ended up being only myself. For a time that was its own trauma, this having to be the woman I was, this having to carry the history I carried. Not to say my self is whole, or I've found some truth in it, but that I shed what I no longer needed, and accept this as the life I have. Because I won't have any others. To know this—to really and truly know it—and to not go on rejecting that life, is a blessing. Because I did go on living, even when I wanted otherwise, and I wake each day feeling blisteringly grateful for this life, for all the possibility that remains to me, for the fact that those men took nothing I couldn't steal back. They faltered; they flopped; thank god, they fucking failed. When I walked down St. Nicholas this morning, the cherry blossoms outside the church had flowered. How does it happen so fast! Already the petals fluttered onto the sidewalk. Delicately, they caught in my hair. An astonishing canopy of pink branched above and around me like a bower, and I tried pointing out the blooms to Olive but she refused to turn her gaze up, she was too busy sniffing at the roots, looking around herself at eye level, she was wagging her tail and pulling us closer to a passing poodle. Yearning. Needful. She's in her life without reservation or resentment, as I'll be now in mine. If there's a tragedy at the close, I think, it's how I still don't know what I want. I never let myself dream such things, I exiled myself from happiness because I couldn't believe I'd warranted any. I divorced my life from desire, for desire, I saw, was futile. Love, as an example; that wasn't *for* me. But I found I was wrong. And I'll never yield that ground again. Still, I'm no expert now; I didn't solve rape—not even my own. Have I answered any questions? Well, have I? The days advance and the sun stoops in the sky until seven; seven thirty; how wondrous, it's nearly eight. All day my bedroom is filled with light. O it is glorious to let the grief go while the world opens, and its opening astounds me, I see it happening at last, as all around me the trees bud and stretch, I hear birdsong in each moment, my whole body is broken up by hope. I have hope again! I do! I don't know my desire, yes, and yet I'm filled with it. And I think, yes, of all I have still to write. Everything left to do. Obliteration is no life. I hold all of me and go on. I think of all the hours and years ahead, however long or short they may be, and they're waiting there, and life is mine, and I want more life, and more life, and more life, and more—

I'm mindful of our time.

Notes

In writing this book from life, I hope I've treated (most of) those who appear here with care and consideration. *Trauma Plot*'s "characters" are, of course, people I have known, though nearly all names and personal details are blurred or altered. The lone exception to my method is "C," who shares a scene with "Jamie H" in the first chapter. "C," rather, is a composite figure—adapted from three men I encountered in the years between high school and my doctoral program. This decision was made so that I could uphold the temporal border of the chapter, to, in other words, ensure I kept that narrative sequence to the span of a single day. "C" is nonetheless based on real people, and the scene is drawn from real experience.

If my rapists are made identifiable by this book, I don't care. I no longer need vengeance, and I hope they rot.

My memories of the Boston Marathon bombing and the Waltham murders are, as I mention in the second chapter, partly culled from my diaries, but I am also indebted to contemporaneous reporting in *The Boston Globe* and *The New York Times,* as well as Masha Gessen's *The Brothers,* Fanny Howe's *The Needle's Eye,* and the documentaries *American Manhunt* and *The Murders Before the Marathon.*

The translation of *The Odyssey* referenced in chapter 2 is by Emily Wilson.

Acknowledgments

For Charlotte Shane and Harron Walker—my women, my rocks. This book could not exist without you, thank you for believing in and carrying me. How blessed I am to have you both in my little world.

For Emily Scanlan, whose tender heart I am honored to hold close. What a thrill to witness you finding the bigness. Break open. I'll be here.

For K, and for our astonishing years. I'll treasure our time together always. Thank you for teaching me how to be loved—what an immense, utterly irreducible gift.

For Olive, who can't read the book's dedication and can't read this either. My daughter, my life, my angel. I hope you know you saved me.

For my mother and sister and little Paxton.

For Emilia Olsen. May we collaborate forever.

For Zach Phillips and Ayla Zuraw-Friedland, who believed in this book in the dark moments when I wasn't able to. I am lucky, also, to call you both my friends. For Lisa Lucas, an early and steadfast champion of *Trauma Plot*—endless thanks also for That Phone Call. You know the one. For Rose Cronin-Jackman and Julianne Clancy, for getting this book in the right hands. For Amelia Zalcman, who gave me the best blurb of all: "This book is tremendous, deeply disturbing, and surprisingly discreet!" For everyone on the teams at Pantheon and Frances Goldin. What author could ask for more?

For my early readers: Charlotte and Harron, again, as well as Rachel Vorona Cote, Natalie Elliott, and Gina Pugliese. For countless others who were indispensable to the production of this book and my way of seeing in this period, crucially among them Torrey Peters, Kate Zambreno, and David O'Neill.

For H, my therapist, who heard the worst of it, and whose listening to that chaos allowed me at last to find a shape for this project.

I'm sure I've forgotten people, but not because you aren't loved. I'm just fuzzy sometimes. Can I still blame the trauma?

And for all the rape girls. Fuck those monsters. We have to live.

ABOUT THE AUTHOR

JAMIE HOOD is a critic, memoirist, poet, and the author of *how to be a good girl*, one of *Vogue*'s Best Books of 2020, and *regards, marcel*, a monthly newsletter on Proust and other miscellany. Her work has appeared in *The Baffler, Bookforum, The Nation, Los Angeles Review of Books, The New Inquiry, The Drift*, and elsewhere. She lives in Brooklyn.

A NOTE ON THE TYPE

The text of this book was set in Sabon, a typeface designed by Jan Tschichold (1902–1974), the well-known German typographer. Based loosely on the original designs by Claude Garamond (ca. 1480–1561), Sabon is unique in that it was explicitly designed for hot-metal composition on both the Monotype and Linotype machines as well as for filmsetting. Designed in 1966 in Frankfurt, Sabon was named for the famous Lyons punch cutter Jacques Sabon, who is thought to have brought some of Garamond's matrices to Frankfurt.

Typeset by Scribe,
Philadelphia, Pennsylvania

Designed by Cassandra J. Pappas